ADVANCE PRAISE FOR
WHAT'S SO GREAT ABOUT CHRISTIANITY

"If there is a purpose for the recent attacks on God and Christianity, it is that these angry assaults have inspired a sober and informative answer of the kind this book provides. This is a timely, important, and illuminating work, scholarly in tone, though accessible to a general audience. Agnostics and atheists will not be able to ignore this challenge."

—Daniel Robinson, Oxford University

"As an unbeliever I passionately disagree with Dinesh D'Souza on some of his positions. But he is a first-rate scholar whom I feel absolutely compelled to read. His thorough research and elegant prose have elevated him into the top ranks of those who champion liberty and individual responsibility. Now he adds Christianity to his formula for the good society, and although non-Christians and non-theists may disagree with some of his arguments, we ignore him at our peril. D'Souza's book takes the debate to a new level. Read it."

—Michael Shermer, publisher of *Skeptic* magazine

"Pastors, teachers, believers, and the sincerely perplexed will find this book indispensable. It sets an example of how to engage vitally important questions without mudslinging and prejudice. D'Souza uses facts and careful reasoning and exposes the atheist attack as intellectually baseless. Rarely have I seen such forceful clarity brought to an issue of such timeliness and importance."

—Dallas Willard, author of *The Divine Conspiracy*

WHAT'S SO GREAT ABOUT CHRISTIANITY

WHAT'S SO GREAT ABOUT CHRISTIANITY

DINESH D'SOUZA

Since 1947
REGNERY
PUBLISHING, INC.
An Eagle Publishing Company • Washington, DC

D'Souza, Dinesh, 1961–
  What's so great about Christianity / Dinesh D'Souza.
  p. cm.
  Includes bibliographical references and index.
  ISBN-13: 978-1-59698-517-9
  1. Christianity—Essence, genius, nature. I. Title.
  BT60.D76 2007
  230—dc22

                                                    200702953

Published in the United States by

Regnery Publishing, Inc.
One Massachusetts Avenue, NW
Washington, DC 20001
www.regnery.com

Manufactured in the United States of America

10 9 8 7 6 5 4

Books are available in quantity for promotional or premium use. Write to Director of Special Sales, Regnery Publishing, Inc., One Massachusetts Avenue NW, Washington, DC 20001, for information on discounts and terms or call (202) 216-0600.

FOR BRUCE SCHOOLEY,
stricken with cancer,
who has found in Jesus Christ
a cure for death

CONTENTS

A NOTE ON THE
INTERPRETATION OF SCRIPTURE

IN THIS BOOK THE **BIBLE** is read in a traditional way—that is, to discover what it actually states and means. This is not biblical literalism. One of the first literalists was the church father Origen, who read in Matthew 19:12 that there were some who made themselves "eunuchs for the sake of the kingdom of heaven." Taking the passage literally, Origen promptly castrated himself. I am not aware of any modern literalists who have put themselves under the knife in this way.

The Bible, however, uses a range of literary techniques. Some of it is straightforward narrative, as in the Gospel accounts of Christ's life. Some of it is parable, as in the stories told by Jesus to illustrate a moral point. Some of it is metaphor, as when Jesus says, "I am the vine and you are the branches," or when he tells his accusers, "Destroy the temple and I will raise it again in three days." (They thought he was speaking literally while he was referring to his bodily resurrection.) How else except as metaphor can we understand Isaiah 55:12, which describes the mountains and the hills breaking into song and the trees clapping their hands?

The church fathers typically understood scripture as operating on multiple levels. The Exodus narrative, for example, was read both as a description of actual events and as a sign of spiritual liberation. (This is how African American slaves understood it, and the hope helped to sustain many of them through the dark night of slavery.) So I reject crude literalism. But equally do I reject the view at the other extreme, which says the Bible should be read through the lens of contemporary secular assumptions. Some people want to reject the parts of scripture they find objectionable and embrace only the parts they like. This is "cafeteria Christianity," and it is worse than literalism. At least the literalist is trying to learn from scripture. The cafeteria Christian simply projects his or her prejudices onto the text.

My way of reading is neither literal nor liberal but rather contextual. Only by examining the text in relation to the whole can we figure out how a particular line or passage is best understood. This will become clear as we get into the argument of the book. At this point let's settle on a simple operating principle: whether you regard the Bible as inspired or not, read the text in context for what it is actually trying to say.

A CHALLENGE TO BELIEVERS—AND UNBELIEVERS

CHRISTIANS ARE CALLED UPON to be "contenders" for their faith. This term suggests that they should be ready to stand up for their beliefs, and that they will face opposition. The Christian is told in 1 Peter 3:15, "Always be prepared to give an answer to everyone who asks you to give the reasons for the hope that is within you." But in order to give reasons, you must first know what you believe. You must also know why you believe it. And you must be able to communicate these reasons to those who don't share your beliefs. In short, you must know what's so great about Christianity.

This is the arena in which many Christians have fallen short. Today's Christians know that they do not, as their ancestors did, live in a society where God's presence was unavoidable. No longer does Christianity form the moral basis of society. Many of us now reside in secular communities, where arguments drawn from the Bible or Christian revelation carry no weight, and where we hear a different language from that spoken in church.

Instead of engaging this secular world, most Christians have taken the easy way out. They have retreated into a Christian subculture where they engage Christian concerns. Then they step back into secular society, where their Christianity is kept out of sight until the next church service. Without realizing it Christians have become postmodernists of a sort: they live by the gospel of the two truths. There is religious truth, reserved for Sundays and days of worship, and there is secular truth, which applies the rest of the time.

This divided lifestyle is opposed to what the Bible teaches. The Bible tells Christians not to be *of* the world, sharing its distorted priorities, but it does call upon believers to be *in* the world, fully engaged. Many Christians have abdicated this mission. They have instead sought a workable, comfortable modus vivendi in which they agree to leave the secular world alone if the secular world agrees to leave them alone. Biologist Stephen Jay Gould proposed the terms for the treaty between the secular and religious worlds when he said that secular society relies on reason and decides matters of fact, while religious people rely on faith and decide questions about values.[1] Many Christians seized upon this distinction with relief. This way they could stay in their subculture and be nice to everyone.

But a group of prominent atheists—many of them evolutionary biologists—has launched a powerful public attack on religion in general and Christianity in particular; they have no interest in being nice. A new set of anti-religious books—*The God Delusion*, *The End of Faith*, *God Is Not Great*, and so on—now shapes public debate. These atheists reject the Gould solution. They say that a religious outlook makes specific claims about reality: there is a God, there is life after death, miracles do happen, and so on. If you are agnostic or atheist, you have a very different understanding of reality, one that is formed perhaps by a scientific or rationalist outlook. The argument of the atheists is that both views of reality cannot be simultaneously correct. If one is true, then the other is false.

The atheists have a point: there are not two truths or multiple truths; there is one truth. Either the universe is a completely closed system and miracles are impossible, or the universe is not a closed system and there is the possibility of divine intervention in it. Either the Big Bang was the product of supernatural creation or it had a purely natural cause. In a larger sense, either the religious view of reality is correct or the secular view is correct. (Or both are wrong.) So far the atheists have been hammering the Christians and the Christians have been running for cover. It's like one hand clapping. A few pastors have stood up to the atheists' challenge, but they have not, in general, fared well. Pastors are used to administering to congregations that accept Christian premises. They are not accustomed to dealing with skilled attackers who call the Christian God a murderer and a tyrant and who reject the authority of the Bible to adjudicate anything.

This is not a time for Christians to turn the other cheek. Rather, it is a time to drive the money-changers out of the temple. The atheists no longer want to be tolerated. They want to monopolize the public square and to expel Christians from it. They want political questions like abortion to be divorced from religious and moral claims. They want to control school curricula so they can promote a secular ideology and undermine Christianity. They want to discredit the factual claims of religion, and they want to convince the rest of society that Christianity is not only mistaken but also evil. They blame religion for the crimes of history and for the ongoing conflicts in the world today. In short, they want to make religion—and especially the Christian religion—disappear from the face of the earth.

The Bible in Matthew 5:13–14 calls Christians to be the "salt of the earth" and the "light of the world." Christians are called to make the world a better place. Today that means confronting the challenge of modern atheism and secularism. This book provides a kind of tool kit for Christians to meet this challenge. The Christianity defended here is not "fundamentalism" but rather traditional Christianity, what C. S. Lewis called "mere Christianity," the common ground of beliefs between Protestants and Catholics. This Christianity is the real target of the secular assault.

I have written this book not only for believers but also for unbelievers. Many people are genuine seekers. They sense there is something out there that provides a grounding and an ultimate explanation for their deepest questions, yet that something eludes them. They feel the need for a higher sense of purpose in their lives, but they are unsure where to find it. Even though they have heard about God and Christianity, they cannot reconcile religious belief with reason and science; faith seems unreasonable and therefore untenable. Moreover, they worry that religion has been and can be an unhealthy source of intolerance and fanaticism, as evidenced by the motives of the September 11 terrorists. These are all reasonable concerns, and I address them head-on in this book.

This is also a book for atheists, or at least for those atheists who welcome a challenge. Precisely because the Christians usually duck and run, the atheists have had it too easy. Their arguments have gone largely unanswered. They have been flogging the carcass of "fundamentalism" without having to encounter the horse kick of a vigorous traditional Christianity. I think that if atheists are genuine rationalists, they should welcome this book. It is an effort to meet the atheist argument on its own terms. Nowhere in this book do I take Christianity for granted. My modus operandi is one of skepticism, to view the claims of religion in the same open-minded way that we would view claims of any other sort. The difference between me and my atheist opponents is that I am skeptical not only of the allegedly irrational claims of religion but also of the irrational claims made in the name of science and of skepticism itself.

Taking as my foil the anti-religious arguments of prominent atheists like Richard Dawkins, Sam Harris, Christopher Hitchens, and the others, in this book I will demonstrate the following:

1. Christianity is the main foundation of Western civilization, the root of our most cherished values.
2. The latest discoveries of modern science support the Christian claim that there is a divine being who created the universe.
3. Darwin's theory of evolution, far from undermining the evidence for supernatural design, actually strengthens it.
4. There is nothing in science that makes miracles impossible.

5. It is reasonable to have faith.
6. Atheism, not religion, is responsible for the mass murders of history.
7. Atheism is motivated not by reason but by a kind of cowardly moral escapism.

I end this book by showing what is unique about Christianity and how our lives change if we become Christians.

If I may address unbelievers directly for a moment, I hope that you will not read this book merely as an intellectual exercise. It seeks to address practical problems that we all face in life. You, like many Christians, live in a split-screen world. You are, I suspect, a Darwinian in your science and an anti-Darwinian in your morals. You revere science and reason but wonder if they give you a full grasp of the world. You are a rationalist at work and a romantic in your personal life. You have been engaged in the pursuit of happiness for a fairly long time; ever wonder why you haven't found it? How long do you intend to continue this joyless search for joy? Older societies had much less and felt abundant; why do you, in the midst of plenty, continue to feel scarcity pressing down upon you? No doubt you, like the believer, know that every breath you take fends off death. Clearly this is something for which you should prepare, but have you? Death forces upon you a choice that you cannot escape. You must choose God or reject Him, because when you die all abstentions are counted as "no" votes. So if you are wondering if this book is an invitation to convert, it is. I hope you will read it as if your life depended on it, because, in a way, it might.

PART I

THE FUTURE OF CHRISTIANITY

CHAPTER ONE

THE TWILIGHT OF ATHEISM: THE GLOBAL TRIUMPH OF CHRISTIANITY

"The era of Western Christianity has passed within our life-times, and the day of Southern Christianity is dawning."[1]

—Philip Jenkins, *The Next Christendom*

GOD HAS COME BACK TO LIFE. The world is witnessing a huge explosion of religious conversion and growth, and Christianity is growing faster than any other religion. Nietzsche's proclamation "God is dead" is now proven false. Nietzsche is dead. The ranks of the unbelievers are shrinking as a proportion of the world's population. Secularism has lost its identification with progress and modernity, and consequently it has lost the main source of its appeal. God is very much alive, and His future prospects look to be excellent. This is the biggest comeback story of the twenty-first century.

If God is back, why don't we see it? The reason is that many of us live in the wrong neighborhood. "Visit a church at random next Sunday," Brent Staples writes in the *New York Times*, "and you will probably encounter a few dozen people sprinkled thinly over a sanctuary that was built to accommodate hundreds or even thousands." Yes, I've seen the "empty pews and white-haired congregants" that Staples describes.[2] But then, Staples lives in New York and I live in California. We live among people who are practically atheist.

Of course my neighbors do not think of themselves as atheist. Very few of them belong to atheist organizations or subscribe to atheist literature. Some of them who are highly educated like to think of themselves as agnostic: they haven't made up their minds because the evidence simply isn't in yet. Others even consider themselves Christian, either because they were born that way or because they attend church occasionally. The distinguishing characteristic of these people is that they live as if God did not exist. God makes no difference in their lives. This is "practical atheism." We all know people like this. Some of us hardly know anyone not like this. And sometimes we live this way ourselves.

If we live in the wrong neighborhood, we risk missing the most important development of our time: the global revival of religion. It's happening on every continent. In my native country of India, Hinduism is undergoing a resurgence. So is Islam. As I have written about Islamic radicalism and terrorism I am often asked, "When will the Muslims understand the importance of secularism? When will we see an Islamic Reformation?" My answer is that Muslims will never understand the importance of secularism. Nor do they need to, because as we shall see, secularism is increasingly unimportant as a global phenomenon. Moreover, Islam *is* in the middle of a reformation. We see a resurgence of Muslim piety not just in the Middle East but also in Indonesia, Malaysia, Bangladesh, Turkey, and East Africa. At one time Turkey provided a model of Islamic secularism, but not any longer. No Muslim country is going the way of Turkey, and in recent years even Turkey has stopped going the way of Turkey.

Some Western analysts describe the religious revivals around the world in terms of the growth of "fundamentalism." This is the fallacy of ethnocentrism, of seeing the world through the lens of our own homegrown prejudices. Remember that *fundamentalism* is a term drawn from Protestant Christianity. It is an American coinage that refers to a group of early twentieth-century Protestant activists who organized against Darwinian evolution and who championed the literal reading of the Bible. Fundamentalism is a meaningless term outside this context.

There are, of course, Hindu militants and Islamic radicals of the bin Laden stripe, and they are indeed a menace to the world. But the growth of religious militancy and the growth of religion are very different. One may seek to benefit from the other, but the two should not be confused. The resurgence I am talking about is the global revitalization of traditional religion. This means traditional Hinduism, traditional Islam, and traditional Christianity. By "traditional" I mean religion as it has been understood and practiced over the centuries. This is the type of religion that is booming.

Traditional religion is the mainstream, but it is not the only form in which religion appears today. There is also liberal religion. One can hardly speak of liberal Islam, as liberalism is essentially a nonexistent force in the Muslim world. But there are liberal Jews, whose Jewishness seems largely a matter of historical memory and cultural habits. Here in the West, there are lots of liberal Christians. Some of them have assumed a kind of reverse mission: instead of being the church's missionaries to the world, they have become the world's missionaries to the church. They devote their moral energies to trying to make the church more democratic, to assure equal rights for women, to legitimize homosexual marriage, and so on. A small but influential segment of liberal Christianity rejects all the central doctrines of Christianity. H. Richard Niebuhr famously summed up their credo: "A God without wrath brought men without sin into a kingdom without judgment through the ministrations of a Christ without a cross."[3]

I have met liberal Christians who are good and sincere people. But their version of Christianity is retreating, in two senses. Liberal Christians are distinguished by how much intellectual and moral ground they concede to the adversaries of Christianity. "Granted, no rational person today can believe in miracles, but...." "True, the Old Testament God seems a mighty vengeful fellow, but...." "Admittedly religion is responsible for most of the conflict and oppression in history, but...."

This yes-but Christianity in full intellectual withdrawal, and it is also becoming less relevant. The liberal churches are losing members in droves. Once these churches welcomed one in six Americans; now they see one in thirty. In 1960 the Presbyterian church had 4.2 million members; now it has 2.4 million. The Episcopal church had 3.4 million; now it has 2.3 million. The United Church of Christ had 2.2 million; now it has 1.3 million.[4] Traditional Christians who remain within liberal churches become increasingly alienated. Some have become so disgusted that they have put themselves under the authority of more traditional clerics based in countries like Nigeria, Ghana, and the Ivory Coast.

Unfortunately the central themes of some of the liberal churches have become indistinguishable from those of the American Civil Liberties Union, the National Organization for Women, and the homosexual rights movement. Why listen to Episcopal bishop John Shelby Spong drone on when you can get the same message and much more interesting visuals at San Francisco's gay pride parade? The traditional churches, not the liberal churches, are growing in America. In 1960, for example, the churches affiliated with the Southern Baptist Convention had 8.7 million members. Now they have 16.4 million.[5]

The growth of traditional religion and the decline of liberal religion pose a serious problem for a conventional way of understanding religious trends. This is the way of secularization: the idea that as an inevitable result of science, reason, progress, and modernization, the West will continue to grow more secular, followed by the rest of the world. The more confident exponents of secularization believe, as Peter Berger puts it, that "eventually Iranian mullahs, Pentecostal preachers, and Tibetan lamas will all think and act like professors of literature at American universities."[6]

For a good part of the last century, this secularization narrative seemed plausible. Secular people believed it and reveled in it, while religious people believed it and bemoaned it. But now we see a problem with the thesis. If secularization were proceeding inexorably, then religious people should be getting less religious, and so conservative churches should be shrinking and liberal churches growing. In fact, the opposite is the case.

Some scholars put this down to "backlash" against secularization, but this only begs the question: what is causing this backlash? The secularization thesis was based on the presumption that science and modernity would satisfy the impulses and needs once met by religion. But a rebellion against secularization suggests that perhaps important needs are still unmet, and so people are seeking a revival of religion—perhaps in a new form—to address their specific concerns within a secular society.

Of course the secularization thesis is not entirely invalid. In Europe, Australia, and Canada, religion has been expunged from the cultural mainstream. It has been largely relegated to a tourist phenomenon; when you go to Chartres and Canterbury, the guides tell you about architecture and art history and little about what the people who created those masterpieces actually believed. According to the European Values Survey, regular churchgoers number, depending on the country, between 10 and 25 percent of the population. Only one in five Europeans says that religion is important in life. Czech president Vaclav Havel has rightly described Europe as "the first atheistic civilization in the history of mankind."[7]

The religious picture in Europe is not unremittingly bleak. Ninety percent of Greeks acknowledge the existence of God, and only 5 percent of Greeks are atheists. Ireland still has church attendance figures of around 45 percent, twice as high as the Continent as a whole, although Irish Catholicism has also weakened in recent decades. Along with Ireland, Poland and Slovakia are two of the most religious countries in Europe.[8] And some commentators have noted that even Europeans who are not religious continue to describe themselves as "spiritual." These analysts argue that Europe has not abandoned religion in general but only "organized" religion.

But if Europe generally supports the secularization thesis, the United States presents a much more problematic case. America has not gone the way of Europe. True, church attendance in the United States has declined in the past three decades. Still, some 40 percent of Americans say they attend church on Sundays. More than 90 percent of Americans believe in God, and 60 percent say their faith is important to them. Surveying the data on religion, Paul Bloom writes in the *Atlantic Monthly* that "well over half of Americans believe in miracles, the devil, and angels. Most Americans believe that after death they will actually reunite with relatives and get to meet God."[9] All of this is a serious difficulty for the secularization thesis, because America is at the forefront of modernity. The thesis would predict that America would be the most secular society in the world. In fact, America is the most religious country in the Western world.

Perhaps the greatest problem for the secularization theory is that in an era of increasing globalization and modernization, the world as a whole is becoming more religious, not less. In a recent survey, Pippa Norris and Ron Inglehart sum up the evidence. Despite the advance of secularization in the West, they write, "The world as a whole now has more people with traditional religious views than ever before, and they constitute a growing proportion of the world's population." Consequently, the West is more secular but "the world as a whole is becoming more religious."[10]

Even more remarkable is that the religious revival is occurring in places that are rapidly modernizing. China and India today have the fastest growth rates in the world, and religion is thriving in both places. Turkey is the one of the most modern of the Muslim countries, and Islam has steadily gained strength there. In Central and South America, the upwardly mobile classes are embracing Pentecostal Christianity.

The global spread of American culture, with the secular values it carries, seems not to have arrested or even slowed the religious upsurge. The reason is that many non-Western cultures are actively resisting secularism. A common slogan in Asia today is "modernization without Westernization." Many people want American prosperity and American technology, but they want to use these to preserve and strengthen their traditional way of life. They want to live in a world of multiple modernities.

We often read that Islam is the fastest-growing religion. Not true. Christianity is the fastest-growing religion in the world today. Islam is second. While Islam grows mainly through reproduction—which is to say by Muslims having large families—Christianity spreads through rapid conversion as well as natural increase. Islam has become the fastest-growing religion in Europe, which for more than a thousand years has been the home of Christianity. Catholic writer Hilaire Belloc wrote in 1920 that "the faith is Europe and Europe is the faith." Belloc was convinced that the future of Christianity lay in Europe.

Ironically, while Europe has moved away from Christianity, the Christian religion has been expanding its influence in Central and South America, in Africa, and in Asia. For the first time in history, Christianity has become a universal religion. It is in fact the only religion with a global reach. Buddhism and Islam, like Christianity, are religions with global aspirations, but these aspirations have not been realized. Buddhism never established itself even in the land of its founding, India, although it found adherents in the cultures of Southern and Eastern Asia. Even though it has a few followers in the West, Buddhism remains a religion with, at best, a regional impact. Islam is vastly stronger, but even Islam is regional, with little or no sway in the United States, Canada, Central and South America, or Australia. By contrast, Christianity is a force on every continent and in every major region of the world, with the sole exception of the heartland of Islam, the Middle East.

The new face of Christianity is no longer white and blond but yellow, black, and brown. "If we want to visualize a typical contemporary Christian," Philip Jenkins writes in *The Next Christendom*, "we should think of a woman living in a village in Nigeria or in a Brazilian favela." The vital centers of Christianity today are no longer Geneva, Rome, Paris, or London. They are Buenos Aires, Manila, Kinshasa, and Addis Ababa. "The era of Western Christianity has passed within our lifetimes," Jenkins observes, "and the day of Southern Christianity is dawning."[11]

In 1900, more than 80 percent of Christians lived in Europe and America. Today 60 percent live in the developing world. More than two out of three evangelical Christians now live in Asia, Africa, and South America. Here are some numbers Jenkins provides: Europe today has

560 million Christians and America has 260 million, yet many of these are Christian in name only. In comparison, there are 480 million Christians in South America, 313 million in Asia, and 360 million in Africa. The vast majority of these are practicing Christians. There are more churchgoing Presbyterians in Ghana than in Scotland.

Oddly enough, this Christian growth occurred after the period of European conquest and colonialism ended. The old boys in pith helmets are long gone, but the faith that first came with them has endured and now thrives without them. It's just like the early times of Christianity. After Constantine converted and Theodosius proclaimed Christianity the state religion toward the end of the fourth century, Christianity was carried by the Roman empire. Yet the faith spread fastest after the collapse of that empire, and soon all of Europe was Christian. We're witnessing a comparable pace of growth for Christianity in the rest of the world.

A century ago, less than 10 percent of Africa was Christian. Today it's nearly 50 percent. That's an increase from 10 million people in 1900 to more than 350 million today. Uganda alone has nearly 20 million Christians and is projected to have 50 million by the middle of the century.[12] Some African congregations have grown so big that their churches are running out of space. While Western preachers routinely implore people to come every Sunday to fill the pews, some African preachers ask their members to limit their attendance to every second or third Sunday to give others a chance to hear the message.

Central and South America are witnessing the explosive growth of Pentecostalism. As David Martin shows in his study *Tongues of Fire*, partly this is a shift within Christianity: millions of South American Catholics have become evangelical Protestants.[13] In Brazil, for example, there are now 50 million evangelical Protestants whereas a few decades ago there weren't enough to count. The movement of Catholics into Protestant evangelicalism should not be considered purely lateral, however, as the conversion of lackadaisical nominal Catholics to an active, energized evangelicalism can perhaps be considered a net gain for Christianity. Even within Catholicism there is an expanding charismatic movement that has grown in response to the success of the Protestant evangelicals. This charismatic Catholicism emphasizes many of the same themes as "born again" Christianity, including a personal relationship with Christ. And the Catholic numbers remain huge: Brazil had 50 million Catholics in 1950, but now it has 120 million.

Despite the limitations imposed by the Chinese government, it is estimated that there are now 100 million Christians in China who worship in underground evangelical and Catholic churches. At current growth rates, David Aikman observes in his book *Jesus in Beijing*, China will in a few decades become the largest Christian country in the world.[14] In Korea, where Christians already outnumber Buddhists, there are numerous mega-churches with more than 10,000 members each. The Yoido Full Gospel Church reports 750,000 members. The Catholic church in the Philippines reports 60 million members, and is projected to have 120 million by mid-century.

What distinguishes these Christians, Philip Jenkins writes, is that they immerse themselves in the world of the Bible to a degree that even devout Western Christians do not. For poor people around the world, the social landscape of the Bible is quite familiar. They, too, live in a world of hardship, poverty, money-lenders, and lepers. The themes of exile and persecution resonate with them. Supernatural evil seems quite real to them, and they have little problem in understanding the concept of hell.[15] Some of them even expect the miracles of ancient times to be witnessed in their own lifetimes. I remember an African preacher who visited a church I used to attend in Northern Virginia. He insisted that through God's grace he had performed innumerable healings. When one of the assistant pastors looked at him a bit doubtfully, he pointed to the Bible and said, "Young man, there is a big difference between you and me. You see this book right here? We believe it."

This Third World Christianity is coming our way. South Korea has become the world's second-largest source of Christian missionaries, with 12,000 preaching the faith abroad. Only the United States sends more missionaries to other countries.[16] We may be seeing the beginning of a startling reversal. At one time Christian missionaries went to the far continents of Africa and Asia, where white priests in robes proclaimed the Bible to wide-eyed and uncomprehending brown and black people. In the future, we may well see black and brown missionaries proclaim the Bible to wide-eyed and uncomprehending white people in the West.

We might think that this preaching will fall on unreceptive ears. But I'm not so sure. The *Washington Post* reports that there are 150 churches in Denmark and more than 250 in Britain run by foreigners as "part of a growing trend of preachers from developing nations coming to Western Europe." Stendor Johansen, a Danish sea captain, seems to reflect the sentiments of many Europeans who are joining the new congregations. "The Danish church is boring," he says. "I feel energized when I leave one of these services."[17] If more people come to share these sentiments then secularization may ultimately be reversed even in Europe.

Peter Berger writes about what he calls the "myth of secularization." He means that the thesis of inevitable secularization has now lost its credibility. In fact, it is going the way of Zeus and Baal. Berger's work points to the reason for this. Ultimately secularization may be reversed even in Europe.

Berger argues that modernization helps people triumph over necessity but it also produces a profound crisis of purpose in modern life. The greater the effects of modernization, the stronger the social anxiety and the striving for "something more." As Wolfhart Pannenberg puts it, "Secular culture itself produces a deep need for meaning in life and therefore also for religion."[18] This may not be religion in the same form in which it is imbibed in Nigeria or Korea, but it is traditional religion all the same, no less vital for having adapted to new circumstances. It is quite possible that a renewed Christianity can improve modern life by correcting some of the deficiencies and curbing some of the excesses of modernity.

I have found this to be true in my own life. I am a native of India, and my ancestors were converted to Christianity by Portuguese missionaries. As this was the era of the Portuguese Inquisition, some force and bludgeoning may also have been involved. When I came to America as a student in 1978, my Christianity was largely a matter of birth and habit. But even as I plunged myself into modern life in the United

States, my faith slowly deepened. G. K. Chesterton calls this the "revolt into orthodoxy." Like Chesterton, I find myself rebelling against extreme secularism and finding in Christianity some remarkable answers to both intellectual and practical concerns. So I am grateful to those stern inquisitors for bringing me into the orbit of Christianity, even though I am sure my ancestors would not have shared my enthusiasm. Mine is a Christianity that is countercultural in the sense that it opposes powerful trends in modern Western culture. Yet it is thoroughly modern in that it addresses questions and needs raised by life in that culture. I don't know how I could live well without it.

In the end, though, my story doesn't matter very much, and neither does it matter whether the West returns to Christianity. Perhaps the non-Western Christians will convert the Western unbelievers, and perhaps they won't. Either way, they are the future, they know it, and now we know it too. Christianity may come in a different garb than it has for the past several centuries, but Christianity is winning, and secularism is losing. The future is always unpredictable, but one trend seems clear. God is the future, and atheism is on its way out.

CHAPTER TWO

SURVIVAL OF THE SACRED: WHY RELIGION IS WINNING

"The vigorous, the healthy, and the happy survive and multiply."[1]

—Charles Darwin, *The Origin of Species*

THE CONTINUED GROWTH OF RELIGION worldwide has not gone unnoticed by leading atheists. Some of these nonbelievers, most of them Darwinists, express candid puzzlement at religion's enduring vitality. These Darwinists are convinced that there must be some biological explanation for why, in every culture since the beginning of history, man has found and continues to find solace in religion. Biologist Richard Dawkins confesses that religion poses a "major puzzle to anyone who thinks in a Darwinian way."[2]

Here, from the evolutionary point of view, is the problem. Scholars like anthropologist Scott Atran presume that religious beliefs are nothing more than illusions. Atran contends that religious belief requires taking "what is materially false to be true" and "what is materially true to be false." Atran and others believe that religion requires a commitment to "factually impossible worlds."[3] The question, then, is why humans would evolve in such a way that they come to believe in things that don't exist.

Philosopher Daniel Dennett states the problem clearly: "The ultimate measure of evolutionary value is fitness—the capacity to replicate more successfully than the competition does."[4] Yet on the face of it religion seems useless from an evolutionary point of view. It costs time and money, and it induces its members to make sacrifices that undermine their well-being for the benefit of others, who are sometimes total strangers.

Religious people build cathedrals and pyramids that have very little utility except as houses of worship and burial. The ancient Hebrews sacrificed their fattest calves to Yahweh, and even today people slaughter goats and chickens on altars. Religious people sometimes forgo certain foods—the cow is holy to the Hindus, and the pig unholy to the Muslims. Christians give tithes and financial offerings in church. The Jews keep holy the Sabbath, as Christians keep Sunday for church. Religious people recite prayers and go on pilgrimages. Some become missionaries or devote their lives to serving others. Some are even willing to die for their religious beliefs.

The evolutionary biologist is puzzled: why would evolved creatures like human beings, bent on survival and reproduction, do things that seem unrelated and even inimical to those objectives? This is a critical question, not only because religion poses an intellectual dilemma for Darwinists, but also because Darwinists are hoping that by explaining the existence of religion they can expose its natural roots and undermine its supernatural authority. Biologist E. O. Wilson writes that "we have come to the crucial stage in the history of biology when religion itself is subject to the explanations of the natural sciences." He expresses the hope that sometime soon "the final decisive edge enjoyed by scientific naturalism will come from its capacity to explain traditional religion, its chief competitor, as a wholly material phenomenon."[5]

So how far have these evolutionary theories progressed in accounting for the success of religion? "The proximate cause of religion might be hyperactivity in a particular node of the brain," Dawkins writes. He also speculates that "the idea of immortality survives and spreads because it caters to wishful thinking."[6] But it makes no evolutionary sense for minds to develop comforting beliefs that are evidently false. Cognitive psychologist Steven Pinker explains, "A freezing person finds no comfort in believing he is warm. A person face to face with a lion is not put at ease by the conviction that he is a rabbit."[7] Wishful thinking of this sort would quickly have become extinct as its practitioners froze or were eaten.

Yet Pinker's own solution to the problem is no better than Dawkins's. He suggests that there might be a "God module" in the brain that predisposes people to believe in the Almighty. Such a module, Pinker writes, might serve no survival purpose but could have evolved as a byproduct of other modules with evolutionary value.[8] This is another way of saying there is no Darwinian explanation. After all, if a "God module" produces belief in God, how about a "Darwin module" that produces belief in evolution?

Still, the question raised by the Darwinists is not a foolish one. Biologists like Dawkins and Wilson say there simply must be some natural and evolutionary explanation for the universality and persistence of religious belief, and they are right. There is such an explanation, and I am pleased to provide one in this chapter. The Reverend Randy Alcorn, founder of Eternal Perspective Ministries in Oregon, sometimes presents his audiences with two creation stories and asks them whether it matters which one is true. In the secular account, "You are the descendant of a tiny cell of primordial protoplasm washed up on an empty beach three and a half billion years ago. You are the blind and arbitrary product of time, chance, and natural forces. You are a mere grab-bag of atomic particles, a conglomeration of genetic substance. You exist on a tiny planet in a minute solar system in an empty corner of a meaningless universe. You are a purely biological entity, different only in degree but not in kind from a microbe, virus, or amoeba. You have no essence beyond your body, and at death you will cease to exist entirely. In short, you came from nothing and are going nowhere."

In the Christian view, by contrast, "You are the special creation of a good and all-powerful God. You are created in His image, with capacities to think, feel, and worship that set you above all other life forms. You differ from the animals not simply in degree but in kind. Not only is your kind unique, but you are unique among your kind. Your Creator loves you so much and so intensely desires your companionship and affection that He has a perfect plan for your life. In addition, God gave the life of His only son that you might spend eternity with Him. If you are willing to accept the gift of salvation, you can become a child of God."

Now imagine two groups of people—let's call them the secular tribe and the religious tribe—who subscribe to these two worldviews. Which of the two tribes is more likely to survive, prosper, and multiply? The religious tribe is made up of people who have an animating sense of purpose. The secular tribe is made up of people who are not sure why they exist at all. The religious tribe is composed of individuals who view their every thought and action as consequential. The secular tribe is made up of matter that cannot explain why it is able to think at all.

Should evolutionists like Dennett, Dawkins, Pinker, and Wilson be surprised, then, to see that religious tribes are flourishing? Throughout the world, religious groups attract astounding numbers of followers and religious people are showing their confidence in their way of life and in the future by having more children. By contrast, atheist conventions draw only a handful of embittered souls. One of the largest atheist organizations, American Atheists, has around 2,500 members. Throw a stone in the faculty parking lot of an elite American or European university and you have a good chance of hitting an atheist. But throw a stone anywhere else and you really have to aim.

The important point is not just that atheism is unable to compete with religion in attracting followers, but also that the lifestyle of practical atheism seems to produce listless tribes that cannot even reproduce themselves. Sociologists Pippa Norris and Ron Inglehart note that many richer, more secular countries are "producing only about half as many children as would be needed to replace the adult population" while many poorer, more religious countries are "producing two or three times as many children as would be needed to replace the adult population." The consequence, so predictable that one might almost call it a law, is that "the religious population is growing fast, while the secular number is shrinking."[9]

Russia is one of the most atheist countries in the world, and abortions there outnumber live births by a ratio of two to one. Russia's birth rate has fallen so low that the nation is now losing 700,000 people a year. Japan, perhaps the most secular country in Asia, is also on a kind of population diet: its 130 million people are expected to drop to around 100 million in the next few decades. Canada, Australia, and New Zealand find themselves in a similar predicament.

Then there is Europe. The most secular continent on the globe is decadent in the quite literal sense that its population is rapidly shrinking. Birth rates are abysmally low in France, Italy, Spain, the Czech Republic, and Sweden. The nations of Western Europe today show some of the lowest birth rates ever recorded, and Eastern European birth rates are comparably low.[10] Historians have noted that Europe is suffering the most sustained reduction in its population since the Black Death in the fourteenth century, when one in three Europeans succumbed to the plague. Lacking the strong religious identity that once characterized Christendom, atheist Europe seems to be a civilization on its way out. Nietzsche predicted that European decadence would produce a miserable "last man" devoid of any purpose beyond making life comfortable and making provision for regular fornication. Well, Nietzsche's "last man" is finally here, and his name is Sven.

Eric Kaufmann has noted that in America, where high levels of immigration have helped to compensate for falling native birth rates, birth rates among religious people are almost twice as high as those among secular people. This trend has also been noticed in Europe.[11] What this means is that, by a kind of natural selection, the West is likely to evolve in a more religious direction. This tendency will likely accelerate if Western societies continue to import immigrants from more religious societies, whether they are Christian or Muslim. Thus we can expect even the most secular regions of the world, through the sheer logic of demography, to become less secular over time.

In previous decades, scholars have tried to give a purely economic explanation for demographic trends. The general idea was that population was a function of affluence. Sociologists noted that as people and countries became richer, they had fewer children. Presumably, primitive societies needed children to help in the fields, and more prosperous societies no longer did. Poor people were also believed to have more children because sex provided one of their only means of recreation. Moreover, poor people are often ignorant about birth control or don't have access to it. From this perspective, large families were explained as a phenomenon of poverty and ignorance.

This economic explanation is partly true, but it falls short of the full picture. Many poor people have large families despite having access to birth control and movie tickets; it turns out they generally *want* larger families. Sure, they are more economically dependent on their children, but on the other hand, rich people can afford more children. Wealthy people in America today tend to have one child or none, but wealthy families in the past tended to have three or more children. The real difference is not merely in the level of income—it is that in the past children were valued as gifts from God, and traditional cultures still view them that way.

Muslim countries, with their oil revenues, are by no means the poorest in the world and yet they have among the highest birth rates. Practicing Catholics, orthodox Jews, Mormons, and evangelical Protestants are by no means the poorest groups in America, and yet they have large families. Clearly religious factors are at work here. The declining birth rates in the West as a whole are, in considerable part, due to secularization. The religious motive for childbearing has been greatly attenuated, and children are now viewed by many people as instruments of self-gratification. The old biblical principle was "Be fruitful and multiply." The new one is "Have as many children as will enhance your lifestyle."

The economic forecasters of the disappearance of religion have proven themselves to be false prophets. Not only is religion thriving, but it is thriving because it helps people to adapt and survive in the world. In his book *Darwin's Cathedral*, evolutionary biologist David Sloan Wilson argues that religion provides something that secular society doesn't: a vision of transcendent purpose. Consequently, religious people develop a zest for life that is, in a sense, unnatural. They exhibit a hopefulness about the future that may exceed what is warranted by how the world is going. And they forge principles of morality and charity that simply make them more cohesive, adaptive, and successful than groups whose members lack this binding and elevating force.[12]

My conclusion is that it is not religion but atheism that requires a Darwinian explanation. Atheism is a bit like homosexuality: one is not sure where it fits into a doctrine of natural selection. Why would nature select people who mate with others of the same sex, a process with no reproductive advantage at all? It seems equally perplexing why nature would breed a group of people who see no higher purpose to life or the universe. Here is where the biological expertise of Dawkins, Pinker, and Wilson could prove illuminating. Maybe they can turn their Darwinian lens on themselves and help us understand how atheism, like the human tailbone and the panda's thumb, somehow survived as an evolutionary leftover of our primitive past.

CHAPTER THREE

GOD IS NOT GREAT: THE ATHEIST ASSAULT ON RELIGION

"Boldness was not formerly a characteristic of atheists as such. But of late they are grown active, designing, turbulent, and seditious."[1]

—Edmund Burke

ALARMED BY THE RISING POWER of religion around the world, atheists in the West today have grown more outspoken and militant. What we are witnessing in America is atheist backlash. The atheists thought they were winning, but now they realize that, far from dying quietly, religion is on the global upswing. So the atheists are striking back, using all the resources they can command. This is not a religious war but a war over religion, and it has been declared by leading Western atheists who have commenced hostilities.

Statistics seem to suggest that in America the number of atheists is growing. The Pluralism Project at Harvard reports that people with no religious affiliation now number nearly forty million. That's almost 15 percent of the population, up from less than 10 percent in 1990, and so a virtual doubling of the atheist ranks in a single decade. Science writer John Horgan boasts that "there are more of us heathens out there than you might guess."[2] It's unclear from the data if there are more atheists, or simply more people who are open about their atheism.

Atheists come in different varieties, making up their own sectarian camps. There are secularists, nonbelievers, non-theists, apatheists, anti-theists, agnostics, skeptics, free thinkers, and humanists. Fine distinctions separate some of these groups. While agnostics say they don't know whether God exists, apatheists say they don't care. Some of these groups are not technically atheist because an atheist is one who declares God does not exist. But even so they are de facto atheists, because their ignorance and indifference amounts to a practical rejection of God's role in the world. In this book I use the term atheist in its broad sense to refer to those who deny God and live as if He did not exist.

The distinguishing element of modern atheism is its intellectual militancy and moral self-confidence. We have seen a spate of atheist books in recent years, like Richard Dawkins's *The God Delusion*, Sam Harris's *The End of Faith*, Victor Stenger's *God: The Failed Hypothesis*, and Christopher Hitchens's *God Is Not Great*. Other writers, like E. O. Wilson, Carl Sagan, Daniel Dennett, and Steven Pinker, have also weighed in with anti-religious and anti-Christian tracts. In Europe, the *Wall Street Journal* reports, philosopher Michel Onfray has rallied the unbelievers with his bestselling *Atheist Manifesto*, which posits a "final battle" against the forces of Christianity.[3]

Never before have we seen what we are seeing now, which is what Dawkins terms a widespread assertion of "atheist pride."[4] Prominent atheists are staging a huge "coming out" party. Two of them, American philosopher Daniel Dennett and British biologist Richard Dawkins, published articles calling on fellow unbelievers to give up the term "atheist," as the term, they suggested, has such negative connotations. Their alternative? Dennett and Dawkins want to be called "brights." Yes, "brights," as in "I am a bright." Dawkins defines a bright as one who espouses "a worldview that is free of supernaturalism and mysticism."[5] According to Dennett, "We brights don't believe in ghosts or elves or the Easter Bunny—or God."[6] Dennett's implication is clear: brights are the smart people who don't fall for silly superstitions.

Brights and other nonbelievers are not impressed with the growth of religious belief around the world. When I published an article in the

San Francisco Chronicle detailing this growth, I received lots of indignant letters. One theme stood out: the stupidity or irrationality of believers. "The reason that religious tribes are growing around the world is that it is much easier to believe in the unproven than to think and to ask questions." "Most of the world is impoverished, uneducated, and plagued by war and disease. So I take little solace that so many of the besieged believe in fairy tales in order to make their lives a little easier." "It's amazing that anyone with an ounce of sense can believe in gods, spooks, and leprechauns. No wonder the world is such a mess with so many irrational people in it." "The world is already overcrowded. So thank heaven we atheists are keeping our number down. The poor, religious people in other countries seem to be breeding like mice."

Yes, there is a bit of arrogance here, but in the view of the atheists and the brights, it is justified. Long considered a marginal and reticent minority, atheists are now lashing out at religion with enormous gusto. Nobel laureate Steven Weinberg writes, "Anything that we scientists can do to weaken the hold of religion should be done and may in the end be our greatest contribution to civilization."[7] Sam Harris in *The End of Faith* condemns what he terms "the lunatic influence of religious belief."[8] Christopher Hitchens writes, "All religions and all churches are equally demented in their belief in divine intervention, divine intercession, or even the existence of the divine in the first place."[9] Dawkins adds, "The great unmentionable evil at the center of our culture is monotheism. From a barbaric Bronze Age text known as the Old Testament, three anti-human religions have evolved: Judaism, Christianity, and Islam."[10]

What gives the atheists such confidence? The answer, in a word, is science. Many atheists believe that modern science—the best known way to accumulate knowledge, the proven technique for giving us airplanes and computers and drugs that kill bacteria—has vindicated the nonbeliever's position. And it seems that a majority of scientists in the United States are atheists. Only 40 percent—a sizable minority, but a minority nevertheless—believe in a personal God. And among members of the elite National Academy of Sciences, only 7 percent of scientists can be counted among the ranks of the believers.[11] These figures have remained generally consistent over several decades, with the proportion of atheists rising slightly.

But what is it about science that supports atheism? For one, science seems to work better than religion. "We can pray over the cholera victim," Carl Sagan writes, "or we can give her 500 milligrams of tetracycline every twelve hours."[12] In such cases, Sagan points out, even Christians are likely to supplement their prayers with medicine. Another reason, according to Steven Pinker, is that "the modern sciences of cosmology, geology, biology, and archaeology have made it impossible for a scientifically literate person to believe that the biblical story of creation actually took place."[13] While science relies on the principle that "nothing is more sacred than the facts," Sam Harris charges that "theology is now little more than a branch of human ignorance. Indeed it is ignorance with wings."[14]

In making their case, the atheists often appeal to the revolutionary influence of Charles Darwin. In his book *The Blind Watchmaker*, Dawkins writes that "Darwin made it possible to be an intellectually fulfilled atheist."[15] He points out that the universe and its creatures show irrefutable evidence of design. Before Darwin, there was no plausible explanation for that design other than to posit a designer. So atheists had no way to account for life's diversity and complexity. Many—including skeptic David Hume—were forced to concede that each creature was fitted with the equipment needed for its survival by some sort of higher being.

The great achievement of Darwin's theory of evolution and natural selection, Dawkins and others say, is that it shows how creatures that appear to be designed have in fact evolved according to the pressures of chance and survival. Atheists now have an alternative explanation for why fish have gills, why birds have wings, and why human beings have brains and arms and lungs. Indeed, in the atheist view, evolution refutes the biblical account of human creation, exposing it as a crude and primitive myth. Carl Sagan remarks that "as science advances, there seems to be less and less for God to do.... Whatever it is we cannot explain lately is attributed to God.... And then after a while, we explain it, and so that's no longer God's realm."[16] This is none other than the God of the Gaps, who is forced by science into ever greater irrelevance. Dawkins argues that contrary to the claims of religion, we humans "are survival machines—robot vehicles blindly programmed to preserve the selfish molecules known as genes."[17]

In his book *Darwin's Dangerous Idea*, Dennett contends that Darwin's theories are a kind of "universal acid" that "eats through just about every traditional concept, and leaves in its wake a revolutionized worldview" about the nature of man and the universe.[18] Specifically, Dennett and others interpret Darwinism to mean that all life can be understood entirely in natural and material terms. Man is nothing more than matter in motion. The soul? A product of fantasy. The afterlife? A myth. Human purpose? An illusion.

Leading biologists spell out some of the implications. As Darwin has shown how life is "the result of a natural process," Francisco Ayala writes, we are "without any need to resort to a Creator."[19] In an essay on evolution and its implications, William Provine writes, "Modern science directly implies that there are no inherent moral or ethical laws, no absolute guiding principles for human society.... We must conclude that when we die, we die, and that is the end of us."[20]

Many scientific atheists portray man as simply a carbon-based machine, a purely material object whose belief in immaterial things is a kind of epiphenomenon or illusion. Biologist Francis Crick, who helped to discover the structure of DNA, writes that all biology is reducible to the laws of physics and chemistry. Life is the product of the same mechanical operations as the inanimate matter in nature. Consciousness is "no more than the behavior of a vast assembly of nerve cells and their associated molecules."[21] Biologist E. O. Wilson writes that the hidden operations of our mental activity give us "the illusion of free will."[22]

For centuries, cognitive scientist Steven Pinker points out, religion has taught men to believe in an immortal soul that inhabits our bodies, a kind of "ghost in the machine." But modern science has, in Pinker's view, destroyed that belief. "The mind is the physiological activity of the brain" and "the brain, like other organs, is shaped by the genes" and those have been "shaped by natural selection and other evolutionary processes." Therefore the mind is nothing more than "an entity in the physical world, part of a causal chain of physical events." When the brain decays through aging or disease, the mind disappears. As for the soul? Pinker ringingly declares that "the ghost in the machine has been exorcised."[23]

This scientific atheism has its roots in the Enlightenment. Leading thinkers of the Enlightenment, like Voltaire, were anti-clerical and anti-religious rather than atheist. Denis Diderot and Baron d'Holbach did, however, introduce a full-fledged atheism to the educated population of Europe. These thinkers viewed science as a privileged form of knowledge based on reason and criticism and testing, and viewed religious doctrine as a form of ignorance rooted in myth, coercion, and fear. As Voltaire put it, "There are no sects in geometry."[24] That's because there are methods of verification that enable all scientifically minded people to agree on the facts.

Modern doctrines of materialism and naturalism, which hold that matter is the only reality and that there are no supernatural influences in nature, have their foundation in the atheistic wing of the Enlightenment. Modern atheists have employed these ideas to formulate their influential theories. Marx, for instance, portrayed religion as the "opiate of the masses," a drug that dulls the mind, preventing it from comprehending the scientific forces acting upon history. Freud, in his 1927 book *The Future of an Illusion*, termed belief in God a comforting illusion invented by human beings to avoid facing the reality of death. When Richard Dawkins states in *The God Delusion* that he holds his beliefs "not because of reading a holy book but because I have studied the evidence," he is placing himself squarely in this tradition of the skeptical Enlightenment.[25]

The Enlightenment critique of religion was not merely an intellectual critique but also a moral critique. This is the case with the atheism of today, which involves a moral denunciation of God's role in the world as well as a condemnation of the evil influence of religion throughout history. Christopher Hitchens writes glibly of the "moral superiority of atheism."[26] The leading figure of this type of atheism was philosopher Friedrich Nietzsche. Nietzsche accepted Darwin's theory of evolution as true, but he detested Darwinism for what he took to be its exaltation of a certain brutish type that survived in nature through raw force. Nietzsche's atheism is of a very different pedigree than Dawkins's. Nietzsche would have taken Dawkins's breed of Darwinism as the mark of a particularly low and unimaginative human type, widely found in England. Nietzsche too was interested in survival of the fittest, but to him this meant the cultural survival of great and noble and artistically imaginative forms of humanity. Nietzsche termed his superior type of human being the *übermensch*, or "over-man."

Nietzsche hated religion, and most of all he hated Christianity. For him, Christianity represented hostility to life, a seething hatred of existence dressed up as faith in another life. Nietzsche also viewed Christianity as a foe of nature, depriving the greater man of his instinctive and rightful desire to subdue and crush the inferior man. In Nietzsche's view Christianity invented morality as a device to keep the strong men of the world in check and to con them into sharing the fruits of their genius with lesser men. Christianity, in short, was a "slave morality" designed for losers, which for Nietzsche explained its immense popularity. Nietzsche's aristocratic atheism has few open advocates today, but many themes from his polemic against Christianity remain influential.

One such theme is that the God of Christianity is an autocrat. Nietzsche's objection was not to His tyranny, but to the fact that He represented the wrong kind of tyranny. Nietzsche condemned the Christian God for humbling the great and exalting the lowly. Modern atheists like Christopher Hitchens also castigate the Christian God for his "desert morality." Slavery and patriarchy are usually mentioned in the indictment, but the real objection is to the moral severity of Christian ethics, which imposes strict commandments and forecasts hell for those who fail to abide by them. Hitchens charges that "the religious impulse lies close to the authoritarian, if not the totalitarian personality," and he especially faults religion for "sexual repression."[27] In this line of thinking, God is condemned in the name of freedom, especially the moral freedom for human beings to evaluate for themselves what is right and what is wrong.

A second major theme of atheist discourse is the historical crimes of religion. The Crusades, the Inquisition, the religious wars, and the witch trials all feature prominently in this moral indictment. "In the so-called ages of faith," Bertrand Russell writes in *Why I Am Not a Christian*, "there was every kind of cruelty practiced upon all sorts of people in the name of religion."[28] In recent years, with the rise of Islamic radicalism and terrorism, atheists commonly invoke bin Laden and his murderous co-conspirators to show that religion in general is a motivating force for violence and oppression. Columnist Wendy Kaminer described the September 11 attacks as a "faith-based initiative."[29] The War on Terror is commonly portrayed as a clash of competing extremisms, with Christian extremists on the one side and Muslim extremists on the other. Sam Harris frets that "we are, even now, killing ourselves over ancient literature."[30]

For atheists, the solution is to weaken the power of religion world-wide and to drive religion from the public sphere so that it can no longer influence public policy. A secular world, in this view, would be a safer and more peaceful world. Philosopher Richard Rorty pro-claimed religious belief "politically dangerous" and declared atheism the only practical basis for a "pluralistic, democratic society."[31] These ideas resonate quite broadly in Western culture today.

One may think that atheism—based as it is on a rejection or nega-tion of God—would be devoid of a philosophy or worldview of its own. Historically it would be virtually impossible to outline anything resembling an atheist doctrine. Today, however, there are common themes that taken together amount to a kind of atheist ideology. We hear hints of this ideology when Dawkins writes of "the feeling of awed wonder that science can give us" as "one of the highest experi-ences of which the human psyche is capable."[32] There is almost a reli-gious sensibility here, but it is framed in secular terms. Consider Carl Sagan's self-proclaimed manifesto, "Better by far to embrace the hard truth than a reassuring fable."[33] This is a statement not of fact but of ethics, a dedication to manly honesty over wishful fantasy, an affirmation of what one ought to believe and on what basis. Strange though it may seem, the best way to understand this ideology is to consult the most villainous character in the Christian story.

The Christian villain, Satan, has now become the atheist hero. Consider Milton's *Paradise Lost*. There Satan is portrayed as a lonely, intrepid figure, deprived of cosmic hope, abandoned to his own wits, navigating his way through the heavens, pitting himself against the unknown, refusing to accept the tyrannical sovereignty of God, rebelling against divine decree, and determined to build out of his own resources a rival empire devoted to happiness in the here and now. "What though the field be lost, all is not lost, the unconquerable will, and study of revenge, immortal hate, and courage never to submit or yield." This is the independence to which contemporary atheists aspire. As Rorty put it, "It is a matter of forgetting about eternity."[34] E. O. Wilson writes, "We can be proud as a species because, having discovered that we are alone, we owe the gods very little."[35]

Modern atheists view themselves as brave pioneers, facing the truths of man's lowly origins and the fact of death with heroic acceptance. They profess to be guided not by blind faith but by the bright (though not infallible) flame of reason. They derive their morality not from external commandments but from an inwardly generated calculus of costs and benefits. Setting aside hopes for eternity, they are dedicated to the welfare of mankind. Science is their watchword, and its practical achievements are the only "miracles" they are willing to countenance. It is an impressive vision, and in the rest of this book I will examine it carefully to see how much sense it makes of our world and whether it can enrich our lives.

CHAPTER FOUR

MISEDUCATING THE YOUNG: SAVING CHILDREN FROM THEIR PARENTS

"Isn't it always a form of child abuse to label children as possessors of beliefs that they are too young to have thought about?"[1]

—Richard Dawkins, *The God Delusion*

IT SEEMS THAT ATHEISTS are not content with committing cultural suicide—they want to take your children with them. The atheist strategy can be described in this way: let the religious people breed them, and we will educate them to despise their parents' beliefs. So the secularization of the minds of our young people is not, as many think, the inevitable consequence of learning and maturing. Rather, it is to a large degree orchestrated by teachers and professors to promote anti-religious agendas.

Consider a timely example of how this works. In recent years some parents and school boards have asked that public schools teach alternatives to Darwinian evolution. These efforts sparked a powerful outcry from the scientific and non-believing community. Defenders of evolution accuse the offending parents and school boards of retarding the acquisition of scientific knowledge in the name of religion. The *Economist* editorialized that "Darwinism has enemies mostly because it is not compatible with a literal interpretation of the book of Genesis."[2]

This may be so, but doesn't Darwinism have friends and support-
ers mostly for the same reason? Consider the alternative: the Darwinists are merely standing up for science. But surveys show that the vast
majority of young people in America today are scientifically illiterate,
widely ignorant of *all* aspects of science.[3] How many high school grad-
uates could tell you the meaning of Einstein's famous equation? Lots
of young people don't have a clue about photosynthesis or Boyle's Law.
So why isn't there a political movement to fight for the teaching of
photosynthesis? Why isn't the ACLU filing lawsuits on behalf of
Boyle's Law?

The answer is clear. For the defenders of Darwinism, no less than
for its critics, religion is the issue. Just as some people oppose the theory of evolution because they believe it to be anti-religious, many others support it for the very same reason. This is why we have Darwinism
but not Keplerism; we encounter Darwinists but no one describes
himself as an Einsteinian. Darwinism has become an ideology.

The well-organized movement to promote Darwinism and exclude
alternatives is part of a larger educational project in today's public
schools. I'll let the champions of this project describe it in their own
words. "Faith is one of the world's great evils, comparable to the small-
pox virus but harder to eradicate," writes Richard Dawkins. "Religion
is capable of driving people to such dangerous folly that faith seems to
me to qualify as a kind of mental illness." While Dawkins recognizes
that many people believe that God is speaking to them or that He
answers prayers, he points out that "many inhabitants of lunatic asy-
lums have an unshakeable inner faith that they are Napoleon...but
this is no reason for the rest of us to believe them."[4]

Columnist Christopher Hitchens, an ardent Darwinist, writes,
"How can we ever know how many children had their psychological
and physical lives irreparably maimed by the compulsory inculcation
of faith?" Religion, he charges, has "always hoped to practice upon the
unformed and undefended minds of the young." He wistfully concludes, "If religious instruction were not allowed until the child had
attained the age of reason, we would be living in a quite different
world."[5]

If religion is so bad, what should be done about it? It should be eradicated. According to Sam Harris, belief in Christianity is like belief in slavery. "I would be the first to admit that the prospects for eradicating religion in our time do not seem good. Still the same could have been said about efforts to abolish slavery at the end of the eighteenth century."[6]

But how should religion be eliminated? Our atheist educators have a short answer: through the power of science. "I personally feel that the teaching of modern science is corrosive of religious belief, and I'm all for that," says physicist Steven Weinberg. If scientists can destroy the influence of religion on young people, "then I think it may be the most important contribution that we can make."[7]

One way in which science can undermine the plausibility of religion, according to biologist E. O. Wilson, is by showing that the mind itself is the product of evolution and that free moral choice is an illusion. "If religion … can be systematically analyzed and explained as a product of the brain's evolution, its power as an external source of morality will be gone forever."[8]

By abolishing all transcendent or supernatural truths, science can establish itself as the only source of truth, our only access to reality. The objective of science education, according to biologist Richard Lewontin, "is not to provide the public with knowledge of how far it is to the nearest star and what genes are made of." Rather, "the problem is to get them to reject irrational and supernatural explanations of the world, the demons that exist only in their imaginations, and to accept a social and intellectual apparatus, science, as the only begetter of truth."[9]

What, then, happens to religion? Philosopher Daniel Dennett suggests that "our religious traditions should certainly be preserved, as should the languages, the art, the costumes, the rituals, the monuments. Zoos are now more or less seen as second-class havens for endangered species, but at least they are havens, and what they preserve is irreplaceable."[10]

How is all this to be achieved? The answer is simple: through indoctrination in the schools. Richard Dawkins has recently issued a set of DVDs called *Growing Up in the Universe*, based on his Royal

Institution Christmas Lectures for children. The lectures promote Dawkins's secular and naturalistic philosophy of life.

Daniel Dennett urges that the schools teach religion as a purely natural phenomenon. By this he means that religion should be taught as if it were untrue. Dennett argues that religion is like sports or cancer, "a human phenomenon composed of events, organisms, objects, structures, patterns."[11] By studying religion on the premise that there is no supernatural truth underlying it, Dennett argues that young people will come to accept religion as a social creation pointing to nothing higher than human hopes and aspirations.

As for atheism, Sam Harris argues that it should be taught as a mere extension of science and logic. "Atheism is not a philosophy. It is not even a view of the world. It is simply an admission of the obvious....Atheism is nothing more than the noises reasonable people make in the presence of unjustified religious beliefs."[12]

Consider a practical example of how this works. In his famous PBS program *Cosmos*, astronomer Carl Sagan developed the trademark slogan "The cosmos is all there is or ever was or ever will be." Sagan's implication was clear: the natural is all that exists, and there is simply no supernatural. This was presented not as a metaphysical claim but as the authoritative finding of science.

The effect of all this indoctrination, leading advocates of atheism argue, is not that religion will disappear but that it will cease to matter. Writer Jonathan Rauch calls this "apatheism," which he defines as "a disinclination to care all that much about one's own religion, and an even stronger disinclination to care about other people's." Rauch argues that even many self-proclaimed Christians today are really apatheists. "It is not a lapse," he contends. "It is an achievement."[13] Rauch hopes to see our whole culture become this way.

If the supernatural ceases to become a subject of devotion, what happens to the religious impulse? Some educators argue that children should be taught to have reverence for science, which can replace religion as the object of human veneration. "We should let the success of the religious formula guide us," urged Carolyn Porco, a research scientist at the Space Science Institute in Colorado, at a 2006 conference on science and religion. "Let's teach our children from a very young age about the story of the universe and its incredible richness and beauty. It is already so much more glorious and awesome—and even comforting—than anything offered by any scripture or God concept I know."[14]

Of course, parents—especially Christian parents—might want to say something about all this. That's why the atheist educators are now raising the question of whether parents should have control over what their children learn. Dawkins asks, "How much do we regard children as being the property of their parents? It's one thing to say people should be free to believe whatever they like, but should they be free to impose their beliefs on their children? Is there something to be said for society stepping in? What about bringing up children to believe manifest falsehoods? Isn't it always a form of child abuse to label children as possessors of beliefs that they are too young to have thought out?"[15]

Dennett remarks that "some children are raised in such an ideological prison that they willingly become their own jailers...forbidding themselves any contact with the liberating ideas that might well change their minds." The fault, he adds, lies with the parents who raised them. "Parents don't literally own their children the way slaveowners once owned slaves, but are, rather, their stewards and guardians and ought to be held accountable by outsiders for their guardianship, which does imply that outsiders have a right to interfere."[16]

Psychologist Nicholas Humphrey argued in a recent lecture that just as Amnesty International works to liberate political prisoners around the world, secular teachers and professors should work to free children from the damaging influence of their parents' religious instruction. "Parents, correspondingly, have no god-given license to enculturate their children in whatever ways they personally choose: no right to limit the horizons of their children's knowledge, to bring them up in an atmosphere of dogma and superstition, or to insist they follow the straight and narrow paths of their own faith."[17]

Philosopher Richard Rorty argued that secular professors in the universities ought "to arrange things so that students who enter as bigoted, homophobic religious fundamentalists will leave college with views more like our own." Rorty noted that students are fortunate to find themselves "under the benevolent *Herrschaft* of people like me, and to have escaped the grip of their frightening, vicious, dangerous parents." Indeed, parents who send their children to college should recognize that as professors "we are going to go right on trying to discredit you in the eyes of your children, trying to strip your fundamentalist religious community of dignity, trying to make your views seem silly rather than discussable."[18]

This is how many secular teachers treat the traditional beliefs of students. The strategy is not to argue with religious views or to prove them wrong. Rather, it is to subject them to such scorn that they are pushed outside the bounds of acceptable debate. This strategy is effective because young people who go to good colleges are extremely eager to learn what it means to be an educated Harvard man or Stanford woman. Consequently their teachers can very easily steer them to think a certain way merely by making that point of view seem fashionable and enlightened. Similarly, teachers can pressure students to abandon what their parents taught them simply by labeling those positions simplistic and unsophisticated.

A second strategy commonly used to promote atheism on campus utilizes the vehicle of adolescent sexuality. "Against the power of religion," one champion of agnosticism told me, "we employ an equal if not greater power—the power of the hormones." Atheism is promoted as a means for young people to liberate themselves from moral constraint and indulge their appetites. Religion, in this framework, is portrayed as a form of sexual repression.

The story of how young people move from a childhood of innocence and piety to a questioning, sexually liberated, and finally cynical adolescence is now a familiar one in Western culture. While this is often represented as a form of enlightenment or liberation, it also represents an ideologically motivated attack on religion and traditional morality. Religion and morality are either excluded from consideration or treated with presumptive disdain. Biologist Kenneth Miller, who has testified in favor of evolution in court trials, admits that "a presumption of atheism or agnosticism is universal in academic life....The conventions of academic life, almost universally, revolve around the assumption that religious belief is something that people grow out of as they become educated."[19]

Children spend the majority of their waking hours in school. Parents invest a good portion of their life savings in college education to entrust their offspring to people who are supposed to educate them. Isn't it wonderful that educators have figured out a way to make parents the instruments of their own undoing? Isn't it brilliant that they have persuaded Christian moms and dads to finance the destruction of their own beliefs and values? Who said atheists weren't clever?

PART II

CHRISTIANITY AND THE WEST

CHAPTER FIVE

RENDER UNTO CAESAR: THE SPIRITUAL BASIS OF LIMITED GOVERNMENT

"Christianity and nothing else is the ultimate foundation of liberty, conscience, human rights and democracy, the benchmarks of Western civilization. We continue to nourish ourselves from this source."[1]

—Jürgen Habermas, "A Time of Transition"

THE EFFORT TO TEACH OUR CHILDREN hostility to religion, and specifically to Christianity, is especially strange considering that Western civilization was built by Christianity. The problem is not that our young people know too much about Christianity, but that they know too little. In America we do not have the problem of the Muslim *madrassas*, where only the Koran is studied. Rather, we live in a religiously illiterate society in which the Bible is rarely taught. Consequently many people in America and the West cannot name five of the Ten Commandments or recognize Genesis as the first book of the Bible. There's no point in even asking about the meaning of the Trinity. One in ten Americans apparently believes that Joan of Arc was Noah's wife.[2] Ignorance of this kind has made many Westerners aliens in their own civilization, as they no longer know the literature, history, and philosophy that made the West the civilization it is today.

There is also a second type of person, in a way more dangerous than the first, that I seem to run into more often. This is the person who thinks he knows the foundations of Western civilization but doesn't. Such people are usually the products of self-education, or cursory reading, or tidbits they have picked up over the years. They have not read Edward Gibbon, but they have somehow absorbed his anti-Christian prejudice. Thus they confidently assert that Greece and Rome represented the high point of ancient civilization. The classical world, they sigh, was then destroyed by Christian barbarians who plunged the world into the Dark Ages. Fortunately, they go on, civilization was saved by the Renaissance, which was a return to classical learning. Then came the Enlightenment, which opened our eyes to the wonders of modern science, the market system of creating wealth, and modern democracy.

Even the names—"Middle Ages," "Dark Ages"—guide such a person in his prejudices. Terms like "Renaissance" and "Enlightenment" are uncritically interpreted as literal descriptions of the spirit of the age. We should remember that the people who lived during the Renaissance did not consider themselves Renaissance figures. The term is a nineteenth-century one that has been retroactively applied.

To the two groups I have mentioned—the ignorant and the half-educated—we must add a third: those who know the West has Christian roots but want to leave them behind. When the drafters of the European Union's constitution excluded any mention of Christianity from their account of Europe's identity, they did so because they wanted to emphasize the degree to which Europe had broken with its Christian past. As George Weigel writes in *The Cube and the Cathedral*, secularism is now one of the banners behind which modern European man wishes to march.[3]

In this and the next few chapters I intend to dispel some modern prejudices and show that Christianity is the very root and foundation of Western civilization. I will also argue that Christianity is responsible for many of the values and institutions secular people cherish most. Consequently, the desire to repudiate the Christian roots of Western culture is not only an act of historical denial, but it also imperils the secular person's moral priorities.

Let us begin by examining how Christianity formed a kind of foundation pillar of Western civilization. Actually, the West was built on two pillars: Athens and Jerusalem. By Athens I mean classical civilization, the civilization of Greece and pre-Christian Rome. By Jerusalem I mean Judaism and Christianity. Of these two, Jerusalem is more important. The Athens we know and love is not Athens as it really was, but rather Athens as seen through the eyes of Jerusalem.

"It was at Rome, on the fifteenth of October 1764, as I sat musing amidst the ruins of the Capitol, while the barefooted friars were singing vespers in the Temple of Jupiter, that the idea of writing the decline and fall of the city first started to my mind."[4] In *The Decline and Fall of the Roman Empire* Edward Gibbon accuses Christianity of replacing classical civilization with religious barbarism. But classical civilization was itself infused with barbarous practices like pederasty and slavery. Moreover, the Christians didn't destroy Roman civilization. The Huns, Goths, Vandals, and Visigoths did. These barbarians, who came from the pagan regions of northern Europe, smashed a Rome that had long been weak and decadent. Fortunately, they eventually converted to Christianity. Over time it was Christianity that civilized these rude people. Christianity didn't overrun and lay waste to a learned civilization. Christianity found a continent that had already been laid waste. The "Dark Ages" were the consequence of Roman decadence and barbarian pillage.

Slowly and surely, Christianity took this backward continent and gave it learning and order, stability and dignity. The monks copied and studied the manuscripts that preserved the learning of late antiquity. Christopher Dawson shows in *Religion and the Rise of Western Culture* how the monasteries became the locus of productivity and learning throughout Europe.[5] Where there was once wasteland they produced hamlets, then towns, and eventually commonwealths and cities. Through the years the savage barbarian warrior became a chivalric Christian knight, and new ideals of civility and manners and romance were formed that shape our society to this day. If Christianity had not been born out of Judaism, Rodney Stark writes, we might still be living in the Dark Ages.[6]

Christianity is responsible for the way our society is organized and for the way we currently live. So extensive is the Christian contribution to our laws, our economics, our politics, our arts, our calendar, our holidays, and our moral and cultural priorities that historian J. M. Roberts writes in *The Triumph of the West*, "We could none of us today be what we are if a handful of Jews nearly two thousand years ago had not believed that they had known a great teacher, seen him crucified, dead, and buried, and then rise again."[7]

Consider the case of Western art. Have you been to the Sistine Chapel? Seen Michelangelo's *Pietà*? Leonardo da Vinci's *Last Supper*? Perhaps you are familiar with Rembrandt's *Christ at Emmaus* or his *Simeon in the Temple*. In Venice you can see the spectacular murals of Veronese, Titian, and Tintoretto. What would Western music be without Handel's *Messiah*, Mozart's *Requiem*, and the soaring compositions of Johann Sebastian Bach? If you haven't, set foot in one of the great Gothic cathedrals and see what those anonymous builders did with stone and glass. Is Western literature even conceivable without Dante, Milton, and Shakespeare? My point is not only that all these great artists were Christian. Rather, it is that their great works would not have been produced without Christianity. Would they have produced other great works? We don't know. What we do know is that their Christianity gives their genius its distinctive expression. Nowhere has human aspiration reached so high or more deeply touched the heart and spirit than in the works of Christian art, architecture, literature, and music.

Even artists who rejected Christianity produced work that was unmistakably shaped by Christian themes. Goethe was a kind of pantheist who viewed God as identical with nature, yet his *Faust* is a profound allegory derived from Christian themes of suffering, transformation, and redemption. Our greatest skeptics and atheists—such as Voltaire and Nietzsche—are inconceivable without Christianity (Voltaire was educated by Jesuits; Nietzsche's father was a pastor and the title of his autobiography, *Ecce Homo*, is a reference to what Pilate said of Christ: "behold the man.")

Today, however, we read books like Susan Jacoby's *Freethinkers* that celebrate the fact that we live in a mostly secular society. We find Sam Harris insisting that it is quite possible to develop morality independent of the Christian religion or religion in general.[8] We read Theodore Schick Jr. in *Free Inquiry* insisting that philosophers as different as John Stuart Mill and John Rawls "have demonstrated that it is possible to have a universal morality without God."[9]

There is a profound confusion here. We get a hint of this when we realize that the term "secular" is itself a Christian term.[10] In Catholicism a priest who joins a contemplative community and retreats from the world is considered to have joined a "religious" order, while a priest who lives in a parish among ordinary people is considered a "secular" priest. As we will see, secularism is itself an invention of Christianity. Secular values too are the product of Christianity, even if they have been severed from their original source.

If all this is true, then our cultural prejudice against acknowledging and teaching the role of Christianity is wrong. Believer and nonbeliever alike should respect Christianity as the movement that created our civilization. We should cherish our Christian inheritance not as an heirloom but as a living presence in our society, and we should worry about what will happen to our civilization if Christianity disappears from the West and establishes itself in non-Western cultures.

Rather than attempt a catalogue of Christianity's achievements, I am going to trace its influence in the West by focusing on three central ideas. The first one is explored in this chapter and the next two in subsequent chapters. First I consider the idea of separating or disentangling the spheres of religion and government. Although this notion has become highly confused and distorted in our time, the original concept is a very good one. We think of separation of religion and government as an American idea or an Enlightenment idea, but long before that it was a Christian idea. Christ seems to be the first one who thought of it. As we read in Matthew 22:21, Christ said, "Render unto Caesar that which is Caesar's, and to God that which is God's."

To see the radicalism of Christ's idea, I turn to the ancient Roman writer Celsus, who in the second century AD wrote an influential attack on Christianity.[11] Celsus's work was lost, but the church father Origen published a refutation, *Contra Celsum*, that helps us reconstruct his argument. Celsus basically accused the Christians of being atheists.

He was serious. For the ancient Greeks and Romans, the gods a man should worship were the gods of the state. Each community had its own deities—it was a polytheistic age—and patriotism demanded that a good Athenian make sacrifices to the Athenian gods and a good Roman pay homage to the gods of Rome. The Christians, Celsus fumed, refused to worship the Roman gods. They did not acknowledge the Roman emperor as a god, even though Caesar had been elevated by the Roman Senate to divine status. Instead the Christians insisted on worshipping an alien god, putting their allegiance to him above their allegiance to the state. What blasphemy! What treason!

I am not suggesting that the ancient Greeks and Romans were especially "religious." Gibbon reports that philosophers and public officials held very different attitudes toward the gods than did ordinary citizens: "The various modes of worship which prevailed in the Roman world were all considered by the people as equally true, by the philosopher as equally false, and by the magistrate as equally useful."[12] Even so, religious identity in the ancient world was indissolubly tied up with your tribe and community. You could not be a good Dinka and not worship the Dinka deities, whether rock or stone or sun. Nor could you be a good Roman and not exalt the Roman deities, whether Apollo, Bacchus, or Jupiter.

Christianity introduced not only a new religion but a new conception of religion. So successful was this cultural revolution in the West that today the ancient paganism lives only in the names of planets and for those who follow astrology charts. Atheists do not bother to disbelieve in Baal or Zeus and invoke them only to make all religion sound silly. The atheists' real target is the God of monotheism, usually the Christian God.

Christianity was not the first monotheistic religion. There are hints of monotheism in the ancient Persian religion of Zoroastrianism. The Persians were henotheists: they seemed to have believed in many gods but with one supreme god who was more powerful than the others. The Jews were the first monotheists, embracing the concept of one God who embodies all the virtues and who is the sole deity deserving of human worship and obedience: "thou shall have no other gods before me." In the Old Testament we can witness the battle raging between Jewish monotheism and the still powerful temptation to polytheism, represented in the episodes of the Israelites who worshipped Baal, Moloch, and the golden calf.

Christianity adopted Jewish monotheism and gave it both a universal and an individualistic interpretation. There was no individualism in the Judaism of ancient Israel; the Jews worshipped Yahweh as a tribe and as a community. Individual Jews were not given a choice in this matter. When Moses came down from the mountain and saw the Israelites worshipping the golden calf, he did not think they were simply choosing to follow a different faith. "Freedom of religion" was not an issue here. Moses's approach was a bit more severe: either embrace Yahweh, the monotheistic God of the Jews, or be killed. Some people imprudently chose to stick with calf worship, and Moses ordered them massacred.

The God of the Old Testament is a universal deity, yet at the same time He seems to be a tribal God. He relates mainly to His chosen people, and the enemies of Israel become His enemies. Egyptians and Romans are not expected to follow Him, even though the Jews regarded Him as superior to the Egyptian and Roman deities. No wonder Jewish monotheism was generally unthreatening to Roman paganism. Indeed, the Romans simply integrated the Jews' god into their pantheon. Judaism was a legal religion in the Roman empire; Christianity was not, at least not until the conversion of the emperor Constantine. The reason for the prohibition and persecution of Christianity was that Christians claimed one God not only for themselves but for the whole world.

Implicit in Christian monotheism was a critique of pagan polytheism. According to the Christians, the Greek and Roman gods were human inventions. Look at the gods of Homer. Each of them seems to embody a human quality: Aphrodite is the goddess of sexual desire, Ares is the god of conflict, and so on. The gods have the same petty vanities and jealousies as their human counterparts. Their virtues are human virtues writ large. As classical scholar Mary Lefkowitz puts it, "The life of the gods is a highly idealized form of what human life would be if mortals were deathless, ageless, and strong."[13] Ironically, this criticism of invented deities, which seemed valid when it was launched against ancient polytheism, is today leveled against Christianity. As Daniel Dennett and Richard Dawkins would have it, the Christians too have invented their God. But the Christian God is not like human beings at all. He is outside space and time. He does not have a body. He is a purely spiritual being. He can be comprehended only dimly by humans, who resort to anthropomorphic images and analogies.

Monotheism was a hugely important idea, but as we can see from how Islam is interpreted today, it is an idea that can be used to justify theocracy. By theocracy I don't mean rule by priests. I simply mean that God's law extends to every sphere of society and human life. This was the case with ancient Israel, and this has indeed been the Islamic tradition. The prophet Muhammad was in his own day both a prophet and a Caesar who integrated the domains of church and state. Following his example, the rulers of the various Islamic empires, from the Umayyad to the Ottoman, saw themselves as Allah's vicegerents on earth, charged with establishing Islamic rule worldwide and bringing all the lands they could under the authority of Islamic holy law. Historian Bernard Lewis writes that "in classical Arabic and in the other classical languages of Islam, there are no pairs of terms corresponding to 'lay' and 'ecclesiastical,' 'spiritual' and 'temporal,' 'secular' and 'religious,' because these pairs of words express a Christian dichotomy that has no equivalent in the world of Islam."[14] Even today in strict Islamic states like Saudi Arabia we see that Islamic law (or *sharia*) extends beyond religious law to commercial law, civil law, and family law.

Not so in Christianity. The reason is spelled out in the church father Augustine's great work *The City of God*. Augustine argued that during our time here on earth, the Christian inhabits two realms, the earthly city and the heavenly city. (Only at the end of time will God integrate these two into a single majestic kingdom ruled by Him.) To each of these realms the Christian citizen has duties, but they are not the same duties. Yes, the Christian gives his ultimate devotion to the heavenly city. But some remarkable conclusions follow from this primary allegiance. It means that the earthly city need not concern itself with the question of man's final or ultimate destiny. It also implies that the claims of the earthly city are limited, that there is a sanctuary of conscience inside every person that is protected from political control, and that kings and emperors, however grand, cannot usurp authority that rightly belongs only to God.

Here we see, in its embryo, the idea of limited government. This idea derives from the Christian notion that the ruler's realm is circumscribed and there are limits beyond which he simply must not go. Those limits were originally set by the church competing with the state and establishing its own realm of authority. Let's remember that the church was not simply a spiritual institution—holding services and administering sacraments—but was also a temporal power, possessing huge properties and in some cases even commanding armies. For centuries the kings and the church fought over how to draw the legitimate dividing line between the two spheres, but both sides agreed that there was a dividing line. The kings have now been replaced by democratic government, but the Christian idea persists that there are some things even elected governments cannot control.

Our modern idea of limited government takes the Christian notion of space that is off-limits to state control and extends it to the whole private sphere. This is the crucial distinction we see in the West between the spheres of state and society. "Society" encompasses the whole range of people's activities, while "state" refers to the specific and delineated sphere of government authority. The state may trespass on territory that has been previously reserved for the private realm, but it cannot take over the private realm altogether. Even an elected government cannot arbitrarily force you to move out of your house or turn over your property to the government. Even a government with 99 percent of the popular support does not have the right to tell the remaining 1 percent of the people that they must all become Republicans, vegetarians, or even Christians. If it does, then legitimate government has become tyrannical government, and the people have the right to oppose and replace it.

If the domain of government is to be limited in this manner, so is the domain of the church. As Christ put it, "My kingdom is not of this world." God has chosen to exercise a limited domain over earthly rule, not because He is limited, but because He has turned over part of His kingdom to humans for earthly supervision. This Christian notion would have been utterly unintelligible not only to an ancient Athenian or Roman but also to an ancient Israelite. In the new framework of Christian universalism, the same God rules over the whole universe, but each country retains its own laws and its own culture.

God's domain is the domain of the church. Here God's laws are supreme, although there must necessarily be earthly interpreters to understand and apply them. Even so, there is also a secular realm that operates outside church control. Here we see how the idea of the "secular" is itself a creation of Christianity.

It is important to recognize that separation of the realms of state and church has operated since the beginning of Christianity. It is not an invention of modernity, although in modern times this separation has been given a new and to some degree perverse form. In the Rome of the Caesars, the rulers were the emperors, and the Christian church was a persecuted minority entirely distinct from the empire. Once Christianity became the official religion of the Roman empire in the late fourth century, the two realms were somewhat integrated. But even so, the church administered the sacraments and the emperor ratified and enforced the laws. Even during the tragic time of the Spanish Inquisition, if you committed heresy you were tried by the church, while if you committed murder you were tried by the state. So church and state have functioned as distinct if overlapping jurisdictions throughout Western history. Thus it is today that we in the West stare in horrified incomprehension when an Islamic government proposes to execute a woman for refusing to wear religiously mandated garb or a man for daring to convert to Christianity.

But this sort of thing did happen in the West, and unfortunately its perpetrators were Christians. Starting from the time that Christianity became the official religion of the Roman empire, all the way through the Spanish Inquisition, and even as late as the seventeenth century,

Christian rulers with the support of the churches used the power of the state to enforce religious orthodoxy. Both Catholics and Protestants were guilty of this. The Puritans who fled England for America were not escaping Catholic persecution but Anglican persecution. Their objective in finding a land of their own was not to allow everyone to have religious freedom but rather to impose their version of orthodoxy on the whole society.

In some ways the motives of all these Christian autocrats are understandable. Sometimes they were even well meaning. Believing themselves to be in possession of the sole truth, they were driven by their concern for others to go to extreme lengths, even to the extent of using imprisonment and coercion to win the unpersuaded over to their side. In doing this, however, they confused Christianity and Christendom. They were trying to establish the heavenly city here on earth, which is precisely what Augustine warned against, as did Christ before him. Moreover, they were violating the principle established by God in the Garden of Eden. God could have easily compelled Adam and Eve to conform to His command, but He didn't. Even though He knew they were making a bad decision, He respected their freedom enough to allow them to make it. The freedom to do good implies the freedom to reject the good.

Early modern thinkers like John Locke were sincere and practical Christians. They invented the concept of religious tolerance not because they wanted to dilute or eliminate the influence of Christianity, but because they saw that the wrong kind of Christianity had come to dominate Western society. Men like Locke were rightly disgusted with some of the abuses that had occurred in the name of Christianity. So for this Christian problem—division and conflict—they developed a Christian solution: religious freedom. This idea developed in stages, the first one of which was religious tolerance. The word *tolerance* is derived from the Latin word meaning "to bear," and to tolerate means "to put up with." Tolerance contains the seeds of disagreement and even contempt: I tolerate you because although I believe you are wrong, I will endure you and let you persist in your erroneous ways. Locke's tolerance extended to most Protestant denominations but not to Catholics.

The American founders extended the concept of tolerance and produced a bold new idea unknown in Europe: freedom of conscience. The Peace of Westphalia (1648) had established the practical rule that the religion of the ruler became the religion of the state. But this was simply a compromise solution aimed at stopping the interminable quarrels among the various Christian sects. In some ways "separation of church and state" also developed in America for the same reason. There were several denominations that wanted to dominate and impose their orthodoxy into law, but none were strong enough to do so everywhere. The Puritans predominated in Massachusetts, but the Anglicans were the majority in Virginia, and there was a substantial Catholic stronghold in Maryland. Ultimately the various groups agreed to leave the central government out of religion. The Establishment Clause of the First Amendment was passed largely with Christian support. As John Courtney Murray once said, it was not an article of faith, but an article of peace.

The genius of the American founders was to go beyond tolerance to insist that the central government stay completely out of the business of theology. Despite its novelty, this idea was a profoundly Christian one. The majority of the founders were devout Christians, although some of them, like Thomas Jefferson, were Deists. But whether they knew it or not, they were following Christ's rule to keep the domains of Caesar and God separate. The founders in no way denied the Christian foundations of the American experiment. Even Jefferson, perhaps the least religious of them, argued that religious faith was the very foundation for liberty itself: "And can the liberties of a nation be thought secure when we have removed their only firm basis, a conviction in the minds of the people that these liberties are the gift of God? That they are not to be violated but with His wrath?"[15] After the Revolutionary War, the founders continued to hold public days of prayer, to appoint chaplains for Congress and the armed forces, and to promote religious values through the schools in the Northwest Territory.

Nor did they seek to insulate the central government from the province of morality. No "wall of separation" was intended here. On the contrary, the founders believed that morality was indispensable for their new form of government to succeed. Most of them shared George Washington's view as expressed in his farewell address: "Let us with caution indulge the supposition that morality can be maintained without religion." John Adams went even further: "Our Constitution was made only for a moral and religious people. It is wholly inadequate to the government of any other."[16] At the same time, the founders recognized that theological differences were the province of revelation and thus not a fit subject for democratic debate. They sought to exclude differences in theology precisely so that there could be reasoned disagreements over issues of morality, and so that the laws could reflect the prevailing moral sentiment of the people.

Visiting America in the early nineteenth century, Alexis de Tocqueville observed that "the sects that exist in the United States are innumerable," and yet "all sects preach the same moral law in the name of God."[17] Tocqueville termed religion the first of America's political institutions, which means that it had a profoundly public effect in regulating morality and mores throughout the society. And he saw Christianity as countering the powerful human instincts of selfishness and ambition by holding out an ideal of charity and devotion to the welfare of others.

Today courts wrongly interpret separation of church and state to mean that religion has no place in the public arena, or that morality derived from religion should not be permitted to shape our laws. Somehow freedom for religious expression has become freedom from religious expression. Secularists want to empty the public square of religion and religious-based morality so they can monopolize the shared space of society with their own views. In the process they have made religious believers into second-class citizens. This is a profound distortion of a noble idea that is also a Christian idea. The separation of the realms should not be a weapon against Christianity; rather, it is a device supplied by Christianity to promote social peace, religious freedom, and a moral community. If we recovered the concept in its true sense, our society would be much better off.

CHAPTER SIX

THE EVIL THAT I WOULD NOT: CHRISTIANITY AND HUMAN FALLIBILITY

"For the good that I would, I do not, but the evil which I would not, that I do."

—St. Paul, Letter to the Romans, 7:19

I **NOW WANT TO EXAMINE** a second major feature of Western civilization that derives from Christianity. This is what philosopher Charles Taylor calls the "affirmation of ordinary life." It is the simple idea that ordinary people are fallible, and yet these fallible people matter. In this view, society should organize itself in order to meet their everyday concerns, which are elevated into a kind of spiritual framework. The nuclear family, the idea of limited government, the Western concept of the rule of law, and our culture's high emphasis on the relief of suffering all derive from this basic Christian understanding of the dignity of fallible human beings.

Let's explore this by considering two related themes that arise from the same Christian root. The first is Paul's statement above. Here Paul in a single phrase repudiates an entire tradition of classical philosophy founded in Plato. For Plato, the problem of evil is a problem of knowledge. People do wrong because they do not know what is right. If they knew what was right, obviously, they would do it. But Paul denies that this is so. His claim is that even though he knows something is wrong, he still does it. Why? Because the human will is corrupt. The problem of evil is not a problem of knowledge but a problem of will.

I also want to focus on the Christian exaltation of the low man, the common man, and the underdog. These groups were not favorites in the world of ancient Greece and Rome. Homer ignored them in his epics, concentrating entirely on life among the ruling class. Lesser men appeared, if at all, as servants. Aristotle too had a job for low men: slavery. Aristotle argued that with low men in servitude, superior men would have leisure to think and participate in the governance of the community. Aristotle cherished the "great-souled man" who was proud, honorable, aristocratic, rich, and (if this were not enough) spoke in a low and measured voice.

But Jesus was not such a man. Jesus was born in a stable and lived most of his life as a carpenter's apprentice. He usually traveled by foot and occasionally by donkey. As literary scholar Erich Auerbach writes, "Christ had not come as a hero and king but as a human being of the lowest social station. His first disciples were fishermen and artisans. He moved in the everyday milieu of the humble folk. He talked with publicans and fallen women, the poor and the sick and children."[1] It may be added that Christ came to a bad end on the cross, hanged like a common criminal and flanked by two actual criminals.

Yet Auerbach notes that despite Christ's undistinguished origins, simple life, and lowly death, everything he did was imbued with the highest and deepest dignity. The fishermen the Greeks would have treated as figures of low comedy were in the Christian narrative embroiled in events of the greatest importance for human salvation. The sublimity of Christ and his disciples completely reversed the whole classical ideal. Suddenly aristocratic pride came to be seen as something preening and ridiculous. Christ produced the transformation of values in which the last became first, and values once scorned came to represent the loftiest human ideals.

Charles Taylor notes that as a consequence of Christianity, new values entered the world. For the first time people began to view society not from the perspective of the haughty aristocrat but from that of the ordinary man. This meant that institutions should not focus on giving the rich and high-born new ways to pass their free time; rather, they should emphasize how to give the common man a rich and meaningful life. Moreover, economic and political institutions should be designed in such a way that sinful impulses—what Kant termed the crooked timber of humanity—could nevertheless be channeled to produce humane and socially beneficial outcomes.

One area where we see this change is in the social importance that is given to marriage and the family. Today we take it for granted that the family is the institution entrusted with the care and rearing of children. Incredible as it seems, the family was not very important in ancient Greece. In fact, Plato proposed an abolition of marriage and the family, envisioning a republic in which the whole business of procreation and care of the young was turned over to the state.

Aristotle, more prudent than Plato, recognized the need for the family. At the same time he described the family as an infrastructural good. Of course family is necessary for the good life, just as it is necessary to eat and sleep every day, but for Aristotle a life devoted to the family is neither a complete nor a noble one. The Greeks viewed the family almost exclusively as a vehicle for procreation. Most marriages were arranged, and the husband and wife were not even expected to be friends. Indeed Aristotle thought women largely incapable of friendship, and he certainly did not expect wives to relate to husbands on a plane of equality. The unimportance of romantic love in ancient Greece can be verified from the fact that of the three dozen or so Greek tragedies we possess, not a single one has love as its subject.[2]

Eros was a powerful force in ancient Greece, but it expressed itself mainly in homosexuality. The practice was common in Athens, but the Spartans were especially notorious for it, encouraging it in their gymnasiums and using homosexual attachments to build solidarity among soldiers in war.[3] Historian Michael Grant writes that Eros was also the basis for the practice of pederasty. He notes that sexual relations between men and boys were "far more favored than homosexual relations between men of the same age."[4] The ancients also erected an educational philosophy based on pederasty. As historian K. J. Dover describes it, the man always played the active role and the boy the passive role. The whole project was conceived of in terms of an exchange; the young boy agreed to sexual relations with an older man and in return he received knowledge and tutoring.[5]

We may worry that the younger boy might be exploited in such a relationship, but the ancients did not. Many of them felt like Pausanius in Plato's *Symposium*, who frets that pederastic arrangements are unfair to older men because young boys, once they have received their mentoring, casually move on to other partners their own age. We can admire the great achievements of classical philosophy, drama, and statesmanship, but when we rhapsodize about "the glory that was Greece and the grandeur that was Rome," we should keep in mind that the sexual practices of these civilizations live on today only in prisons and in the ideology of marginal groups like the North American Man/Boy Love Association.

In the Christian era, pederasty and homosexuality were considered sinful. Instead, Christianity exalted heterosexual monogamous love, which would provide the basis for a lasting and exclusive relationship between husband and wife, oriented toward the rearing of children. We take the family so much for granted—it remains such a powerful ideal in our society, even when actual family life falls short—that we forget the central premises on which it is based. Those premises were introduced by Christianity into a society to which they were completely foreign.

First, Christianity made family life important in a way that it wasn't before. No longer was family life subordinated to the life of the city, as both Plato and Aristotle thought it should be. Indeed, the family came to be viewed for the first time as the central venue for the fulfillment of life's main satisfactions. This change began with the elevation of marriage to a Catholic sacrament, giving it religious prestige beyond its social necessity. An equally significant shift was wrought by the Protestant Reformation. The Catholics had revered the celibate priest, modeled on a celibate Christ, as the exemplar of virtue, but Martin Luther disputed this interpretation, insisting that the ordinary Chris-

tian who took a wife and had children by her was also fulfilling a vocation or "calling" from God.

Second, Christendom developed a new notion of romantic love,
which is today one of the most powerful forces in our civilization.
While marriages continued to be arranged in the West, especially
among the more affluent classes, a new and alternative ideal emerged
in the Middle Ages. This was the idea of love as the basis for getting
married and also for preserving a happy marriage. I am not saying that
people did not "fall in love" before the medieval era. But "falling in
love" was previously considered a mild form of insanity, something
that could not and should not be the basis for enduring marriage. The
medieval Christians began to understand marriage between a man
and a woman as a relationship similar to that between Christ and the
church. The Bible portrays this relationship as intimate and passion-
ate, certainly not as some kind of a mercenary bargain. So Christians
began to view marriage as an intimate companionship enlivened by
romantic passion.

Romantic love is today considered to be little more than a feeling,
but that is a pale shadow of its original meaning. It was meant to be
the culmination of a quest, to represent the high ideals of personal
sacrifice and service to another. The concept was at first confined to
the aristocracy, but it soon spread throughout society. The first hint of
romance as an important social value emerges in the courtly love
poems that fused erotic and spiritual love and focused it on a beautiful woman, usually unavailable. This literature of longing implanted
the dream of romance in the mind of the West.

Third, Christianity introduced consent on the part of both the man
and the woman as the prerequisite for marriage. Again, we take this
for granted today, but you have only to go to Asia, Africa, or the Middle East to see that people there are frequently pressured into marriage against their will. I grew up in India, where marriages even today
are often arranged by the parents. The West, however, since the early
days of Christianity, has had marriage by choice and mutual agreement. This did not originate because of "equality between the sexes."

Rather, it originated because of the Christian idea that each of us has a partner God made for us. Romantic feeling was perceived as an activity of the soul guiding us to find this lifelong companion. As fallible human beings we can be wrong about a lot of things, but we cannot be wrong in how we feel about someone else. At the same time, Christianity emphasized that free choice should also be binding choice. As we have consented to marry without coercion, we should live up to our vows and preserve marriage as a lifelong commitment.

The Christian priority of extending respect to ordinary persons—while taking into account human failings and shortcomings—can also be seen in the emergence in the West of new political institutions. These political institutions existed nowhere else in the world, and they did not exist in ancient Greece or Rome. Something changed within the West to give rise to them. That something is Christianity. Consider our modern concept of "rule of law." In his book *Law and Revolution* Harold Berman argues that the modern Western legal system is "a secular residue of religious attitudes and assumptions which historically first found expression in the liturgy and rituals and doctrine of the church, and thereafter in the institutions and concepts and values of the law."[6] This is quite true, but there is much more to the story.

Plato says that the highest form of law is discretion. This sounds strange to us, but it is correct. The best form of justice is to give each person his appropriate deserts. In the family, for example, you don't treat your children exactly alike by establishing "laws" for them. You adapt your instructions and requirements in keeping with their individual personalities and situations. So it is, according to Plato, in politics. The best form of government is a benign monarchy or aristocracy ruling by discretion and dispensing justice in each individual case.

But we don't do this in the West. Consider the simple example of speeding on the highway. We establish fixed rules—such as a limit of seventy miles per hour—and then enforce them. This does not, however, seem like the best system. Some people drive safely at eighty miles per hour. Others are a danger to themselves and others at fifty miles per hour. So why don't we let the authorities decide each case on its merits? The simple answer is that we don't trust the policeman to do this. We consider him a fallible human being who may be guided by prejudices. We would rather all live under a uniform rule that applies to everyone.

This idea that power should be very cautiously entrusted to fallible human beings became the basis of the modern liberal idea of laws. The people choose the government, but the American system imposes "separation of powers" and "checks and balances" as internal mechanisms to keep the government honest and accountable. The American founders devised a structure that deliberately fostered economic and political rivalries in order to prevent unhealthy concentrations of power. In *The Federalist* 51, Publius describes such measures collectively as "supplying, by opposite and rival interests, the defect of better motives." Moreover, in the West we insist that the people who make the laws be subject to them and to the recall of the people on whose behalf they are making them.

Christianity enhanced the notion of political and social accountability by providing a new model: that of servant leadership. In ancient Greece and Rome no one would have dreamed of considering political leaders anyone's servants. The job of the leader was to lead. But Christ invented the notion that the way to lead is by serving the needs of others, especially those who are the most needy. Mark 10:43 quotes Christ: "Whoever wants to become great among you must be your servant... for even the Son of Man did not come to be served but to serve." And in Luke 22:27 we hear Jesus say, "Who is greater, the one who is at the table or the one who serves? Is it not the one who is at the table? But I am among you as one who serves." In the new Christian framework, leaders are judged by how well they respond to the concerns and welfare of the people. Over time, people once known as "followers" or "subjects" become "customers" and "constituents." As a consequence of the new ideal, the job of the political leader, the merchant, and the priest becomes serving the people by attending to their political, material, and spiritual needs.

The system of modern capitalism arose in the West. To some it is surprising that capitalism developed so easily in conjunction with a

Christian ethic. But capitalism satisfied the Christian demand for an institution that channels selfish human desire toward the betterment of society. Some critics accuse capitalism of being a selfish system, but the selfishness is not in capitalism—it is in human nature. As Adam Smith put it in *The Wealth of Nations*, the desire to better our condition "comes with us from the womb, and never leaves us till we go into the grave."[7] Selfishness, like lust, is part of the human condition. It is hopeless to try to root it out, although some zealous utopians have certainly tried. Over the centuries, Christianity came up with a much better solution. The Bible is often quoted to say that money is the root of all evil, but the relevant passage actually says that "love of money is the root of all evil." This is a condemnation of a certain human attitude to wealth, not a condemnation of either wealth or commerce.

The effect of capitalism is to steer human selfishness so that, through the invisible hand of competition, the energies of the capitalist produce the abundance from which the whole society benefits. Moreover, capitalism encourages entrepreneurs to act with consideration for others even when their ultimate motive is to benefit themselves. So while profit remains the final goal, entrepreneurs spend the better part of each day figuring out how better to serve the needs of their actual and potential customers. They are operationally, if not intentionally, altruistic. As Samuel Johnson once put it, "There are few ways in which a man can be more innocently occupied than in getting money."[8] One may say that capitalism civilizes greed in much the same way that marriage civilizes lust. Both institutions seek to domesticate wayward or fallen human impulses in socially beneficial ways.

And when it came to capitalism, Christian civilization created the basic rules of modern economics. In the Middle Ages, Rodney Stark shows, people first realized that prices should be determined through supply and demand. In the past, prices had been set by law or custom. But Albertus Magnus, a thirteenth-century Dominican friar, explained that prices reflect "what goods are worth according to the estimate of the market at the time of sale."[9] And this of course is what we believe now.

In his classic work *The Protestant Ethic and the Spirit of Capitalism*, Max Weber traces the rise of capitalism to a spirit of calling or election introduced by Calvinism. But as in the case of market pricing, the core elements of capitalism all predate the Reformation. Some scholars have traced them to the monastery communities of the early Christian era, in which bands of monks demonstrated a strong work ethic, practiced specialization and division of labor, borrowed and lent money, and engaged in long-distance trade involving a fairly wide range of foodstuffs and other commodities. Stark argues that "all of the essential features of capitalism ... are to be found from the twelfth century on, in the city republicans of Italy, such as Venice, Genoa, or Florence."[10]

My goal here is not to settle the issue of which Christians got there first. Capitalism grew in stages, each of them influenced by a different aspect of Christianity. When Francis Bacon and Descartes called for a technological system in which man becomes a master and possessor of nature, they made their case in terms of recovering the prosperity of the Garden of Eden. When Locke defended property rights and the cultivation of nature by practical intelligence, he saw humans as imitating the creativity of God and thus acting "in His image." Even today we think of work in terms of a "calling" or "vocation." In this Christian understanding, we receive our talents from God and use them to benefit ourselves, our families, and our society in line with God's will for us.

With capitalism and prosperity came something new: the idea of progress. This is the notion that things are getting better and will continue to get better in the future. History is seen as moving in a straight line, onward and upward. In the past century the idea of progress has seen some strange and ugly manifestations, such as "survival of the fittest" and the supposedly inevitable "revolution of the proletariat." Tarred as it now may be, the ideal of progress endures, and in some form it is now part of the furniture of the modern mind. Most of us, for example, fully expect our children to live better than we do. We also tend to believe in moral progress. The abolition of slavery, for instance, seems to be an irreversible moral achievement. We hope that future generations will be more morally enlightened than we are, take better care of the planet, and stop killing the unborn.

This is not, however, the way the Greeks and the Romans—or the Chinese and the Indians—saw it. Most cultures believe that history moves in cycles. Things go up and then they go down. An alternative view is that things were better in the past, and the further you go back, the better they get. As J. B. Bury shows in *The Idea of Progress*, Westerners think of progress not in terms of cycles but arrows. Our modern ideas of "development" and "progress" are a secular version of the Christian idea of providence.[11] The Christian narrative of history guided by God from beginning to end—a story of creation, incarnation, and last judgment—is converted into a story of human advancement. Thus through human effort we fulfill a kind of spiritual mandate to continually make things better.

A final aspect of the Christian legacy of human fallibility and ordinary satisfaction should be stressed. This is our culture's powerful emphasis on compassion, on helping the needy, and on alleviating distress even in distant places. If there is a huge famine or reports of genocide in Africa, most people in other cultures are unconcerned. As the Chinese proverb has it, "the tears of strangers are only water." But here in the West we rush to help. Massive relief programs are organized. The rock singer Bono launches a campaign to raise funds. Sometimes even military intervention is considered as a last resort to stop the killing. Part of the reason why we do this is because of our Christian assumptions. Those people are human like us. They too deserve a chance to be happy. If we are more fortunate than they are, we should do what we can to improve their lot.

The ancient Greeks and Romans did not believe this. They held a view quite commonly held in other cultures today: yes, that is a problem, but it's not our problem. Aristotle, who came closest to the Christian view, wrote that the great-souled man does in fact assist those in need. But in Aristotle's view he does so out of liberality, in order to demonstrate his magnanimity and even superiority to those beneath him. Ancient aristocrats funded baths, statues, and parks that prominently bore their names and testified to their family nobility and personal greatness. This is not the Christian view, which demands that we act out of compassion, which means "suffering with others." We help starving infants in Haiti and Rwanda not because we are better than they are but because we are, humanly speaking, all in the same boat. Christian humility is the very opposite of classical magnanimity.

It was the Christian spirit of mutual love and communal charity that astonished and impressed the pagans and the Romans. The emperor Julian, seeking to revive paganism in the fourth century, professed admiration for the way in which Christians looked after their poor, their widows and orphans, and their sick and dying. However paradoxical it seems, people who believed most strongly in the next world did the most to improve the situation of people living in this one.

In the West, the Christians built the first hospitals. At first they were just for Christians, but eventually they were open to everyone, even Muslims who had entered Christian lands with the aim of conquest. Today many hospitals have Christian names—St. John's Hospital, St. Luke's Hospital, Methodist Hospital, Lutheran Hospital, and so on—and relief organizations like the Salvation Army and the Red Cross bear, sometimes lightly, the Christian influence that brought them into existence. So do organizations like the Rotary Club, the Kiwanis Club, and the YMCA, all of which are involved in civic and charitable activities.

Christianity has also produced many great figures, from Vincent de Paul to Mother Teresa, who have dedicated their lives to the service of the poor and sick. Nowhere else—not in other religions nor in secular society—do we find anything like this. One does not have to be a Christian or even a believer to acknowledge that this Western faith has done an incredible amount to improve human life and reduce human suffering.

CHAPTER SEVEN

CREATED EQUAL: THE ORIGIN OF HUMAN DIGNITY

*"Another Christian concept, no less crazy: the concept of
equality of souls before God. This concept furnishes the
prototype of all theories of equal rights."*[1]

—Friedrich Nietzsche, *The Will to Power*

IN PREVIOUS CHAPTERS I have discussed how Christianity is responsible for important ideas and institutions that remain central to our lives. Of course, not all these Christian innovations are valued by everyone. Some may object to Christianity precisely because it has given us capitalism or the traditional two-parent family. But here I discuss a Christian legacy that virtually all secular people cherish: the equality of human beings. This Christian idea was the propelling force behind the campaign to end slavery, the movement for democracy and popular self-government, and also the successful attempt to articulate an international doctrine of human rights. My celebration of Christianity's role in shaping these great social changes comes with a sober corollary: if the West gives up Christianity, it will also endanger the egalitarian values that Christianity brought into the world. The end of Christianity also means the systematic erosion of values like equal dignity and equal rights that both religious and secular people cherish.

When Thomas Jefferson wrote in the Declaration of Independence that "all men are created equal" he claimed that this was a self-evident truth. But it is not evident at all. Indeed, most cultures throughout history, and even today, reject the proposition. On the face of it, there is something absurd in claiming human equality when all around us we see dramatic evidence of inequality. People are unequal in height, in weight, in strength, in stamina, in intelligence, in perseverance, in truthfulness, and in about every other quality. Inequality seems to be the self-evident reality of human nature.

Jefferson knew this. He was asserting human equality of a special kind. Human beings, he was claiming, are moral equals. They don't all behave equally well, but each of their lives has a moral worth no greater and no less than that of any other. According to this strange doctrine, the worth of a street sweeper on the streets of Philadelphia was as great as that of Jefferson himself. Each life is valuable, and no one's life is more valuable than another's.

The preciousness and equal worth of every human life is a Christian idea. Christians have always believed that God places infinite value on each human life He creates and that He loves each person equally. In Christianity you are not saved through your family or tribe or city. Salvation is an individual matter. Moreover, God has a "vocation" or calling for every one of us, a divine plan for each of our lives. During the Reformation, Martin Luther stressed the individualism of the Christian journey. Not only are we each judged as individuals at the end of our lives, but throughout our lives we also relate to God as individuals. Even religious truth is not just handed down to us but is worked out through individual study and prayer. These ideas have had momentous consequences.

We are often told that modern notions of democracy and equal rights trace back to ancient Greece and Rome, but the American founders were not so sure. Alexander Hamilton wrote that it would be "as ridiculous to seek for models in the simple ages of Greece and Rome as it would be to go in quest of them among the Hottentots and Laplanders."[2] In *The Federalist* we read that the classical idea of liberty decreed "to the same citizens the hemlock on one day and statues on the next.... Had every Athenian citizen been a Socrates, every Athenian assembly would still have been a mob."[3] While the ancients had direct democracy, supported by large-scale slavery, we have something quite different: representative democracy, with full citizenship and the franchise extended in principle to all. Let us try to understand how this great change came about.

In ancient Greece and Rome, human life had very little value. The Spartans left weak children to die on the hillside. Infanticide was common, as it is even today in many parts of the world. Fathers who wanted sons had few qualms about drowning their newborn daughters. Human beings were routinely bludgeoned to death or mauled by wild animals in the Roman gladiatorial arena. The greatest of the classical thinkers, from Seneca to Cicero, saw nothing wrong with these practices. Christianity banned them, and Christianity introduced the moral horror we now feel when we hear about them.

Women had a very low status in ancient Greece and Rome, as they do today in many cultures, notably in the Muslim world. Aristotle expressed the view of many when he wrote that in men reason finds its full expression. In children, according to Aristotle, reason is present but undeveloped. In women, he wrote, reason is present but unused. Such views are common in patriarchal cultures. And, of course, they were prevalent in the Jewish society in which Jesus lived. But Jesus broke the taboos. From society's point of view and even from some of his male disciples' point of view, Jesus scandalously permitted women (even of low social status) to travel with him and be part of his circle of friends and confidantes.

Christianity did not contest patriarchy, but it elevated the status of women within it. The Christian prohibition of adultery—a sin viewed as equally serious for men and women—placed a moral leash on the universal double standard that commanded women to behave themselves while men did as they pleased. Unlike Judaism and Islam, which treated men and women unequally in matters of divorce, Christian rules on the matter were identical for women and men. So dignified was the position of the woman in Christian marriage that women predominated in the early Christian church, as in some respects they do even today. As a result, the Romans scorned Christianity as a religion for women.

We encounter in the Middle Ages a new development—the idea of courtly love. For the first time in history, the woman who was a knight's object of love was raised to a high status. In fact, her status was higher than that of the man pursuing her. Women were increasingly viewed as companions whose conversation was prized and whose company was avidly sought. Chaucer's independent-minded Wife of Bath is inconceivable in any other culture of the fourteenth century. Courtesy, the habit of treating women with deference, was invented by Christianity. Social life involving men and women began in the late Middle Ages. Moreover, as family life came to be seen as the central locus of human happiness, the role of the mother in preserving the household and ensuring the education of children became more highly valued.

Against these advances, atheists counter with another issue: slavery. "Consult the Bible," Sam Harris writes in *Letter to a Christian Nation*, "and you will discover that the creator of the universe clearly expects us to keep slaves."[4] Steven Weinberg notes that "Christianity...lived comfortably with slavery for many centuries."[5] These atheist writers are certainly not the first to fault Christianity for its alleged approval of slavery. But slavery pre-dated Christianity by centuries and even millennia. It was widely practiced in the ancient world, from China and India to Greece and Rome, and most cultures regarded it as an indispensable institution, like the family. For centuries, slavery needed no defenders because it had no critics.[6] Even the Bible does not condemn slavery outright, with Paul in Ephesians 6:5 and other passages urging slaves to obey their masters and urging masters to be kind to their slaves.

Even so, Christianity from its very beginning discouraged the enslavement of fellow Christians. We read in one of Paul's letters that Paul himself interceded with a master named Philemon on behalf of his runaway slave. "Perhaps this is the reason he was separated from you for a while," Paul says, "so that you might have him back forever, no longer as a slave, but as a brother." How can a slave also be a brother? Christians began to see the situation as untenable. Slavery, the foundation of Greek and Roman civilization, withered throughout medieval Christendom and was replaced by serfdom, which was not the same thing. While slaves were "human tools," serfs were human beings who had rights of marriage, contract, and property ownership that were legally enforceable. Medieval feudalism was based on a hierarchical system of reciprocal rights and duties between lords and serfs.

Moreover, Christians were the first group in history to start an antislavery movement. The movement started in late eighteenth-century Britain, spread to other parts of Europe, and then gathered force in the United States, where the economy of the South was heavily dependent on slave labor. In England, William Wilberforce spearheaded a campaign that began with almost no support and was driven entirely by his Christian convictions—a story effectively told in the film *Amazing Grace*. Eventually Wilberforce triumphed, and in 1833 slavery was outlawed in Britain. Pressed by religious groups at home, England then took the lead in repressing the slave trade abroad.

The debate over slavery in America was essentially a religious debate. All sides claimed the authority of the Bible and the Christian tradition. The slaveowners invoked Paul and pointed to the fact that slavery had existed in Christian countries since the time of Christ. Free blacks who agitated for the emancipation of their fellow blacks invoked the narrative of liberation in the Book of Exodus, in which Moses led the captive Israelites to freedom: "Go down, Moses, way down to Egypt land and tell old Pharaoh, let my people go."

It's not entirely surprising that a group would oppose slavery for its own members. Throughout history people have opposed slavery for themselves but have been perfectly happy to enslave others. Indeed there were several thousand black slaveowners in the American South. What is remarkable is for a group to oppose slavery in principle. The Quakers were the first people in America to oppose slavery, and the evangelical Christians soon followed. These groups gave a political interpretation to the biblical notion that all are equal in the eyes of God. From this spiritual truth they derived a political proposition:

because human beings are equal in God's sight, no man has the right to rule another without his consent. This doctrine is the moral root of both abolitionism and democracy.

The great sweep of American history can be understood as a struggle to realize this Christian principle. For those who think of American history in largely secular terms, it may come as news that the greatest events of our history were preceded by massive religious revivals. The First Great Awakening, a Christian revival that swept the country in the mid-eighteenth century, created the moral foundation of the American Revolution. The revival emphasized that people should not merely know about Christ, but that they should also develop a personal relationship with him. The leading figures here were George Whitefield, the Oxford-educated clergyman who led the newly founded Methodist movement, and Jonathan Edwards, the Yale-educated Congregationalist minister who was president of Princeton University. Historian Paul Johnson writes that the American Revolution is "inconceivable...without this religious background."[7]

The First Great Awakening supplied the assumptions that Jefferson and the American founders relied on during the Revolution. Remember that Jefferson asserted his proposition of human equality as both "self-evident" and a gift from God: we are endowed by our Creator with inalienable rights. Indeed there is no other source for such rights. But how could Jefferson have so confidently claimed that his doctrine was "self-evident"? He could because he knew that most Americans already believed it. He was, as he put it, merely giving expression to something already in the American grain. John Adams later wrote, "What do we mean by the American Revolution? The war? That was no part of the Revolution; it was only an effect and consequence of it. The Revolution was in the minds of the people...a change in their religious sentiments."[8] Those religious sentiments were forged in the fiery sermons of the First Great Awakening.

The Second Great Awakening, which started in the early nineteenth century and coursed through New England and New York and then through the interior of the country, left in its wake the temperance movement, the movement for women's suffrage, and most important, the abolitionist movement. It was the religious fervor of men like Charles Finney, the Presbyterian lawyer who became president of Oberlin College, that drove the abolitionist cause and set off the chain of events that produced the Civil War, the end of slavery, and America's "new birth of freedom."

Fast-forward now to the twentieth century, and consider the Reverend Martin Luther King's famous claim that he was submitting a promissory note to America and demanding that it be cashed.[9] A Southern segregationist might have asked, "What promissory note? What's he talking about?" King was appealing to the Declaration of Independence. Remarkably, this champion of freedom was resting his case on a proclamation issued two hundred years earlier by a Southern slaveowner! Yet King, in doing this, was appealing to the principle he and Jefferson shared, the principle of the equal worth of all human beings. Both men, the twentieth-century pastor and the eighteenth-century planter, were reflecting the long reach of Christianity.

Or recall King's famous dream of a day when human beings will be judged "not by the color of their skin but by the content of their character."[10] Many writers—and I am one of them—have in the past interpreted this as a call to meritocracy: we should be judged on our intelligence and talents. But this is not what King says. He hopes for a day when we will be judged by the content of our *character*. Not intellectual achievement, but ethical achievement, seems to be what matters to King. Here, too, we see the strong echo of Christianity, which assesses human worth not through power and possessions but through the virtue that we integrate into our daily lives.

As Nietzsche suggested in the quotation at the beginning of this chapter, the Christian doctrine of human equality is also the basis for all modern doctrines of human rights. True, today we have a host of rights doctrines from secular sources, but you only have to prod them a little to uncover their Christian foundations. Philosopher John Rawls argued that we should devise a social system by imagining ourselves behind a "veil of ignorance" in which we have no idea whether we will be smart or stupid, rich or poor.[11] An interesting concept, but why should we place ourselves behind this hypothetical veil? Why should we negate our current privileges?

Rawls's ideas make no sense without a prior belief that each life counts as much as every other. He takes for granted the notion that we have no automatic right to our privileges, that we are not intrinsically better than others, and that we might just as easily have occupied another's position in life, and they ours. Or consider Jeremy Bentham's famous utilitarian theory of rights. Bentham is committed to seeking "the greatest good of the greatest number," but that's because he presumes that every human being has a right to happiness, and that the happiness of each person counts equally.[12] Otherwise my happiness alone could count more than that of everyone else put together, and Bentham's utilitarianism is in ruins.

Today there are two types of human rights doctrines: moral doctrines and legal doctrines. Both are products of Christianity. Consider a moral theory like the doctrine of "just war." It specifies the ethical conditions under which wars should operate. The radicalism of this concept can be gleaned by reading the Melian Dialogue in Thucydides' *Peloponnesian War*. There the Athenians dismiss the moral arguments of the Melians with the cool insistence that in war "the strong do what they have the power to do and the weak accept what they have to accept." When the Melians eventually surrendered, the Athenians killed all the men and sold the women and children into slavery. This has been, as the Athenian ambassador told the Melians, the way of the world. If it horrifies us today, that's because our social conscience has been molded by Christianity.

The Christian "just war" principles say that even in war you should not deliberately kill civilians. It also says that war should be waged defensively: you should not attack first. A just war should be a last resort, undertaken only when other measures have been exhausted and when there is a reasonable chance of success. Moreover, retaliation should be proportionate to the original offense. If someone raids your tribe and kills ten people, you are not justified in raiding theirs and killing ten thousand people. The "just war" doctrine is a product of Christianity. It has its roots in Augustine, was developed further by

Aquinas, and was then given its first modern expression by such thinkers as Francisco de Vitoria, Hugo Grotius, and John Locke.

Now consider a legal doctrine such as the Declaration of Human Rights in the charter of the United Nations. This declaration, adopted on December 10, 1948, by the UN General Assembly without a single dissenting vote, asserts rights common to all people on earth.[13] Everyone has the right to freedom of conscience. The will of the people shall be the basis of the authority of governments. Each adult person has the right to marry a person of the opposite sex through free consent and to form a family. No one shall be subjected to torture or inhuman punishment. All are equal before the law. Everyone has the right to life, liberty, and property. There shall be equal pay for equal work. These ringing declarations are a standing indictment to tyranny and oppression everywhere.

Yet the universalism of this declaration is based on the particular teachings of Christianity. The rights in the declaration are based on the premise that all human lives have worth and that all lives count equally; this is not the teaching of all the world's cultures and religions. Even so, it is entirely appropriate that a doctrine Christian in origin should be universal in application because Christianity articulates its message in universal terms. As Paul writes in Galatians 3:28, "There is neither Jew nor Greek, there is neither slave nor free, there is neither male nor female, for you are all one in Christ Jesus." Here Christian individualism is combined with Christian universalism, and the two together are responsible for one of the great political miracles of our day, a global agreement on rights held to be inviolable.

Finally, Christianity is also responsible for our modern concept of individual freedom. There are hints of this concept both in the classical world and in the world of the ancient Hebrews. One finds, in such figures as Socrates and the Hebrew prophets, notable individuals who have the courage to stand up and question even the highest expressions of power. But while these cultures produced great individuals, as other cultures often do even today, none of them cultivated an appreciation for individuality. It is significant that Socrates and the Hebrew prophets all came to a bad end. They were anomalies in their societies, and their societies moved swiftly to get rid of them.

In his essay "The Liberty of the Ancients Compared with That of the Moderns," Benjamin Constant made a vital distinction between how the Greeks and Romans viewed freedom and how we in the modern era view freedom.[14] Constant noted that for the ancients, freedom was the right to participate in the making of laws. Greek democracy was direct democracy in which every citizen could show up in the *agora*, debate issues of taxes and war, and then vote on what action the *polis* should take. This was real power, the power of the citizen to shape the decisions of the society. Thus the Greeks exercised their freedom through active involvement in the political and civic life of the city. There was no other kind of freedom.

Indeed Constant reports that in most ancient cities "all private actions were submitted to a severe surveillance. No importance was given to individual independence, neither in relation to opinions, nor to labor, nor, above all, to religion. The right to choose one's own religious affiliation, a right which we regard as one of the most precious, would have seemed to the ancients a crime and a sacrilege. There was hardly anything the laws did not regulate. Thus among the ancients the individual, almost always sovereign in public affairs, was a slave in all his private relations."

Of all ancient cities, only Athens permitted its citizens reasonable latitude in personal decisions. Athens could do this, Constant argues, largely because of its massive slave population. That the Athenians did not entirely depart from the practices of other ancient cities can be seen in their practice of ostracism, which Constant notes "rested upon the assumption that society had complete authority over its members." Each year, citizens would be asked to write on a ballot the names of persons who, in their view, deserved to be expelled from the city. Anyone who received more than a specified number of votes would be sent away, sometimes for a period of ten years, sometimes permanently.[15] When the Athenians inexplicably voted to ostracize one of their best men, Aristides the Just, the only explanation given by the citizens was that they were tired of hearing him called "the Just."

All this, Constant writes, is entirely different from the modern idea of freedom. We don't have direct democracy; we have representative democracy. Yes, we vote on election day, but even then our vote is one of a hundred million, so each citizen's influence on the overall outcome is very slight. This is not the kind of freedom most important to us today. Rather, the modern idea of freedom means the right to express your opinion, the right to choose a career, the right to buy and sell property, the right to travel where you want, the right to your own personal space, and the right to live your own life. This is the freedom we are ready to fight for, and we become indignant when it is challenged or taken away.

This modern concept of freedom we inherit from Christianity. Christianity emphasizes the fact that we are moral agents. God has freely created us in His own image, and He has given us the power to take part in His sublime act of creation by being architects of our own lives. But God has also granted to other human beings the same freedom. This means that in general we should be free to live our lives without interference from others as long as we extend to others the same freedom. My freedom to swing my fist has to stop at your nose. John Stuart Mill's influential doctrine of liberty, which so many of us take for granted, is a direct inheritance from Christianity. It is no use responding that Mill was a product of the Enlightenment understanding of human freedom and equality. That notion was itself a product of Christianity. Where else do you think the Enlightenment thinkers got it?

I end this chapter with the warning I alluded to at the beginning. It's a warning that was first issued by Nietzsche. The life of the West, Nietzsche said, is based on Christianity. The values of the West are based on Christianity. Some of these values seem to have taken a life of their own, and this gives us the illusion that we can get rid of Christianity and keep the values. This, Nietzsche says, is an illusion. Our Western values are what Nietzsche terms "shadows of gods." Remove the Christian foundation, and the values must go too.

True, values like equal dignity and equal rights will persist for a period out of sheer unthinking habit. But their influence will erode.

Consider the example of secular Europe. Secularization has been occurring in Europe for well over a century, and for a while it seemed as if the decline of Christianity would have no effect on Western morality or Western social institutions. Yet if Nietzsche is right we would expect to see the decline of Christianity also result, over time, in the decline of one of the great legacies of Christianity, the nuclear family. We would expect to see high rates of divorce and births out of wedlock. And this is what we do see. Secular trends in America have produced the same results, which are not as advanced in America because Christianity has not eroded as much here as it has in Europe.

As secularism continues, Nietzsche forecasts that new values radically inconsistent with the Christian ones—the restoration of infanticide, demands for the radical redefinition of the family, the revival of eugenic theories of human superiority—will begin to emerge. These, too, are evident in our day. And they are some of the motives for attacking Christianity and insisting that its values are outmoded and should be replaced.

Unfortunately for the critics of Christianity, even values they care about will, according to Nietzsche, eventually collapse. Consider our beliefs in human equality and the value of human life. We may say we believe in human equality, but why do we hold this belief? It is the product of the Christian idea of the spiritual equality of souls. We may insist we believe that all human life has dignity and value, but this too is the outgrowth of a Christian tradition in which each person is the precious creation of God. There is no secular basis for these values, and when secular writers defend them they always employ unrecognized Christian assumptions.

In sum, the death of Christianity must also mean the gradual extinction of values such as human dignity, the right against torture, and the rights of equal treatment asserted by women, minorities, and the poor. Do we want to give these up also? If we cherish the distinctive ideals of Western civilization, and believe as I do that they have enormously benefited our civilization and the world, then whatever our religious convictions, and even if we have none, we will not rashly try to hack at the religious roots from which they spring. On the contrary, we will not hesitate to acknowledge, not only privately but also publicly, the central role that Christianity has played and still plays in the things that matter most to us.

PART III

CHRISTIANITY AND SCIENCE

CHAPTER EIGHT

CHRISTIANITY AND REASON: THE THEOLOGICAL ROOTS OF SCIENCE

"We shall first try to manifest the truth that faith professes and reason investigates, setting forth demonstrative and probable arguments, so that the truth may be confirmed and the adversary convinced."[1]

—Thomas Aquinas, *Summa Contra Gentiles*

WE HAVE SEEN IN THE previous chapters how Christianity forms the heart of Western civilization, shaping ideas and institutions that have persisted for two millennia. In the next few chapters I will examine the relationship between Christianity and science. Specifically, I will consider whether there is an inherent antagonism between the two; atheist writers often portray an ongoing war between them. The conflict, Sam Harris writes, is "zero sum."[2] E. O. Wilson proclaims it an "insoluble" enmity,[3] and the popular media breathlessly publicizes this theme of combat, as when *Time* magazine titled its cover story on November 13, 2006, "God vs. Science."[4]

Yet science as an organized, sustained enterprise arose only once in human history. And where did it arise? In Europe, in the civilization then called Christendom. Why did modern science develop here and nowhere else? In his September 12, 2006, speech in Regensburg, Germany, Pope Benedict XVI argued that it was due to Christianity's emphasis on the importance of reason. The pope argued that reason

is a central distinguishing feature of Christianity. While the Regensburg address became controversial because of the pope's remarks
about Islam, on his point about Christianity and reason he was right.
An unbiased look at the history of science shows that modern science
is an invention of medieval Christianity, and that the greatest break-
throughs in scientific reason have largely been the work of Christians.
Even atheist scientists work with Christian assumptions that, due to
their ignorance of theology and history, are invisible to them.

Before religion as we understand the term, there was animism,
which was based on the idea of an enchanted universe. Every river,
every tree, and every stone was thought to be populated by spirits. The
world was mysterious, capricious, unpredictable, and uncontrollable.
Then came the various polytheistic religions, like those of the Babylonians, the Egyptians, and the Greeks. Each of these religions posited
divine beings—sometimes immortal, sometimes not—who involved
themselves in the daily workings of nature, creating storms and earthquakes, turning humans into stags, and so on. Then appeared the
great religions of the East, Hinduism and Buddhism, followed by the
three great monotheistic religions, Judaism, Christianity, and Islam.

Of these, only one—Christianity—was from the beginning based on
reason. Judaism and Islam are primarily religions of law; there is a
divine lawgiver who issues edicts that are authoritative both for nature
and for human beings. In the case of Judaism these edicts apply mainly
to God's chosen people, the Jews. In the case of Islam they apply to
everyone. In both cases, however, the laws are divinely revealed and
humans must follow them. Both Jews and Muslims may engage in
extensive debates, but these are confined to the best way to interpret
and apply the written codes. Christianity, by contrast, is not a religion
of law but a religion of creed. Christianity has always been obsessed
with doctrine, which is thought to be a set of true beliefs about man's
relationship to God.

Philosopher Ernest Fortin writes that while the highest discipline
in Judaism and Islam is jurisprudence, the highest discipline in Christianity is theology.[5] The Christian theologian is charged with employing reason to understand the ways of God. There are no theologians in

Hinduism and Buddhism because human beings are not called to investigate God's purposes in this manner.

But what is a theologian good for? We can answer this question by looking at the church father Augustine. Augustine was faced with a deep and serious theological problem: Before today, there was yesterday, and before yesterday, there was the day before yesterday, and so on. But how can this be? Does the series of yesterdays extend infinitely into the past? If so, then how could God have created a universe that has always existed? If not, there must have been a beginning, but what had been going on before that? If the universe was created by God, then what was God doing before He created the universe?

To these questions Augustine gave an astounding answer that does not seem to have occurred to anyone before him: God created time along with the universe. In other words, "before" the universe there was no time. The universe is like a series, which may or may not extend infinitely backward and forward in time. But God stands outside the series, and this is what we mean when we say God is "eternal." Eternal does not mean "goes on forever"; it means "stands outside of time." Notice that Augustine was not engaging in vague theological speculation. He was making a radically counterintuitive claim about the nature of physical reality. Today we know from modern physics and astronomy that Augustine was correct; time is a property of our universe, and time came into existence with the universe itself. Augustine's reflections on the nature of time, which were generated entirely through theological reasoning, are some of the most penetrating insights in the history of thought.

In order to get a sense of how Christians reasoned about God, I'd like to consider two famous arguments for the existence of God and match the wits of ancient Christian thinkers against those of their modern atheist detractors. The first is Aquinas's argument based on causation. Aquinas argues that every effect requires a cause, and that nothing in the world is the cause of its own existence. Whenever you encounter A, it has to be caused by some other B. But then B has to be accounted for, so let us say it is caused by C. This tracing of causes, Aquinas says, cannot continue indefinitely, because if it did, then nothing would have come into existence. Therefore there must be an original cause responsible for the chain of causation in the first place. To this first cause we give the name God.

Leading atheists are unimpressed. "If God created the universe," Sam Harris writes, "what created God?"[6] His sentiments are echoed by several atheist writers: Richard Dawkins, Christopher Hitchens, Carl Sagan, Steven Weinberg. They raise the problem of infinite regress. Yes, there has to be a chain of causation, but why does it have to stop with God? Why can't it go on forever? Dawkins makes the further point that only a complex God could have created such a complex universe, and we cannot account for one form of unexplained complexity (the universe) by pointing to an even greater form of unexplained complexity (God). Consequently Dawkins concludes that "the theist answer has utterly failed" and he sees "no alternative but to dismiss it."[7]

The real force of Aquinas's argument, however, is not that every series must have a beginning but that every series, in order to have being or existence, must depend on something outside the series. It is no rebuttal to say that as everything must have a cause, who caused God? Aquinas's argument does not use the premise that everything needs a cause, only that everything that exists in the universe needs a cause. The movement and contingency of the world cannot be without some ultimate explanation. Since God is by definition outside the universe, He is not part of the series. Therefore the rules of the series, including the rules of causation, would not logically apply to Him.

Think of God as the author of a novel. The events in the narrative have a certain coherence and logic. Something that occurs in the beginning of the story causes a crisis for one of the characters in the middle of the story. Raskolnikov's actions in *Crime and Punishment* cause the death of the old woman. But the author is the cause of the story on an entirely different level. The rules of causation that apply within the novel do not apply to its creator. It makes sense to ask of a character that suddenly appears, "Where did he come from? How do you account for him?" It makes no sense in this context, however, to ask, "Where did this fellow Dostoevsky come from? How do you account for him?" The author is outside the narrative, and his act of creation cannot be understood as an episode within it.[8] From this discussion it should be evident that Harris and Dawkins have not even come close to answering Aquinas's argument.

Next I turn to Anselm's ontological argument for the existence of God.[9] Anselm begins whimsically with the passage from Psalm 13:1, "The fool has said in his heart that there is no God." Anselm intends to demonstrate that those who deny the existence of God are indeed fools. They are fools because once you understand the meaning of the term *God*, you are rationally compelled to assent to God's existence. Anselm is not joking about this.

Unlike the inductive argument of Aquinas, Anselm's argument is purely deductive and relies on no data from experience. Anselm defines God as "that than which no greater can be thought." Presumably, this is a reasonable and widely accepted definition. Even an atheist should have no problem with it. We all understand the idea of God to correspond to a supreme being that stretches—even transcends—the limits of our imagination. Anselm proceeds to say that as we acknowledge and understand the definition, we must have some idea of God in our mind. He doesn't mean a pictorial representation. He simply means that our minds comprehend as a logical possibility the idea of God as "that than which no greater can be thought."

But if this is true, Anselm says, then God exists. We have proved God's existence. Why? Because if "that than which no greater can be thought" exists in the mind, then it must also exist in reality. The reason is that to exist in reality is, according to Anselm, "greater" than to exist merely in the mind. What is possible and actual is obviously greater than what is merely possible. Anselm gives the example of a portrait painter whose portrait, actually painted, is the realization of an intuition or idea in his head; thus the actual painting is "greater" than the mere intuition or idea of it. In the same way, in order for "that than which no greater can be thought" to satisfy its own definition, it must exist. Otherwise it would be "that than which a greater *can* be thought." Anselm claims to have shown not only that God exists, but that He exists necessarily. If He existed only in fact and not by necessity,

He would be a great being indeed, but He would not be "that than which no greater can be thought."

I offer Anselm's proof not because it is immediately convincing—we feel sure that Anselm has drawn a theological rabbit out of a rhetorical top hat—but because it is notoriously hard to refute. Descartes and Leibniz considered the argument to be a valid one, and produced their own versions of it. Yet in his book *God Is Not Great* Christopher Hitchens seeks to expose Anselm's shortcomings. He offers the example of a child in a novel who is asked why she believes in dragons. The child replies, "If there is a word dragon, then once there must have been dragons." Clearly it is childish reasoning to infer the object from the mere idea of it. Hitchens triumphantly proclaims Anselm's argument "overthrown."[10]

Hitchens's argument was first made by a contemporary of Anselm, a monk named Gaunilo, and Gaunilo's version is much more effectively argued than Hitchens's. Gaunilo accused Anselm of making an illicit transition from the conceptual to the existential. Gaunilo's point was that just because we can imagine unreal things like unicorns, mermaids, and yellow flying dogs does not mean that any of these creatures exist. Anselm answered Gaunilo by pointing out his ontological argument does not say that everything we can imagine in our heads necessarily exists. The argument merely insists that "that than which no greater can be thought" exists and exists by necessity. In other words, Anselm is only making his claim in one particular case. It is precisely the character of "that than which no greater can be thought" to exist necessarily: there is nothing in the definition of unicorns and yellow flying dogs that confers existence on them, much less necessary existence.[11]

There have been other objections to Anselm, and I don't propose to discuss them here. My point is that theology gives evidence of a high order of reason at work, and one cannot, as many atheists do, dismiss these arguments as unreasonable even if you don't agree with them. Consider many of the famous arguments in philosophy, say, Locke's argument about private property or Wittgenstein's argument about the possibility of a private language. Whether or not we think these arguments successful, it can hardly be said that they are irrational. Rather, they represent powerful rational claims about the nature of reality.

So it is with Aquinas and Anselm. In proving God's existence they at no point appeal to supernatural revelation. Theirs are arguments based on reason alone. They were, of course, devised in a very different historical and philosophical context than the one we now inhabit, so they need to be updated to be persuasive. And when they are reformulated in modern terms, they are persuasive. I intend, as you will see, to make an argument very similar to Aquinas's in a later chapter on the origin of the universe. My point is that the kind of reasoning about God that we see in Augustine, Aquinas, and Anselm is typical of Christianity. There is very little of this in any other religion. And out of such reasoning, remarkably enough, modern science was born.

CHAPTER NINE

FROM LOGOS TO COSMOS: CHRISTIANITY AND THE INVENTION OF INVENTION

"So vast, without any question, is the divine handiwork of the Almighty Creator!"[1]

—Nicolaus Copernicus

LISTS OF THE GREAT IDEAS of modern science typically contain a major omission. On such lists we are sure to find Copernicus's heliocentric theory, Kepler's laws, Newton's laws, and Einstein's theory of relativity, yet the greatest idea of modern science is almost never included. It is such a big idea that it makes possible all the other ideas. And it is invisible to us because it is an assumption taken for granted rather than a theory that has been formulated. Oddly enough, the greatest idea of modern science is based not on reason but on faith.

Faith is not a highly acclaimed word in the scientific community. "I do not believe that the scientist can have that same certainty of faith that very deeply religious people have," writes physicist Richard Feynman in *The Meaning of It All*.[2] Astronomer Neil deGrasse Tyson complains that "the claims of religions rely on faith" and boasts that "the claims of science rely on experimental verification."[3] Feynman and Tyson seem quite unaware that at the heart of their cherished scientific enterprise is a faith-based proposition no less mysterious than any religious dogma. This is the presumption, quite impossible to prove, that the universe is rational.

Scientists today take for granted the idea that the universe operates according to laws, and that these laws are comprehensible to the human mind. Science is based on what author James Trefil calls the principle of universality: "It says that the laws of nature we discover here and now in our laboratories are true everywhere in the universe and have been in force for all time."[4] Physicist Steven Weinberg writes, "All my experience as a physicist leads me to believe that there is order in the universe.... As we have been going to higher and higher energies and as we have studied structures that are smaller and smaller, we have found that the laws, the physical principles, that describe what we learn become simpler and simpler.... The rules we have discovered become increasingly coherent and universal.... There is a simplicity, a beauty, that we are finding in the rules that govern matter that mirrors something that is built into the logical structure of the universe at a very deep level."[5]

The laws that govern the universe seem to be written in the language of mathematics. The greatest scientists have been struck by how strange this is. In his essay "The Unreasonable Effectiveness of Mathematics in the Natural Sciences," physicist Eugene Wigner confesses that the mathematical underpinning of nature "is something bordering on the mysterious and there is no rational explanation for it."[6] Feynman confesses, "Why nature is mathematical is a mystery.... The fact that there are rules at all is a kind of miracle."[7]

This astonishment springs from the recognition that the universe doesn't have to be this way. There is no special reason why the laws of nature we find on earth should also govern a star billions of light years away. It is easy to imagine a universe in which conditions change unpredictably from instant to instant, or even a universe in which things pop in and out of existence. There is no logical necessity for a universe that obeys rules, let alone one that abides by the rules of mathematics.

Yet the universe seems to be ordered. I say "seems" because there is no way to prove this is so. There are peculiar things going on in quantum physics that call into question the premise that the universe follows stable rules. Even so, scientists cling to their long-held faith in the fundamental rationality of the cosmos. Convinced in advance that rules exist, and that human reason is up to the task of uncovering those rules, scientists continue to try to find them. These articles of faith are essential for science to function. Without the "irrational" belief that we live in an ordered universe, modern science is impossible. Science also relies on the equally unsupported belief that the rationality of the universe is mirrored in the rationality of our human minds.

So where did Western man get this faith in a unified, ordered, and accessible universe? How did we go from chaos to cosmos? My answer, in a word, is Christianity.

Christianity did not invent the idea of a rational cosmos. That idea was invented by the pre-Socratics, such men as Thales, Parmenides, Heraclitus, and Pythagoras. These men had some very strange ideas, but their greatest contribution was to posit a universe that operates through discoverable rules of cause and effect. Before the pre-Socratics there were mythical cosmologies such as the Egyptian account of the sun god, Ra, who periodically traveled in his chariot across the heavens. Even the Greeks attributed storms and earthquakes to the wrath of Poseidon, god of the sea.

The pre-Socratics replaced the idea of an "enchanted universe" with that of a "disenchanted" cosmos accessible to unassisted human reason. They may not have known what caused eclipses and earthquakes, but they didn't look to Ra and Poseidon for explanations. This was a radical shift of consciousness. Unfortunately, their influence was short-lived. This is partly due to Socrates, who argued that philosophy should not bother with the regularities of nature but should instead focus on those of human nature. The pre-Socratics were also defeated by the deities of Greek paganism, who were believed to operate capriciously to fulfill their own inscrutable purposes.

Christianity reinvigorated the idea of an ordered cosmos by envisioning the universe as following laws that embody the rationality of God the creator. "In the beginning was the Word, and the Word was with God, and the Word was God." The term used here for *word* is *logos*, a Greek term meaning "thought" or "rationality." God is sacred and made the universe, and the universe operates lawfully in accordance with divine reason. At the same time Christianity held that the universe itself is not sacred. The Bible says, "God made the two great lights, the greater light to rule the day and the smaller one to rule the night." For Christians the sun is not an object of worship; it is merely a great lamp. The Christian universe is ordered and yet disenchanted. Moreover, Christianity (adopting here the legacy of Judaism) teaches that man was made in the "image" and "likeness" of God. This means that there is a spark of the divine reason in man, setting him apart from other things and giving him the special power of apprehending them. According to Christianity, human reason is derived from the divine intelligence that created the universe.

True, Christians believe in miracles, which can be seen as departures from the orderliness of nature. But miracles are notable because they are exceptional. Miracles inspire wonder because they are believed to be the product of a natural order that is, in rare cases, suspended. By contrast, Islam doesn't emphasize miracles because everything in the universe is seen as miraculous. Medieval Muslim theologian Abu Hamed al-Ghazali claimed that God intervenes at every moment to make the events in the universe happen as they do. There is no question of laws; everything is the product of ceaseless divine intrusion.[8] Historian Joseph Needham explains that despite the wealth and sophistication of China in ancient and medieval times, science never developed there because "there was no confidence that the code of nature's laws could ever be unveiled and read, because there was no assurance that a divine being, even more rational than ourselves, had ever formulated such a code capable of being read."[9] In his classic book *Science and the Modern World* Alfred North Whitehead concludes that "faith in the possibility of science ... is an unconscious derivative from medieval theology."[10]

The medieval era in Europe saw the founding of the university, which would have a crucial role in the growth of modern science. At first monks labored in monasteries, working tirelessly to retrieve the classical knowledge destroyed when the barbarians overran the Roman Empire and spread chaos throughout the continent. For several centuries monasteries were the only institutions in Europe for the acquisition, preservation, and transmission of knowledge.

Then the churches began to build schools, first at the elementary and then at the secondary level. Eventually these became more advanced until, in the twelfth century, the first universities were founded in Bologna and Paris. Oxford and Cambridge were founded in the early thirteenth century, followed by universities in Rome, Naples, Salamanca, Seville, Prague, Vienna, Cologne, and Heidelberg. These institutions might be affiliated with the church, but they were independently governed and operated. The curriculum was both theological and secular, so that the new scientific knowledge of early modern times could be accommodated. As Alvin Schmidt points out, many of America's earliest colleges and universities—Harvard, the College of William and Mary, Yale, Northwestern, Princeton, Dartmouth, Brown—began as Christian institutions.[11]

Robert Grosseteste, a Franciscan bishop who was the first chancellor of Oxford University, proposed that knowledge be accumulated through an inductive, experimental method. A couple of centuries later Francis Bacon—a devoutly religious man who wrote treatises on the Psalms and on prayer—used the inductive method to record experimental outcomes. Bacon argued that through the God-given power of discovery man could fulfill the divine mandate to establish dominion over creation and even restore a new kind of Eden.[12] Today Bacon is considered the founder of the scientific method, the "inventor of invention." It was under the auspices of the church that the first medical research institutions and the first observatories were built and supported. From the Middle Ages to the Enlightenment, a period of several centuries, the church did more for Western science than any other institution.

We often hear that science was founded in the seventeenth century in revolt against religious dogma. In reality, science was founded between the thirteenth and fourteenth centuries through a dispute between two kinds of religious dogma. The first kind held that scholastic debate, operating according to the strict principles of deductive reason, was the best way to discover God's hand in the universe. The other held that inductive experience, including the use of experiments to "interrogate nature," was the preferred approach. Science benefited from both methods, using experiments to test propositions and then rigorous criticism and argumentation to establish their significance.

Historian Lynn White shows how the new scientific method launched an explosion of innovations and inventions starting in the thirteenth century. The fourteenth century was, according to Jean Gimpel, "one of the great inventive eras of mankind."[13] The technological revolution described by White and Gimpel was unlike anything known in classical times. Between the trial-and-error agricultural techniques of the monasteries and the new theoretical and experimental study of the universities, Europe developed a new way of understanding nature and making it work to human purposes. A continent once desolate was soon dotted with schools, farms, and workshops, all taking learning and agricultural production and trade to a new level. Inventions of the period included the waterwheel, the windmill, the chimney, eyeglasses, and the mechanical clock. Humble these may seem, but they are responsible for launching a civilization that would soon, in learning, affluence, and power, dwarf the other cultures of the world.[14]

The first professional scientists can be traced to the late Middle Ages, and since this period the overwhelming majority of them have not only been Christians, but have also viewed their work as a fulfillment of Christian objectives. Morris Kline writes that "the Renaissance scientist was a theologian with nature instead of God as his subject."[15] This does not mean the Renaissance scientist was on a secular path. On the contrary, he saw himself as achieving God's purpose in a new and better way, by going beyond God's holy book and exploring His creation.

In the sixteenth century the Reformation introduced a new idea. This was the notion that knowledge is not simply the province of ecclesiastical institutions but that, especially when it comes to matters of conscience, each man should decide for himself. The "priest-hood of the individual believer" was an immensely powerful notion because it rejected the papal hierarchy, and by implication all institu-tional hierarchy as well. Ultimately it was a charter of independent thought, carried out not by institutions but by individuals. The early Protestants didn't know it, but they were introducing new theological concepts that would give new vitality to the emerging scientific cul-ture of Europe.

Here is a partial list of leading scientists who were Christian: Copernicus, Kepler, Galileo, Brahe, Descartes, Boyle, Newton, Leibniz, Gassendi, Pascal, Mersenne, Cuvier, Harvey, Dalton, Faraday, Herschel, Joule, Lyell, Lavoisier, Priestley, Kelvin, Ohm, Ampere, Steno, Pasteur, Maxwell, Planck, Mendel. A good number of these scientists were cler-gymen. Gassendi and Mersenne were priests. So was Georges Lemaitre, the Belgian astronomer who first proposed the "big bang" theory for the origin of the universe. Mendel, whose discovery of the principles of heredity would provide vital support for the theory of evolution, spent his entire adult life as a monk in an Augustinian monastery. Where would modern science be without these men? Some were Protestant and some were Catholic, but all saw their sci-entific vocation in distinctively Christian terms.

Copernicus, who was a canon in the cathedral of Krakow, cele-brated astronomy as "a science more divine than human" and viewed his heliocentric theory as revealing God's grand scheme for the cos-mos. Boyle was a pious Anglican who declared scientists to be on a divinely appointed mission to serve as "priests of the book of nature." Boyle's work includes both scientific studies and theological treatises. In his will he left money to fund a series of lectures combating athe-ism. Newton was virtually a Christian mystic who wrote long com-mentaries on biblical prophecy from both the book of Daniel and the book of Revelation. Perhaps the greatest scientist of all time, Newton viewed his discoveries as showing the creative genius of God's handi-work in nature. "This most beautiful system of sun, planets, and comets," he wrote, "could only proceed from the counsel and domin-ion of an intelligent and powerful being."[16] Newton's God was not a divine watchmaker who wound up the universe and then withdrew from it. Rather, God was an active agent sustaining the heavenly bodies in their positions and solicitous of His special creation, man.

The example of Kepler shows that the Christian convictions of these towering figures of science were not incidental to their work. Rather, these convictions were the scientists' guiding inspiration. "For a long time," Kepler wrote, "I wanted to become a theologian. Now, however, behold how through my effort God is being celebrated through astronomy." A strong advocate of Copernicus's heliocentrism, Kepler held that the sun-centered cosmos was an image of the Holy Trinity, with God represented by the sun, Christ by the stars and planets, and the Holy Spirit by the motions of the heavenly bodies.[17] When Kepler discovered that planets do not move in circular but rather in elliptical orbits, he was criticized by some theologians as rejecting the beauty of God's creative plan. These theologians reasoned that surely God would have used perfect circles to choreograph the planetary motions!

Kepler, however, was certain, based on his deep Christian faith, that God had employed an even more beautiful pattern, and he labored hard to decipher it. When he discovered what it was—his three laws of planetary motion—he experienced something of a spiritual epiphany. Kepler announced that his laws showed that God had used a far simpler and more elegant scheme than the one previously delineated in the Ptolemaic system of cycles and epicycles. In a prayer concluding *The Harmony of the World*, Kepler implored God "graciously to cause that these demonstrations may lead to thy glory and to the salvation of souls."[18]

Kepler's laws posit uncanny relationships. For instance, Kepler's third law states that the square of the time of a planet's revolution is proportional to the cube of its mean distance from the sun. How could anyone have figured that out? Kepler did in large part because he was convinced that there had to be a beautiful mathematical relationship there hidden and waiting for him. Part of his Christian vocation was to find it and promulgate it to the greater glory of God. Kepler's success leads to the surprising recognition that religious motivation can sometimes result in breakthrough discoveries that change the course of scientific history.

This may seem like an outdated view today, but it is not. Scientists commonly search for new patterns and order in nature, and they use what may appear to be peculiar criteria to determine if they are on the right path. They often ask whether a relationship is "simple" or whether it is "beautiful." Patterns that are overly cumbersome or "ugly" are often rejected on those grounds alone.

Why? Because even the most secular scientist presumes that nature embodies not only order but simplicity and beauty. This, I would argue, is the Christian residue of modern science. It is the little whisper, if we will hear it, that our science even today rests on religious foundations. Even secular scientists cannot get away from these Christian assumptions, and some of the most perceptive of them have recognized this. Einstein confessed that "in every true searcher of nature there is a kind of religious reverence."[19] Biologist Joshua Lederberg recently told *Science* magazine, "What is incontrovertible is that a religious impulse guides our motive in sustaining scientific inquiry."[20] That impulse came originally from Christianity.

CHAPTER TEN

AN ATHEIST FABLE:
REOPENING THE GALILEO CASE

*"I believe the idea that Galileo's trial was a kind of Greek
tragedy, a showdown between blind faith and enlightened
reason, to be naively erroneous."*[1]

—Arthur Koestler, *The Sleepwalkers*

DESPITE THE ROLE OF **C**HRISTIANITY in the origin and development
of science, the theme of the warfare between science and religion persists. What gives this narrative its enduring power? It is the reported cases of church persecution of scientists like Copernicus and Galileo. Atheist writers have taken up this theme with a vengeance. Daniel Dennett singles out the Catholic church and faults "its unfortunate legacy of persecution of its own scientists."[2] Bruce Jakosky writes, "Copernicus's views were not embraced by the church; the history of his persecution is well known."[3] Carl Sagan portrays Galileo "in a Catholic dungeon threatened with torture" for his "heretical view that the earth moved about the sun."[4] Noting that Galileo was "not absolved of heresy until 1992," Sam Harris recalls the Christian tradition of "torturing scholars to the point of madness for merely speculating about the nature of the stars."[5]

There is a *Star Wars* quality to the science versus religion narrative. It is typically portrayed as a battle between good and evil: The good guys developed a new way of acquiring knowledge based on testing and evidence. The forces of darkness were captive to old doctrines derived from sacred books, such as the long-held belief that earth is flat. Despite their ignorance, the forces of darkness occupied the seats of political power. Fearful that their old way of superstition was threatened, the dark forces suppressed and persecuted those who dissented from orthodoxy. A terrible battle ensued. Many good people were accused of heresy merely for advancing valid scientific theories. Giordano Bruno was burned at the stake for saying the universe is infinite. Copernicus and Galileo were persecuted for showing that the earth revolves around the sun. Fortunately, this sad history now is behind us; the forces of light have prevailed over the forces of darkness. Today science is on the advance and religion is on the retreat. Scientists can now work unmolested and the Catholic church has even apologized for its treatment of Galileo. The moral of the story is that we should always be grateful for the rise of science and vigilant in guarding against the fanaticism of religion.

This thrilling drama suffers from only one limitation: it is not true. Historian David Lindberg writes, "There was no warfare between science and the church." Indeed, historians are virtually unanimous in holding that the whole science versus religion story is a nineteenth-century fabrication.[6] The names of the fabricators are known. The first is John William Draper, who introduced the "warfare" model in his popular 1874 book *History of the Conflict between Religion and Science*. This book is full of whoppers and lies, and is today read mostly as a case study in *fin de siècle* anti-religious prejudice. The second source is Andrew Dickson White, the first president of Cornell University, whose 1896 two-volume study *History of the Warfare of Science with Theology in Christendom* is a more sophisticated warfare account, but no less misleading than Draper's.

The source documents have now been discredited, but their tune continues to be sounded by leading atheist writers. This tune is now hummed throughout our modern culture, even by people who know very little about the details of the issues involved. To this day many people believe that the medieval church held that the earth was flat until modern science demonstrated to an exasperated clergy the roundness of the globe. In reality the ancient Greeks and the medieval Christians all knew that the earth was round. They observed that the hull of a ship sailing from shore disappears before the top of the mast. They also saw that during a lunar eclipse the earth casts a circular shadow on the moon. Dante's medieval cosmology was based on the idea of a spherical earth. So the idea that the church or educated Christians believed in the flat-earth theory is a concoction of the nineteenth-century "warfare" propagandists.

Other well-known episodes in the great war also require serious revision. Do you recall hearing about the famous debate between the bishop of Oxford, Samuel Wilberforce, and Darwin's ally Thomas Henry Huxley, in which the ignorant bishop taunted Huxley and Huxley shot back with a crushing rebuttal? "The exchange quickly became legendary," notes Edward Larson in his book *Evolution*.[7] As Larson and others tell the story, Wilberforce inquired of Huxley whether it was through his grandfather or grandmother that he was descended from a monkey. Huxley replied with great dignity that he would rather have a miserable ape for a relative than a bishop who used the authority of his office to ridicule scientific debate on a serious question. So widely reported was this exchange that historians who checked the transcripts of the British Association were surprised to discover that it never happened. Darwin's friend Joseph Hooker was present at the debate, and he reported to Darwin that Huxley made no response to Wilberforce's arguments. Larson's use of "legendary" acquires a quite literal meaning in this context.

For most people, no single episode more dramatically illustrates the conflict between science and religion than the Galileo case. In the late 1930s Bertolt Brecht wrote a brilliant play, *Life of Galileo*, that was made into a film in 1975 by American director Joseph Losey. Brecht's play is the account of priestly malevolence and scientific virtue. It is a canonization of Galileo as a secular saint. And this is the place that Galileo has come to occupy in our culture today, a martyr for the cause of science.

When atheist writers speak of the church's "history" of persecution of scientists, they are usually referring to the Galileo case. Copernicus was never persecuted by the church. The freethinker Giordano Bruno was burned at the stake, but as historian Thomas Kuhn points out, "Bruno was not executed for Copernicanism but for a series of theological heresies centering on his view of the trinity."[8] Bruno's execution was a terrible injustice, but it has nothing to do with the conflict between religion and science. Prior to the twentieth century and the purges of Stalin and Hitler, only one noted scientist was executed by government decree. That was the great chemist Antoine Lavoisier, a devout Catholic who was guillotined by the Jacobins during the French Revolution.

So we are back to Galileo. In this chapter I want to draw on historical scholarship to reopen the Galileo case.[9] If the atheist version of this case cannot withstand scrutiny, then the whole melodrama of science in conflict with religion is exploded as a farce. Prior to the sixteenth century, most educated people accepted the theories of the Greek astronomer Ptolemy, who held that the earth was stationary and the sun revolved around it. The geocentric universe was a classical, not a Christian, concept. The Christians accepted it, though not because of the Bible. The Bible never says that the sun revolves around the earth. It is silent on this scientific question. There are a few passages that refer to the sun rising and setting, but these can be understood as a spiritual text using ordinary understandable language. (Even your local weatherman, who knows all about the earth going around the sun, employs the same colloquial terminology: "Sunrise tomorrow will be at 5:00 AM") The reason the Christians accepted Ptolemy was because he had a sophisticated theory that was supported by common sense and that gave reasonably accurate predictions about the motions of heavenly bodies.

Interestingly, there was a Greek thinker, Aristarchus of Samos, who had proposed the heliocentric theory as far back as the third century BC. "Aristarchus has been celebrated for his anticipation of Copernicus," historian David Lindberg writes. But were Aristarchus and his followers good scientists? To avoid the retroactive fallacy of using current knowledge to judge the merits of past scientific claims, we have to examine the data available at the time. As Lindberg puts it, "The

question is not whether *we* have persuasive reasons for being helio-
centrists, but whether *they* had any such reasons, and the answer is
that they did not."[10]

The data right up to Galileo's day favored Ptolemy. Kuhn notes that
throughout the Middle Ages there were people who proposed the
heliocentric alternative. "They were ridiculed and ignored," Kuhn
writes, adding, "the reasons for the rejection were excellent." Consider
some examples he gives. The earth does not appear to move, and we
can all witness the sun rise in the morning and set in the evening. If
the earth moves at high speeds around the sun, then birds and clouds
and other objects not attached to the ground should be left behind. A
stone hurled into the sky would land many miles away from the spot
at which it was thrown, as the earth would have traveled a considerable distance while the object was in the air. Human beings standing
on the ground would be flung about. As none of this was observed, the
earth was held to be stationary.[11]

Galileo was a Florentine astronomer highly respected by the
Catholic church. Once a supporter of Ptolemy's geocentric theory,
Galileo became persuaded that Copernicus was right that the earth
really did revolve around the sun. Copernicus had advanced his theory
in 1543 in a book dedicated to the pope. Copernicus admitted that he
had no physical proof, but the power of the heliocentric hypothesis
was that it produced vastly better predictions of planetary orbits.
Copernicus's new ideas unleashed a major debate within the religious
and scientific community, which at that time overlapped greatly. The
prevailing view half a century later, when Galileo took up the issue,
was that Copernicus had advanced an interesting but unproven
hypothesis, useful for calculating the motions of heavenly bodies but
not persuasive enough to jettison the geocentric theory altogether.

Galileo's contribution to the Copernican theory was significant but
not decisive. This is a crucial point to keep in mind because of the elaborate mythology surrounding Galileo, mostly based on incidents that
never occurred. Kuhn takes up the story we all learned in school about
how Galileo went to the top of the leaning Tower of Pisa and dropped
light and heavy objects to the ground. He supposedly discovered that,

contrary to intuition, the objects all hit the ground at the same time. One simple experiment, the story goes, had refuted a millennium of medieval theorizing.

In reality, Galileo didn't perform the experiment in Pisa or anywhere else; the experiment was done by one of his students. Moreover, the heavier bodies did actually hit the ground first. Today we understand why this was the case. Only when such experiments are conducted in the absence of air resistance do all bodies fall at the same speed. "In the everyday world," Kuhn writes, "heavy bodies do fall faster than light ones.... Galileo's law is more useful to science...not because it represents experience more perfectly, but because it goes behind the superficial regularity disclosed by the senses to a more essential, but hidden, aspect of motion. To verify Galileo's law by observation demands special equipment. Galileo himself got the law not by observation...but by a chain of logical arguments."[12]

Having developed a more powerful telescope than others of his day, Galileo made important new observations about the moons of Jupiter, the phases of Venus, and spots on the sun that undermined Ptolemy and were consistent with Copernican theory. Galileo took these observations to the Jesuits, who were among the leading astronomers of the day, and they agreed with him that his sightings had strengthened the case for heliocentrism. The Jesuits told Galileo that the church was divided, with many clergy supporting Ptolemy but others holding that Copernicus was right. Even so, the Jesuits concluded that the question was still open and they did not think that Galileo had clinched the case. Tyco Brahe, the greatest astronomer of the period, agreed that Galileo's proofs were insufficient and continued to support the geocentric theory. So great was Brahe's reputation that it prevented the conversion of many astronomers to Copernicanism until after his death.

It may surprise some readers to find out that the pope was an admirer of Galileo and a supporter of scientific research that at the time was conducted mostly in church-sponsored observatories and universities. So was the head of the Inquisition, the learned theologian Cardinal Robert Bellarmine. When Galileo's lectures supporting the heliocentric theory were reported to the Inquisition, most likely by one of Galileo's academic rivals in Florence, Cardinal Bellarmine met with Galileo. This was not normal Inquisition procedure, but Galileo was a celebrity. In 1616 he came to Rome with great fanfare, where he stayed at the grand Medici villa, met with the pope more than once, and attended receptions given by various bishops and cardinals.

What Bellarmine observed in connection with Galileo is both memorable and telling. "While experience tells us plainly that the earth is standing still," Bellarmine wrote, nevertheless "if there were a real proof that the sun is in the center of the universe...and that the sun does not go round the earth but the earth round the sun, then we should have to proceed with great circumspection in explaining passages of scripture which appear to teach the contrary, and rather admit that we did not understand them than declare an opinion to be false which is proved to be true. But this is not a thing to be done in haste, and as for myself, I shall not believe that there are such proofs until they are shown to me."[13]

This is a model of sensible procedure. Bellarmine assumed that there could be no real conflict between nature and scripture, which is what Christianity has always taught. Consequently, he argued, if we have been reading scripture one way and the natural evidence shows that we were wrong, then we need to revise our interpretation of scripture and acknowledge our mistake. But first let us make sure that there is in fact conclusive scientific proof before we start changing scriptural interpretations that have been taught for a very long time. Bellarmine proposed a solution. Given the inconclusive evidence for the theory and the sensitivity of the religious issues involved, Galileo should not teach or promote heliocentrism. Galileo, a practicing Catholic who wanted to maintain his good standing with the church, agreed. Bellarmine issued an injunction and made a record of the proceeding that went into the church files.

For several years Galileo kept his word and continued his experiments and discussions without publicly advocating heliocentrism. Then he received the welcome news that Cardinal Maffeo Barberini had been named Pope Urban VIII. Barberini was a scientific "progressive," having fought to prevent Copernicus's work from being placed on the index of prohibited books. Equally significant, Barberini was a fan of Galileo and had even written a poem eulogizing him. Galileo was confident that now he could openly preach heliocentrism. But the new pope's position on the subject was a complicated one. Urban VIII held that while science can make useful measurements and predictions about the universe, it cannot claim to have actual knowledge of reality known only to God. This theory, which sounds a bit strange, is actually quite close to what some physicists now believe, and as we shall see, it is entirely in line with Kant's philosophical demonstration of the limits of reason.

So when Galileo in 1632 published his *Dialogue Concerning the Two Chief World Systems*, the church found itself in a quandary. First, Galileo claimed to have demonstrated the truth of heliocentrism, but in fact his proof was wrong. One of Galileo's main arguments was that the rapid motion of the earth around the sun was responsible for the ocean tides. This was questionable at the time, and we now know that the moon is primarily responsible for tides. Galileo also assumed, as did Copernicus, that planets move in circular paths, even though by Galileo's time Kepler had shown that the planetary orbits are elliptical. Galileo contended that Kepler was wrong

Second, Galileo embarrassed the pope by constructing his "dialogue" between two figures, one representing himself and the other representing the pope. To dramatize the contrast, Galileo gave his pope character the name Simplicio, which in Italian means "simpleton." The dialogue basically consists of foolish claims by Simplicio elegantly refuted by the character speaking for Galileo. The pope was not amused.

Galileo's third mistake was that his writings were not confined to scientific issues; he also advanced his own theory of scriptural interpretation. Galileo argued that the Bible was largely allegorical and required constant reinterpretation to excavate its true meaning. The Jesuits had warned him not to venture into this territory. Scripture, they told Galileo, is the province of the church. With the hubris and imprudence not unknown among great men of science, Galileo ignored this counsel. So when he was again reported to the Inquisition, his opponents were able to fault him not only on scientific grounds but also on the grounds that he was undermining the religious teaching of the church.

Finally, this was the age of the Reformation. Protestant thinkers were attacking the Catholic church for not taking the Bible seriously enough. Urban VIII was eager to demonstrate the Vatican's fidelity to scripture, and geocentrism was an interpretation on which there was agreement in the official positions of both Catholics and Protestants. Had the Reformation occurred a century before or after, Richard Blackwell writes, "the Galileo affair would probably not have happened."[14] Under the prevailing circumstances, however, the pope agreed to let the Galileo case proceed.

In 1633 Galileo returned to Rome, where he was again treated with respect. He might have prevailed in his trial, but during the investigation someone found Cardinal Bellarmine's notes in the files. Galileo had not told the Inquisition—actually he had not told anyone—of his previous agreement not to teach or advocate Copernicanism. Now Galileo was viewed as having deceived the church as well as having failed to live up to his agreements. Even his church sympathizers, and there were several, found it difficult to defend him at this point.

But they did advise him to acknowledge that he had promoted Copernicanism in violation of his pact with Bellarmine, and to show contrition. Incredibly Galileo appeared before the Inquisition and maintained that his *Dialogue* did not constitute a defense of heliocentrism. "I have neither maintained or defended in that book the opinion that the earth moves and that the sun is stationary but have rather demonstrated the opposite of the Copernican opinion and shown that the arguments of Copernicus are weak and not conclusive."

It has been widely repeated that Galileo whispered under his breath, "And yet it moves."[15] But the remark is pure fabrication. In fact, there are no reports that Galileo said anything of the sort. One should be charitable toward Galileo's motives here. Perhaps he made his statement denying heliocentrism out of weariness and frustration. Even so, the Inquisitors can also be excused for viewing Galileo at this point as a flagrant liar. Galileo's defense, Arthur Koestler writes, was so "patently dishonest that his case would have been lost in any court."[16] The Inquisition concluded that Galileo did hold heliocentric views, which it demanded he recant. Galileo did, at which point he was sentenced to house arrest.

Contrary to what some atheist propagandists have said, Galileo was never charged with heresy, and he was never placed in a dungeon or tortured in any way. After he recanted Galileo was released into the custody of the archbishop of Siena, who housed him for five months in his magnificent palace. Then he was permitted to return to his villa in Florence. Although technically under house arrest, he was able to visit his daughters at the convent of San Matteo. The church also permitted him to continue his scientific work on matters unrelated to heliocentrism, and he published important research during this period. Galileo died of natural causes in 1642. It was during subsequent decades, Kuhn reports, that newer and stronger evidence for the heliocentric theory emerged, and scientific opinion, divided in Galileo's time, became the consensus that we share today.

What can we conclude about the Galileo episode? "The traditional picture of Galileo as a martyr to intellectual freedom and a victim of the church's opposition to science," writes historian Gary Ferngren, "has been demonstrated to be little more than a caricature."[17] The case was an "anomaly," historian Thomas Lessl writes, "a momentary break in the otherwise harmonious relationship" that had existed between Christianity and science.[18] Indeed there is no other example in history of the Catholic church condemning a scientific theory.

Galileo was a great scientist who had very little sense. He was right about heliocentrism, but several of his arguments and proofs were wrong. The dispute his ideas brought about was not exclusively between religion and science, but also between the new science and the science of the previous generation. The leading figures of the church were more circumspect about approaching the scientific issues, which were truly unsettled at the time, than the impetuous Galileo. The church should not have tried him, but his trials were conducted with considerable restraint and exemplary treatment. Galileo himself acted badly, which no doubt contributed to his fate. Even so, his fate was not so terrible. Alfred North Whitehead, a noted historian of science, concludes from the case that "the worst that happened to men of science was that Galileo suffered an honorable detention and a mild reproof, before dying peacefully in his bed."[19]

PART IV

THE ARGUMENT FROM DESIGN

CHAPTER ELEVEN

A UNIVERSE WITH A BEGINNING: GOD AND THE ASTRONOMERS

"It would be very difficult to explain why the universe should have begun in just this way, except as the act of a God who intended to create beings like us."[1]

—Stephen Hawking, *A Brief History of Time*

IN THE NEXT FEW CHAPTERS I explore whether the latest findings in modern science support or undermine the case for the existence of God. The argument will engage physics, astronomy, and biology, although no specialized knowledge of any of these is expected. Here I draw on the findings of classical physics to explore what we know about the origin of the universe and the implications of those discoveries. The question at issue is whether the design of nature points to a creator or whether that design can be given a purely naturalistic explanation.

Earlier we encountered astronomer Carl Sagan's assertion that "the cosmos is all there is, or was, or ever will be." Physicist Steven Weinberg argues that "as far as we have been able to discover the laws of nature, they are impersonal, with no hint of a divine plan or any special status for human beings."[2] I intend to show that these statements are factually wrong. Indeed, I wish to take up a challenge issued by biologist E. O. Wilson, who said, "If any positive evidence could be

found of a supernatural guiding force...it would be one of the greatest discoveries of all time."[3] In recent decades, in one of the most spectacular developments in physics and astronomy, such evidence has
indeed been found.

In a stunning confirmation of the book of Genesis, modern scientists have discovered that the universe was created in a primordial
explosion of energy and light. Not only did the universe have a beginning *in* space and time, but the origin of the universe was also a beginning *for* space and time. Space and time did not exist prior to the
universe. If you accept that everything that has a beginning has a
cause, then the material universe had a nonmaterial or spiritual cause.
This spiritual cause brought the universe into existence using none of
the laws of physics. The creation of the universe was, in the quite literal meaning of the term, a miracle. Its creator is known to be a spiritual, eternal being of creativity and power beyond all conceivable
limits. Mind, not matter, came at the beginning. With the help of science and logic, all this can be rationally demonstrated.

The story begins about a century ago, as scientists began to look
for evidence that our universe—not just our planet or our galaxy but
all the matter that exists—had a beginning. The reason for the search
is that one of the most universal laws of physics, the second law of
thermodynamics, predicts such a beginning. The law simply states
that, left to themselves, things break down. We see this all around us:
highways and buildings decay and collapse, people age and die, metals
rust, fabrics become threadbare, rocks and coastlines suffer erosion. If
you haven't studied physics, you might think that the second law is
refuted by the evidence of people who build new highways and buildings, but this is not the case. Materials and power are used up in the
construction process. More resources and energy are required to
maintain these highways and buildings. So even here things are running down and wearing out. Scientists use the term *entropy* as a measure of the level of disorder, and the second law shows that the total
entropy in the universe is continually increasing.

The second law has a startling implication. Consider the example
of the sun. As time passes its fuel reserves decline, so that eventually

the sun will run out of heat and go cold. But this means the fires of the sun must have been ignited at some point. The sun has not been burning forever. And this is also true of other stars. They too are gradually burning out, suggesting that they too were set aflame some time ago. As the great English astronomer Arthur Eddington once put it, if the universe can be compared to a clock, the fact that the clock is continually running down leads to the conclusion that there was a time when the clock was fully wound up. The universe originated with its full supply of energy and that is the fund that has been dissipating ever since. These facts were known as far back as the eighteenth century, but scientists didn't know what to make of them.

In the early twentieth century, Albert Einstein published his equations of general relativity and a Dutch astronomer, Willem de Sitter, found a solution to them that predicted an expanding universe. This, too, was a highly significant prediction because if the universe has been expanding and if galaxies are moving farther apart, this implies that in the past they once were closer together. If the universe has been "blowing up" for the duration of its existence, that means that it must have had an actual beginning.

Einstein, who didn't realize that his equations suggested an expanding universe, was distressed to hear about this implication of his famous theory. When Russian mathematician Alexander Friedmann tried to persuade him, Einstein sought to prove Friedmann wrong. Actually Einstein was wrong. The great physicist was, by his own account, "irritated" by the idea of an expanding universe. He went so far as to invent a new force, the "antigravity" force, as well as a number called the "cosmological constant," to try to disprove the notion of a beginning. Later Einstein admitted his errors and called his cosmological constant the biggest mistake of his life.[4]

In the late 1920s, astronomer Edwin Hubble, peering through the hundred-inch telescope at Mount Wilson Observatory in California, observed through the "red shift" of distant nebulae that galaxies were moving rapidly away from each other. The number of stars involved in this galactic dispersal suggested an astoundingly vast universe, much bigger than anyone had thought. Some galaxies were millions of light years away. The impression that many people had long held of the still-ness and changelessness of space was an illusion. Hubble noticed that planets and entire galaxies were hurtling away from one another at fantastic speeds. Moreover, space itself seemed to be getting bigger. The universe wasn't expanding into background space, because the universe already contains all the space there is. Incredibly, space itself was expanding along with the universe. Hubble's findings, subse-quently confirmed by numerous others, generated great excitement in the scientific community.

Scientists realized right away that the galaxies were not flying apart because of some mysterious force thrusting them away from each other. Rather, they were moving apart because they were once flung apart by a primeval explosion. Extrapolating backward in time, all the galaxies seem to have had a common point of origin approxi-mately fifteen billion years ago. Scientists projected a moment in which all the mass in the universe was compressed into a point of infi-nite density. The entire universe was smaller than a single atom.

Then in a single cosmic explosion—the Big Bang—the universe we now inhabit came into existence. "The universe was filled with light," Steven Weinberg writes. In fact, "it was light that then formed the dominant constituent of the universe." The temperature was about a hundred trillion degrees Centigrade. Then, in a process vividly described by Weinberg in *The First Three Minutes*, the first protons and neutrons began to form into atoms. Once matter was formed, gravitational forces began to draw it into galaxies and then into stars. Eventually heavier elements like oxygen and iron were formed and, over billions of years, gave birth to our solar system and our planet. Crazy though it may seem, our terrestrial existence, indeed the very matter of which we are made, owes itself to a "creation event" that occurred around fifteen billion years ago.[5]

This theory of an expanding universe was consistent not only with the second law of thermodynamics but also with Einstein's theory of relativity. Hubble found that the farther away a galaxy is from us, the faster it is receding from us. This is now called Hubble's Law, and it ful-fills a prediction that was made on the basis of Einstein's theory. The expanding universe theory also solved an old conundrum that had been frustrating scientists for decades: why the galaxies continued to stay apart from each other. Why had the force of gravity not pulled them together? The reason was that they had been hurled apart in a primordial explosion whose force continued to thrust them farther and farther away from each other. Astronomer John Barrow calls Hubble's finding "the greatest discovery of twentieth-century science."[6]

Even so, many scientists were visibly upset by the concept of a Big Bang. Robert Jastrow cites a number of examples in his book *God and the Astronomers*.[7] Astronomer Arthur Eddington called the concept "preposterous...incredible...repugnant." Physicist Philip Morrison of MIT confessed, "I find it hard to accept the big bang theory. I would like to reject it." Allan Sandage of Carnegie Laboratories said the idea was "such a strange conclusion" that "it cannot really be true." Like Einstein, prominent scientists began to advance theories that would eliminate the need for a beginning. They worked very hard to find a scientifically credible way for the universe to have existed forever.

Jastrow argues that the reason several leading scientists were troubled by the notion of a big bang is because, if true, it would imply that there was a "moment of creation" in which everything—the universe and its laws—came into existence. It is very important to recognize that before the Big Bang, there were no laws of physics. In fact, the laws of physics cannot be used to explain the Big Bang because the Big Bang itself produced the laws of physics. The laws of science are a kind of grammar that explains the order and relationship of objects in the universe. Just as grammar has no existence outside the words and sentences whose operations it defines, so too the laws of science cannot exist outside the universe of objects whose relationships they describe.

Scientists call the starting moment of the universe a "singularity," an original point at which neither space nor time nor scientific laws are in effect. Nothing can be known scientifically about what came before such a point. Indeed the term *before* has no meaning since time itself did not exist "prior to" the singularity. Once upon a time there was no time. Jastrow's implication was that such concepts, which border on the metaphysical, give scientists a very queasy feeling. If the universe was produced outside the laws of physics, then its origin satisfies the basic definition of the term *miracle*. This term gives scientists the heebie-jeebies.

Imagine the relief of these scientists when astronomers Hermann Bondi, Thomas Gold, and Fred Hoyle advanced what became known as the "steady state" universe. Their theory was that the universe was infinite in age. Basically Bondi, Gold, and Hoyle hypothesized that as energy burns up over time, new energy and new matter are somehow created in intergalactic space. So despite entropy and the second law of thermodynamics, everything remains in balance and on an even keel, and thus it is possible that the universe has always existed. Space and time are also eternal. The steady state theory quickly gained popularity and became the most favored explanation for the universe among scientists in Europe and America. As late as 1959, it commanded the support of two-thirds of astronomers and physicists.[8]

In a way, the steady state theory built on a very old foundation. The notion of an eternal universe has been around since the ancient Greeks. Greek philosophers and natural scientists had a wide range of views on the origin of the world, but they all generally agreed on the principle that something cannot be produced out of nothing: *ex nihilo, nihil*: "out of nothing there is nothing." It takes matter to give shape to matter. Therefore, as the material universe could not possibly have arisen out of "thin air," it has always been there. Matter is forever. Newton's discoveries in the eighteenth century generally supported the idea of an eternal universe. For Newton, space was a three-dimensional volume stretching without limit in every direction, and time was a single dimension extending indefinitely into the past and into the future. It was this concept of the eternal universe that the steady state theory sought to confirm, as an alternative to the Big Bang theory.

The implications of the steady state theory, its advocates freely conceded, were largely atheistic. If the universe has always existed, then no one created it. It has simply been there all along. Newton himself sought to avoid this implication. While the universe may operate according to mechanical laws, perhaps even laws that have always existed, Newton argued that there was an external creator of those laws and he "certainly is not mechanical" but rather "incorporeal, living, intelligent, omnipresent."[9] But by the early twentieth century most scientists viewed Newton's argument as the special pleading of a religious man who simply could not abide the full significance of his own laws. The scientific consensus seemed to incline toward the view of Pierre-Simon Laplace, who was asked by Napoleon what place his nebular theories had for God and reportedly replied, "I have no need of that hypothesis." The steady state theory had the virtue for many scientists of dispensing with the God hypothesis.

In the 1960s, however, the steady state theory suffered a devastating blow when two radio engineers working at Bell Labs, Arno Penzias and Robert Wilson, discovered some mysterious radiation coming from space. This radiation was not coming from a particular direction; rather, it was coming equally from all directions. In fact, it appeared to be coming from the universe itself. Penzias and Wilson soon learned that scientists had been predicting that, if the universe began in a single explosion around fifteen billion years ago, then some of the radiation from that fiery blast would still be around. This radiation was expected to have a temperature of around five degrees above absolute zero. Penzias and Wilson's radiation measured slightly less than this number, and they realized to their astonishment that they had encountered a ghostly whisper from the original moment of creation.

Numerous other findings—including data from NASA's Cosmic Background Explorer (COBE) satellite—have now confirmed the existence of this primordial background radiation. Based on the Big Bang theory, scientists are able to predict how much hydrogen, lithium, deuterium, and helium should exist in the universe. These predictions are in remarkable congruence with the actual amounts of those elements that we find today. In 1970 physicist Stephen Hawking and mathematician Roger Penrose wrote a famous paper that proved that, given general relativity and the amount of matter in the universe, the universe must have had a beginning. As Hawking states in *A Brief History of Time*, "There must have been a Big Bang singularity."[10] Astronomer Martin Rees notes that numerous lines of evidence have now converged that have discredited the steady state theory and confirmed the Big Bang theory.[11]

"In the beginning," the Bible says in the book of Genesis, "God created the heavens and the earth." The Bible is unique among the documents of ancient history in positing an absolute beginning. In Buddhism, we learn from the Dalai Lama that "there are multiple world systems...in constant state of coming into being and passing away."[12] The Bible also asserts clearly that time is finite. By contrast, Hinduism and Buddhism posit endless cycles of time stretching into the indefinite past. The Greeks and Romans, like other cultures of antiquity, believed in the eternity of history. As Leon Kass notes in his study of Genesis, the biblical writers didn't need to venture into this territory. They could have started with the Garden of Eden and left out the account of creation.[13] Instead the biblical narrative brazenly insists that the universe came into existence at a particular instant in time as an act of voluntary creation by an already existing supernatural being.

It is important here to clear up a common misunderstanding. Many secular writers seem to think that the orthodox Christian position is that the universe and the earth were literally made in six calendar days. But the Bible uses a Hebrew term that could mean a day or a season or an era. We also read in 2 Peter 3:8 that "with the Lord a day is like a thousand years, and a thousand years are like a day." From earliest Christian times, the leading church authorities from Irenaeus to Origen to Augustine gave a figurative interpretation to the "days" in the book of Genesis. Most traditional Christians have no problem with a creation account that extends over millions, even billions, of years.

Remarkably, Jews and Christians have always believed not only that God made the universe, but also that He made it out of nothing: "in the beginning was the Word." With this the Bible implies that the universe was literally spoken into existence.[14] For nearly two thousand years this made no rational sense. We experience time and space in such a way that we cannot imagine them having a beginning or an end. Nature suggests no beginning or end in itself. In the creation myths of most other religions, gods typically fashion the world out of some preexisting stuff. Logic would seem to be on the side of the ancient Greeks: *ex nihilo, nihil*. But now modern science tells us that the Bible is right. The universe was indeed formed out of nothing. And how was it formed? We do not know and may never know, because the creator used processes that are not now operating anywhere in the natural universe.

Even more strange is that Jews and Christians have long held that God made space and time along with the universe. We have seen how the church father Augustine, when confronted with the question of why God sat around for such a long time before deciding to create the universe, answered that the question was meaningless. There was no time before the creation, Augustine wrote, because the creation of the universe involved the creation of time itself. Modern physics has confirmed Augustine and the ancient understanding of the Jews and Christians.

The Big Bang resolves one of the apparent contradictions in the book of Genesis. For more than two centuries, critics of the Bible have pointed out that in the beginning—on the first day—God created light. Then on the fourth day God separated the night from the day. The problem is pointed out by philosopher Leo Strauss: "Light is presented as preceding the sun."[15] Christians have long struggled to explain this anomaly but without much success. The writer of Genesis seemed to have made an obvious mistake.

But it turns out that there is no mistake. The universe was created in a burst of light fifteen billion years ago. Our sun and our planet came into existence billions of years later. So light did indeed precede the sun. The first reference to light in Genesis 1:3 can be seen to refer to the Big Bang itself. The separation of the day and the night described in Genesis 1:4 clearly refers to the formation of the sun and the earth. Day and night—which we experience as a result of the earth's rotation—were indeed created much later than the universe itself. The Genesis enigma is solved, and its account of the creation is vindicated not as some vague parable but as a strikingly accurate account of how the universe came to be.

Let's remember that the Old Testament was written more than 2,500 years ago by people who essentially contended that God told them what He did. Gerald Schroeder notes, "These commentaries were not composed in response to cosmological discoveries as an attempt to force an agreement between theology and cosmology.... Theology presents a fixed view of the universe. Science, through its progressively improved understanding of the world, has come to agree with theology."[16]

Leading scientists have, sometimes reluctantly, endorsed this conclusion. Arthur Eddington, who finally conceded the veracity of the Big Bang, acknowledged that "the beginning seems to present insuperable difficulties unless we agree to look at it as frankly supernatural."[17] Arno Penzias, who won the Nobel prize for his discovery of the cosmic background radiation that corroborated the Big Bang, said, "The best data we have are exactly what I would have predicted had I nothing to go on but the five books of Moses, the Psalms, and the Bible as a whole."[18]

Astronomer Robert Jastrow puts it even more vividly. "For the scientist who has lived by his faith in the power of reason, the story ends like a bad dream. He has scaled the mountains of ignorance; he is about to conquer the highest peak. As he pulls himself over the final rock, he is greeted by a band of theologians who have been sitting there for centuries."[19]

I am not citing the Bible to prove that God created the universe. I am citing it to show that the biblical account of how the universe was created is substantially correct. The Bible is not a science textbook. It does not attempt, as science does, to give a detailed account of how the universe and the earth were formed into their current shapes. But what it does say about creation—about the fact of creation and about the order of creation—turns out to be accurate. In a manner that once would have seemed impossible, the Bible has been vindicated by the findings of modern science.

Now it is time to supply the "missing link" and show that the universe did have a creator. The proof is extremely simple. Everything that begins to exist has a cause. The universe began to exist. Therefore the universe has a cause. That cause we call God. For a long time the denial of a creator was based on denying the second proposition. No, the atheists insisted, pointing to Newtonian science as their evidence, the universe does not have a beginning. It's a kind of perpetual motion machine. It has always been there. Science has now removed that argument.

So atheists—including atheist scientists—are reduced to denying the first proposition. Everything that has a beginning doesn't necessarily have a cause. The universe simply is and there's nothing more we can say about it. Philosopher Bertrand Russell adopted this position in a debate on the existence of God. He said, "The universe is just there, and that's all."[20] Physicist Victor Stenger says the universe may be "uncaused" and may have "emerged from nothing."[21] Even David Hume, one of the most skeptical of all philosophers, regarded this position as ridiculous. For all his skepticism, Hume never denied causation. Hume wrote in 1754, "I have never asserted so absurd a proposition as that anything might arise without cause."[22]

If every effect in nature has a cause, what is the cause of nature itself? Who or what put the matter and energy into the universe? Is it even remotely reasonable to suggest that nature created itself? If for even a single instant there was nothing in existence—no matter, no universe, no God—then how could there be anything at all? When events occur—we see a huge crater where level ground used to be, a famous movie star is found with his head cut off—we immediately ask what caused these things to happen. It would hardly be considered a reasonable or scientific explanation to say, "Well, they just happened. There is no cause." We know that something caused the crater to show up. We know that someone cut off the movie star's head. We may not know the identity of the person who committed the act, but we know that someone did it.

Similarly we may not know what kind of creator made the universe, but we do know that it was made, and that someone made it. Our world looks so physical, and yet we know with scientific certainty that it was the result of a force beyond physics. This is the literal meaning of the term *metaphysics*—that which is after or beyond physics. Science has discovered a reality that it had previously consigned to the domain of faith. But today it takes no faith to recognize that the origin of the universe is metaphysical. The universe that came into being in a primeval explosion fifteen billion years ago did not cause itself. It was caused or created, which means there had to be a creator. To that creator we give the name God.

It seems at this point that we have established the existence of a creator, but nothing can be known about the nature of that creator. I submit that this is not so. Many attributes of the creator remain unknown or hidden, but there are some conclusions that we can reasonably draw from what we know. As the universe was produced by a creative act, it is reasonable to infer that it was produced by some sort of mind. Mind is the origin of matter, and it is mind that produced matter, rather than the other way around. As the universe comprises the totality of nature, containing everything that is natural, its creator must necessarily be outside nature. As the creator used no natural laws or forces to create the universe, the creator is clearly supernatural. As space and time are within the universe, the creator is also outside space and time, which is to say, eternal. As the universe is material, the creator is immaterial, which is to say, spiritual. As the universe was created from nothing, the creator is incomprehensibly powerful or, as best as we can tell, omnipotent.

Is the cosmos all there is, or was, or ever will be? Of course not. That idea is complete nonsense, and from a man who should have known better. The laws of nature give "no hint" of a divine plan or creator? How could Steven Weinberg have made an assertion as foolish as that? To the dogmatic atheist, it seems like science fiction, or a recurrent nightmare. But there's no getting around the scientific fact. The finding of modern physics that the universe has a beginning in space and in time meets E. O. Wilson's litmus test for one of the most important scientific discoveries ever made. It provides, for all who take the trouble to understand and reflect upon it, powerful and convincing evidence of the existence of an eternal, supernatural being that created our world and everything in it.

CHAPTER TWELVE

A DESIGNER PLANET: MAN'S SPECIAL PLACE IN CREATION

*"We will never know completely who we are until we under-
stand why the universe is constructed in such a way that
it contains living things."*[1]

—Lee Smolin, *The Life of the Cosmos*

COPERNICUS IS DEAD. Yes, I know the famous astronomer died in 1543. That's not what I mean. Nor do I mean that the Coperni-can theory—that the earth revolves around the sun, and not the other way around—is dead. But Copernicus's heliocentric revolution was not merely a scientific revolution. It also became (in hands other than his) an intellectual revolution that denied that man has a special place in the cosmos. New discoveries, however, are reversing the les-son of Copernicus. We seem to live in a universe in which we do have a special position of importance. The latest scientific research shows that we apparently inhabit a world specifically crafted for us.

From leading atheists we see familiar expressions of the conven-tional wisdom about the Copernican revolution. In his recent book *God: The Failed Hypothesis*, physicist Victor Stenger writes, "It is hard to conclude that the universe was created with a special, cosmic purpose for humanity."[2] Physicist Steven Weinberg writes, "The human race has had to grow up a good deal in the last five hundred years to confront the fact that we just don't count for much in the grand scheme of things."[3] Astronomer Carl Sagan invokes the Copernican revolution to challenge "our posturings, our imagined self-importance, the delusion that we have some privileged position in the universe."[4]

Although these are not scientific statements, they are invoked with the full authority of science. What we have here is a metaphysical narrative about science that shapes the way many scientists approach the world and the way in which our culture understands what science has demonstrated. The Copernican revolution can be understood as establishing the principle of mediocrity. This principle simply says that we human beings are nothing special. We inhabit a tiny insignificant planet in a relatively undistinguished galaxy in a distant suburb of an unimaginably vast universe.

The principle of mediocrity, derived from the Copernican revolution, has had profound theological implications. The heliocentric revolution was not revolutionary because it contradicted the claim of the Bible that the earth is at the center of the universe. The Bible makes no such claim. Nor did the medieval Christians believe that the earth occupies the most important place in creation. For Christians, no place can be more important than heaven. The earth was viewed as occupying an intermediate position, with the heavens above and hell below. This was the portrait of the cosmos that we find in Dante's *Divine Comedy*. I mention this cosmology not to defend it, but rather to challenge the false presumption that Copernicus undermined some fundamental Christian doctrine of earth's special place in the universe.

Yet in a deeper sense the religious worldview was threatened by the Copernican revolution. After all, it is a core belief of the major religions of the world—specifically Judaism, Christianity, and Islam—that man has a privileged status in God's creation. The universe was, in this view, made with us in mind, perhaps even for our sake. How can these traditional beliefs be reconciled with the discovery that we live in a vast universe with numerous other planets, innumerable other galaxies, and hundreds of billions of stars, some of them so far away that they are completely burned out by the time their light reaches the earth? When we look through a telescope we feel the eerie emptiness of space and with it a hint of cosmic alienation. It's hard to avoid the question: if man is so central to God's purposes in nature, why do we live in such a marginal speck of real estate in such a big, indifferent universe?

In recent years, physics has given this question a resounding answer that overthrows the principle of mediocrity and affirms man's special place in the cosmos. It turns out that the vast size and great age of our universe are not coincidental. They are the indispensable conditions for the existence of life on earth. In other words, the universe has to be just as big as it is and just as old as it is in order to contain living inhabitants like you and me. The entire universe with all its laws appears to be a conspiracy to produce, well, us. Physicists call this incredible finding the anthropic principle, which states that the universe we perceive must be of precisely such a nature as will make possible living beings who can perceive it. The Copernican narrative has been reversed and man has been restored to his ancient pedestal as the favored son, and perhaps even the *raison d'être*, of creation.

Physicists stumbled upon the anthropic principle by asking a simple question: why does the universe operate according to the laws it does? Think about it: the universe seems to follow a very specific set of rules, and yet it didn't *have* to have these rules. So why these rules and not other rules? To take a simple example, the various forces in nature, such as the force of gravity, operate in ways that can be measured. Why is the gravitational force just this strong, and not stronger or weaker? Or consider that the universe is approximately fifteen billion years old and at least fifteen billion light years in size. What would have happened if the universe was much older and bigger or much younger and smaller?

The physicists who asked these questions arrived at a remarkable conclusion. In order for life to exist—in order for the universe to have observers to take notice of it—the gravitational force has to be precisely what it is. The Big Bang had to occur exactly when it did. If the basic values and relationships of nature were even slightly different, our universe would not exist and neither would we. Fantastic though it seems, the universe is fine-tuned for human habitation. We live in a kind of Goldilocks universe in which the conditions are "just right" for life to emerge and thrive. As physicist Paul Davies puts it, "We have been written into the laws of nature in a deep and, I believe, meaningful way."[5]

The anthropic principle is now widely accepted among physicists, and there are several good books that explain it in comprehensive detail. John Barrows and Frank Tipler's *The Anthropic Cosmological Principle* is the most thorough and detailed exposition. In his introduction to that book, physicist John Wheeler writes that "a life-giving factor lies at the center of the whole machinery and design of the world."[6] If you want a shorter and more readable version of the same argument, try astronomer Martin Rees's *Just Six Numbers*. Rees argues that six numbers underlie the fundamental physical properties of the universe, and that each is an exact value required for life to exist. If any one of the six (say the gravitational constant, or the strong nuclear force) were different "even to the tiniest degree," Rees says, "there would be no stars, no complex elements, no life." Although he disavows the religious implications, Rees does not hesitate to call the values attached to the six numbers "providential."[7]

Astronomer Lee Smolin imagines God as a kind of master technician who is sitting at a control panel with a set of dials in front of Him. One dial sets the mass of the proton, another the charge of the electron, a third the gravitational constant, and so on. God spins the dials randomly. What, Smolin asks, is the probability that this random spinning would result in a universe with stars and planets and life? "The probability," he answers, "is incredibly small."[8] How small? Smolin's estimate is one chance in ten to the power of 229. Smolin's point is reinforced by a single example from physicist Stephen Hawking: "If the rate of expansion one second after the Big Bang had been smaller by even one part in a hundred thousand million million, the universe would have recollapsed before it even reached its present size."[9] So the odds against us being here are, well, astronomical. And yet we are here. Who is responsible for this?

We read in Psalm 19:1 that "the heavens declare the glory of God and the firmament shows His handiwork." Paul writes in verse twenty of his first letter to the Romans that "ever since the creation of the world, His invisible nature, namely His eternal power and deity, has been clearly perceived in the things that have been made." In the anthropic principle we seem to have a thrilling confirmation of these ancient passages. Not only does the anthropic principle suggest a creator who is incomparably intelligent and resourceful, but it also suggests a creator who has special concern for us. This is a personal creator, not some abstract "first mover" who uncorked the universe without any evident care for the creatures who would eventually inhabit our planet. Through science we are witnessing powerful evidence that our human destiny seems to be an intrinsic part of a divine plan. No longer do we need to be intimidated by the vast empty spaces of the cosmos. They exist, in a sense, for our sake. Contrary to the principle of mediocrity, we live in a meaningful and purposeful universe. The anthropic principle suggests that human beings are part of the intended handiwork of God.

Leading scientists have acknowledged the far-reaching implications of the anthropic principle. "A commonsense interpretation of the facts," writes astronomer Fred Hoyle, "suggests that a super-intellect has monkeyed with the laws of physics."[10] Physicist Freeman Dyson says, "The more I examine the universe and study the details of its architecture, the more evidence I find that the universe in some sense must have known we were coming."[11] Astronomer Owen Gingerich writes that the anthropic principle "means accepting that the laws of nature are rigged not only in favor of complexity or just in favor of life, but also in favor of mind. To put it dramatically, it implies that mind is written into the laws of nature in a fundamental way."[12] Astronomer Robert Jastrow observes that the anthropic principle "is the most theistic result ever to come out of science."[13]

As you might expect, the anthropic principle has provoked a huge debate and a strong reaction. In this debate there are three positions, which for simplicity I call Lucky Us, Multiple Universes, and the Designer Universe. Let's examine them in sequence. The first response,

Lucky Us, attributes the fine-tuning of the universe to incredible coincidence. "The universe," writes physicist Victor Stenger in *Not By Design*, "is an accident."[14]

An accident? Steven Weinberg and Richard Dawkins are not impressed by how improbable this is. According to Steven Weinberg, "You don't have to invoke a benevolent designer to explain why we are in one of the parts of the universe where life is possible: in all the other parts of the universe there is no one to raise the question."[15] Richard Dawkins concurs. "It is no accident that our kind of life finds itself on a planet whose temperature, rainfall, and everything else are exactly right. If the planet were suitable for another kind of life, it is that kind of life that would have evolved here."[16] In science this is called a "selection effect." Since we are here, we know that—whatever the odds—the game of cosmic chance must have worked out in our favor.

There is a problem with this reasoning that I'd like to dramatize by giving an example from philosopher John Leslie. Imagine a man sentenced to death, standing before a firing squad of ten shooters. The shooters discharge their rifles. Somehow they all miss. Then they shoot again and one more time they fail to hit their target. Repeatedly they fire and repeatedly they miss. Later the prisoner is approached by the warden, who says, "I can't believe they all missed. Clearly there is some sort of conspiracy at work." Yet the prisoner laughs off the suggestion with the comment, "What on earth would make you suggest a conspiracy? It's no big deal. Obviously the marksmen missed because if they had not missed I would not be here to have this discussion." Such a prisoner would immediately, and rightly, be transferred to the mental ward.

What the example shows is that you cannot explain an improbability of this magnitude by simply pointing to our presence on the scene to ponder it. There is still a massive improbability that needs to be accounted for. Remember that the anthropic principle does not say that, given the billions of stars in the universe, it's remarkable that life turned up on our planet. Rather, it says that the entire universe with all the galaxies and stars in it had to be formed in a certain way in order for it to contain life at all. It's hard to disagree with the conclusion drawn by philosopher Antony Flew. Long a champion of atheism—he is one of the most frequently cited figures in atheist literature—Flew finally concluded that the fine-tuning of the universe at every level is simply too perfect to be the result of chance. Flew says that in keeping with his lifelong commitment "to go where the evidence leads," he now believes in God.[17]

Flew recognizes that the anthropic principle requires a better explanation than Lucky Us. So does astronomer Lee Smolin, who writes that "luck will certainly not do here. We need some rational explanation of how something this unlikely turned out to be the case."[18] The odds of us being here in the universe are so fantastic that some kind of a serious explanation is required. One suspects that, deep down, Weinberg and Dawkins know this.

Consequently, many atheists have fled to the second explanation for the anthropic principle: Multiple Universes. Actually, an infinity of universes. Each universe operates according to its own set of laws. Consequently one universe may have an inverse-square law of gravity and another may have an inverse-cube law of gravity. Indeed, under conditions of true infinity, we would expect that every physical condition, every possible arrangement of matter and energy, is realized. Everything that can happen does happen. In this remarkable situation—the argument goes—we can finally account for our privileged universe. As there are an infinite number of universes, it's entirely possible that one has developed in a way that permits observers like us.

There are several versions of the Multiple Universes theory. One is that we live in an oscillating universe that goes through an infinite number of cycles, in which big bangs are followed by big crunches. If the constants of nature vary in each cycle, at some point a particular combination will be realized by chance, like a winning number in a casino slot machine. A second version is that the Big Bang spawned multiple universes, each with its own set of laws. These universes are like separately expanding balloons that cannot relate to one another. Each has its own set of laws. A third version, sometimes called the parallel worlds theory, holds that at each act of quantum measurement the world splits into a series of parallel universes. In fact, universes are springing up even as you read this sentence. Don't ask where; the universes are disconnected from each other and we have access only to our own universe. Another idea, presented by Smolin, is that our universe emerged from a black hole in a previous universe, and indeed the black holes in our universe are even now generating other universes. Smolin has even raised the possibility of the Darwinian principle of natural selection applying to universes, in which some universes adapt and survive and others don't. (Not surprisingly, Darwinian hounds like Dawkins and Dennett have rushed to praise this theory.) In all these versions an infinite horizon of possibilities is invoked in order to allow for the possibility that our universe could have arisen purely by chance.

What is one to make of all this? As with all scientific theories, we begin by asking for the evidence. So what is the empirical evidence for oscillating and parallel and multiple universes? Actually, there isn't any. As Weinberg admits, "These are very speculative ideas ... without any experimental support."[19] Smolin is even more candid. He calls his ideas "a fantasy.... It is possible that all I have done here is cobble together a set of false clues that only seem to have something to do with each other.... There is every chance that these ideas will not succeed."[20] I appreciate this candor, and I am reminded of that old Ptolemaic remedy for problematic data: "just add epicycles." Now we are in the realm of "just add universes."

It seems worth pointing out here what Harvard astronomer Owen Gingerich seems to be the first to have noticed: anyone who can believe in multiple universes should have no problem believing in heaven and hell. Just think of them as alternate universes, operating outside space and time according to laws that are inoperative in our universe. Even the atheist should now be able to envision a realm in which there is no evil or suffering and where the inhabitants never grow old. These traditional concepts, which have long been dismissed as preposterous based on the rules of our world, should be quite believable and perhaps even mandatory for one who holds that there are an infinite number of universes in which all quantum possibilities are realized.

There is a principle of logic, widely accepted in science, called the principle of Occam's razor. It means that when there are a variety of possible explanations, go with the one that requires the fewest assumptions. In other words, if you're trying to get from point A to point B, try to avoid the zigzag route. Applying Occam's razor, Carl Sagan urges that "when faced with two hypotheses that explain the data equally well, choose the simpler."[21] Biologist E. O. Wilson writes that the difficult thing about this principle for many people is that it "grants less license for New Age dreaming...but it gets the world straight."[22]

Imagine if I find a coin and begin flipping it and, every single time, it comes up heads. I try this ten thousand times, and it never fails to show me heads. There are two possibilities. The first and obvious one is that the coin is rigged in some way; somebody "fixed" it to come up heads every time. There is also a second possibility. Perhaps there are an infinite number of coins in circulation, and given infinite tossing and infinite time one set of tosses was bound to show this result. Now which of these two explanations should a rational person choose? Occam's razor says choose the first one.

It is a serious objection to all theories of multiple universes that they violate Occam's razor. They invent a fantastically complicated set of circumstances to explain a single case when there is a much simpler, more obvious explanation right at hand. Yes, I am referring to the third possible response to the anthropic principle. It says, quite simply, that our universe is designed for life because someone designed it that way. The Designer Universe approach has this benefit: you don't need to make up the idea of a hundred billion universes that you know nothing about in order to account for the only universe you can possibly experience. Yet this third response seems to be anathema to some people, and here we see how strongly modern atheism relies on "New Age dreaming."

Physicist Stephen Hawking falls right into the New Age trap. As we saw in the previous chapter, Hawking recognizes that the evidence of the Big Bang and the anthropic principle point directly to a creator. However, he seems eager to have a different explanation. Recently he has advanced a proposal no less outlandish that that of an infinity of universes. Hawking's solution begins with the mathematical concept of "imaginary time." The distinguishing feature of imaginary time is that it requires no past, no present, and no future. Time is viewed merely as a dimension of space. In his book *A Brief History of Time*, Hawking uses imaginary time, together with quantum fluctuations in which literally anything can happen, to postulate multiple universes, all of which have no spatial or temporal boundaries. He envisions universes coming into being as baby universes popping out of wormholes in other universes. The reason none of this can be witnessed, as you may have surmised by now, is that it all occurs in imaginary time. Hawking triumphantly notes that because he has dispensed with a time dimension for universes he has also dispensed with the notion of a beginning, and as there is no beginning, there is no need for a creator.

Once again, where's the evidence for this theory? Hawking admits that there is none, and he doesn't expect to ever find any. Imaginary time is invoked to stipulate imaginary universes. Naturally, with so much imagining going on, there is no need to go overboard and imagine a creator. So rather than consider these theories scientific, it seems entirely reasonable to label them versions of a religious doctrine. Hawking, Weinberg, Dawkins, and the others are all members of the Church of Infinite Worlds, where new worlds with new sets of laws have to be invented in order to avoid one inconvenient admission. For members of this church, the dogmas of infinite universes, baby universes, and the rest of it seem to be largely motivated by the desire to avoid a supernatural creator. As physicist Stephen Barr puts it, "It seems that to abolish one unobservable God, it takes an infinite number of unobservable substitutes."[23]

As one of its longtime residents, I'd like to bring us back to earth and conclude with a final point. Whether we believe in imaginary time and multiple universes or not, those are only concepts. Even if they describe our universe, they do not explain why there is a universe in the first place. As Hawking himself once asked, who put the fire into the equations? Who made them, as it were, "come to life"? Moreover, the atheist viewpoint cannot explain the profound lawfulness of nature itself. Paul Davies writes, "If the divine underpinning of the laws is removed, their existence becomes a profound mystery. Where do they come from? Who sent the message? Who devised the code?"[24]

Indeed the question can be posed in a deeper way. How can inanimate objects like electrons follow laws? Our experience as humans is that only rational and conscious agents can obey instructions. It remains deeply mysterious how things can do anything whatsoever, let alone abide by mathematical rules. And what rules! Throughout the history of science its practitioners have found that anomalies in known laws are usually accounted for by even deeper and more beautiful laws that seem to underlie the workings of nature.

"So where did the laws of physics come from?" Victor Stenger asks. "They came from nothing."[25] I grant that this is an answer, but what kind of an answer? Even scientists who are not religious believers are nevertheless awed by what biologist Ursula Goodenough has called "the sacred depths of nature," and their attitude toward it borders on the mystical. Here, I believe, is where many believers and nonbelievers can find common ground, in their shared reverence for the grandeur of creation. Yet the mind that reflects on nature's intricate order is irresistibly propelled to ask how this order came to be. Why is reality structured in this way? Doesn't the lawful order of nature require some ultimate explanation? If it does, then clearly the best explanation for why the universe is so orderly and intelligible and favorable for life is that an intelligent being made it that way.

CHAPTER THIRTEEN

PALEY WAS RIGHT: EVOLUTION AND THE ARGUMENT FROM DESIGN

"The ancient covenant is in pieces. Man at last knows that he is alone in the unfeeling immensity of the universe, out of which he has emerged only by chance."[1]

—Jacques Monod, *Chance and Necessity*

IN HIS BOOK ***NATURAL THEOLOGY,*** published in 1802, Anglican theologian William Paley made what was regarded for more than a century as an irrefutable argument for the existence of God. "In crossing a heath," Paley wrote, "suppose I pitched my foot against a *stone*, and were asked how the stone came to be there, I might possibly answer, for anything I knew to the contrary, it had lain there forever." But suppose, Paley continued, "I found a *watch* upon the ground, I should hardly think of the answer I had given before."[2] Paley's point was that you don't have to be a horologist to see right away that the watch was intentionally designed. You may not know who designed it, but you know that someone did. Paley proceeded to show, with an intricate tapestry of informed detail, how the earth and its life forms, including human beings, display in their constitution the unquestionable marks of design. Such design, he concluded, demonstrates the presence of a designer who may be considered the divine "watchmaker" of creation.

About two decades ago, biologist Richard Dawkins published his book *The Blind Watchmaker*, in which he asserts that Paley was "gloriously and utterly wrong." Dawkins argued that Charles Darwin had discovered a way for nature to produce the appearance of design—yes, even minute and complex design—without the intervention of a creator. Dawkins declared the "blind, unconscious, automatic process" of natural selection "the explanation for the existence and apparently purposeful form of all life.... It is the blind watchmaker."[3]

Dawkins's argument—widely embraced by biologists—has been hailed as a decisive refutation of the argument from design, one of the oldest arguments for the existence of God. Numerous leading biologists now understand and teach evolution in precisely these terms. They see evolution as undermining the argument for God and discrediting the Christian idea of man created in God's likeness. These views are now part of our culture. In his book *Revolution in Science*, a historical account of the impact of science, Bernard Cohen notes that "the Darwinian revolution sounded the death knell of any argument about design in the universe or in nature."[4] In a recent article in *Harper's*, David Quammen attributed to Darwin a "big scary idea which contradicted...the whole framework of pious beliefs about mankind made in God's image."[5] And Michael Shermer, the publisher of *Skeptic* magazine, is typical of many people who were once Christian but who say they lost their religious faith upon embracing Darwin's account of evolution.

The American public is dubious about evolution. A Gallup survey in February 2001 had 45 percent of responding adults agreeing that "God created human beings pretty much in their present form at one time." Similar surveys over the past two decades show no real shift in people's opinions.[6] These figures are a source of consternation and distress to many scientists. It would be one thing if a few yahoos, what H. L. Mencken termed the "ignorant yokels from the cow states," stood obstinately against evolution. Some of these people may not yet have come around to accepting that the earth is round. But almost half the American population! Many scientists and others have expressed their bafflement that there are so many "creationists" out there who simply refuse to accept the findings of modern science.

Creationists come in different shapes and sizes. Most are biblical literalists, who uphold without qualification the biblical claim that God created the earth and all living things in six days. A quite distinct creationist belief—not always shared by those in the first group—is that the earth is only six thousand years old. This figure is derived by tabulating the genealogies listed in scripture. Many creationists fight evolution with a desperate intensity, because they fear that if any part of the Bible is proven wrong then none of it will be believed. I respect the dedication and moral fervor of the creationists, although I do not agree with their reading either of scripture or the scientific evidence. Moreover, the broader anxiety about Darwinism in the culture is not simply a product of creationism.

It is said that the wife of a London aristocrat, when informed about Darwin's claim that man is descended from an ape-like creature, responded, "My dear, let us hope that it is not true, but if it is, let us pray that it may not become widely known." This woman was raising an interesting question: what does it do to man to teach him that he is nothing more than an animal? Perhaps he will start acting like an animal! Consider this disquieting thought. If your neighbor entered your house by force, killed or stupefied you with blows, and then dragged your daughter to his own place to forcibly mate with her, most people would consider that an outrage. But that kind of behavior is common, natural, and expected in the animal kingdom.

We know that for more than half a century social Darwinists used ideas of "natural selection" and "survival of the fittest" to justify racist and inhumane policies like eugenics, anti-immigration laws, and forced sterilization. William Jennings Bryan—a religious conservative who was also a political progressive—championed the creationist cause at the Scopes trial largely because of his abhorrence of this political program. Today's champions of evolution are quick to declare social Darwinism a crude distortion of Darwin's theories. As one of my college professors put it, "They were using science for ideological ends. That's not going on today."

But it is. According to biologist Francisco Ayala, Darwin "completed the Copernican Revolution....Darwin discovered that living beings can be explained as a result of a natural process—natural selection—without resorting to a Creator."[7] Biologist E. O. Wilson writes, "If humankind evolved by Darwinian natural selection, genetic chance and environmental necessity, not God, made the species."[8] Biologist Stephen Jay Gould invokes evolution to show that "no intervening spirit watches lovingly over the affairs of nature...whatever we think of God, his existence is not manifest in the products of nature."[9] Douglas Futuyma asserts in his textbook *Evolutionary Biology*, "By coupling undirected, purposeless variation to the blind, uncaring process of natural selection, Darwin made theological or spiritual explanations of life processes superfluous."[10] Biologist William Provine boasts that "evolution is the greatest engine of atheism."[11]

So there is an anti-religious thrust in Darwinism, and this is the main reason many Americans refuse to embrace it. They view Darwinism as atheism masquerading as science. They also suspect that Darwin's theories are being used to undermine traditional religion and morality. Many parents are concerned that their children will go to school and college as decent Christians and come out as unbelievers and moral relativists. As we can see from the quotations above, these concerns about contemporary Darwinism are justified. Evolution in the way that it is promoted and taught today seems to promote a social agenda that is anti-religious and amoral.

But doesn't evolution contradict the claims of the Bible? Let us look carefully at what the book of Genesis actually says. We read in Genesis 2:7 that "the Lord God formed man from the dust of the ground and breathed into his nostrils the breath of life." Right away we notice something significant: the Bible says that the universe was created out of nothing but it does not say man was created out of nothing. Rather, it says that man was made or shaped from the existing substance of nature. "Dust thou art and to dust thou shall return." So the Bible is quite consistent with the idea that man is made up of atoms and molecules and shares the same DNA found in earthworms, whales, and monkeys.

It is true, however, that the creation account in Genesis does not prepare us for the discovery that man has about 98 percent of his DNA in common with apes. In his *Descent of Man*, Darwin writes that "man...still bears in his bodily frame the indelible stamp of his lowly origin."[12] Our resistance to this is not religious; it is because we sense a significant chasm between ourselves and chimpanzees. Of course Darwin is not saying that man is descended from chimpanzees, only that apes and man are descended from a common ancestor. Whatever the merits of this theory, there is no reason to reject it purely on biblical grounds. Christians since medieval times have agreed with Aristotle that man is an animal—a "rational animal," but still an animal.

What makes man different, according to the Bible, is that God breathed an immaterial soul into him. Thus there is no theological problem in viewing the bodily frame of man as derived from other creatures. The Bible stresses God's resolution, "Let us make man in our image." Christians have always understood God as a spiritual rather than a material being. Consequently if man is created in the "likeness" of God, the resemblance is clearly not physical. When Jared Diamond in his book *The Third Chimpanzee* refers to humans as "little more than glorified chimpanzees," he is unwittingly making a Christian point.[13] We may have common ancestors with the animals, but we are *glorified* animals.

But didn't the main opposition to Darwin's theory of evolution come from religious people, specifically Christians? Actually, no. Hindus, Jews, and Muslims have never really had a problem with evolution because they have always understood their creation stories as parables. Historian Gertrude Himmelfarb writes that when Darwin published his *Origin of Species*, one group rejected the theory of evolution because of the perception that it undermines Christianity, and another group embraced it for the same reason.[14] Darwin's leading defender, the intellectual "bulldog" Thomas Henry Huxley, belonged to the second group. A lifelong hater of the Catholic church, he acknowledged that he found the new theory appealing because he saw it undermining ecclesiastical doctrine. "One of its greatest merits in my eyes is the fact that it occupies a position of complete and irreconcilable antagonism to...the Catholic church."[15]

But these "irreconcilables," as Himmelfarb calls them, were outnumbered by other groups: scientists who raised non-religious objections to Darwin's theory and religious people who saw no conflict between evolution and Christianity. There were in fact intelligent objections to natural selection raised by British naturalist Richard Owen and Harvard zoologist Louis Agassiz. Ernst Mayr, a longtime champion of evolution, writes that when Darwin published the *Origin of Species* "he actually did not have a single clear-cut piece of evidence for the existence of natural selection."[16] Another Darwin enthusiast, Jonathan Weiner, concedes that despite its title, Darwin's book "does not document the origin of a single species."[17]

Then there was the problem of the age of the earth. Renowned physicist Lord Kelvin published thermodynamic calculations that showed the earth was far too "young" to give evolution time to take place along Darwinian lines. Kelvin turned out to be wrong because the physicists of his day had not discovered radioactivity and nuclear processes that generate energy and heat, prolonging the earth's cooling process. Today we know that the earth is around 4.5 billion years old, giving natural selection more time to produce its transformations. But Darwin and his scientific contemporaries didn't know that. The best physics of the day seemed incompatible with Darwinism.

Even so, many Christians rallied to Darwin's side. The *Dublin Review*, an influential Catholic journal, praised Darwin's book while registering only minor objections. Darwin's leading supporter in the United States was Harvard biologist Asa Gray, who saw evolution not as a denial of God's creation but as a documentation of how He had gone about it. Darwin himself wrote that Gray's interpretation "pleases me especially, and I do not think anyone else has ever noticed the point." But they soon did, and over the years some of Darwin's most prominent defenders, like Theodosius Dobzhansky and R. A. Fisher, have been Christians. While a minority of Christians proclaimed evolution a heresy from the outset, most Christian leaders sought to reconcile Darwin's theory with the biblical story of creation.

Darwin himself was an agnostic, but when he died he was buried in Westminster Abbey with the approval of the Anglican Church. A few years ago, Pope John Paul II moved the Catholic church closer to an endorsement of evolution by proclaiming it "more than a hypothesis." Christian apologist C. S. Lewis had no problem with it. And several of today's leading evolutionists, such as biologist Kenneth Miller and geneticist Francis Collins, are practicing Christians.

What, then, are we to make of the furious intellectual battles that we see, both in the courts and in the media, between the Darwinists and the anti-Darwinists? There is now a school of thought that goes by the name of "intelligent design." Its leading figures are William Dembski, Jonathan Wells, Michael Behe, and Phillip Johnson. Trained in mathematics, biochemistry, and law, these critics are in an entirely different league than the self-styled "creationists." And they have raised important questions: How to account for the complexity of the eye? Why was there an "explosion" of new forms of life, entirely unanticipated in the fossil record, during the Cambrian era? Despite a long history of experimentation, breeders have never been able to breed across species lines and produce new species, so how can random mutations achieve what carefully orchestrated cross-breeding has failed to do? While the fossil record shows evidence of microevolution (one type of finch evolves into another type of finch), where is the evidence for macroevolution (one species evolves into a different species)?

The critics have exposed some of the weak points in the theory of evolution. The fossil record is inadequate, as Darwin himself realized.[18] Biologists routinely debate what caused the Cambrian "explosion," and there are competing theories and much that remains to be discovered. On the other hand biologists have shown that a complex eye can evolve and has evolved—actually on several independent occasions—from simpler forms of light-sensitive cells. Once you see how much change can be produced within a species, it's not hard to see how evolution can transform one species into another. Is it such a stretch to believe that the lion and the tiger evolved from a common ancestor, even if there is no way to see this process occur? I am not a biologist, but what impresses me is that virtually every biologist in the world accepts the theory of evolution. While the debate goes on, it seems improbable that the small group of intelligent design advocates is right and the entire community of biologists is wrong. Consider what two leading Christian biologists say about evolution. Kenneth Miller writes, "Evolution is as much a fact as anything we know in science,"[19] and Theodosius Dobzhansky famously said, "Nothing in biology makes sense except in the light of evolution."[20]

The great strength of evolution as a scientific theory is that it makes sense of two huge facts about life. On the one hand, all living things from trees to cats to humans are formed from the same genetic material. Beyond this, it is evident that many groups of organisms show similar characteristics. So there is a unity to life. At the same time, living creatures exhibit incredible diversity. There are literally millions of living species with widely varying characteristics. Evolution accounts both for the similarities and the differences. It accounts for common characteristics by positing that the creatures possessing them descended from the same ancestor. It explains differences by suggesting that creatures evolved new traits over a long period of time under the pressures of survival.

One of the strongest proofs for evolution is that the geological record, for all its imperfections, shows a single invariant trajectory. The oldest rocks contain only single-celled creatures. Later strata show the appearance of invertebrates. Then we see the first fishes, then amphibians, then reptiles, and finally mammals. Man appears latest on the scene. The fossils are found in exactly the places and at exactly the times that we would expect if Darwin's theory is correct. Not a single fossil has ever been found in a place where it is not supposed to show up. If we ever discover the fossil of a single reptile in a rock so old that fishes had not yet arrived, or if we find human skeletons at the time when dinosaurs also lived, then Darwin's theory will be proven false and biologists will have to come up with a new one.

Until this happens—and I don't think it will—evolution remains the best and most persuasive account of our origins. It is impossible to deny the theory's explanatory power. Evolution by natural selection helps us to explain why pesticides and antibiotics frequently result in the pests and bacteria developing new strains more resistant to human efforts to wipe them out. In a word, they evolve. Without evolution it would not be easy to understand features of living creatures that seem poorly designed or serve no functional purpose. We see snakes with tiny legs buried inside their skins and flightless beetles with wings. We humans possess an unnecessary appendix. How to explain these vestigial organs? Evolution says it is because snakes, flightless beetles, and humans are all descended from creatures that needed those organs to survive.

Still, evolution remains a theory with clear limits. When Dawkins subtitles one of his books "How the Evidence of Evolution Reveals a Universe Without Design" he shows no awareness of these limits. When Dennett invokes evolution as an all-purpose explanation in cosmology, psychology, culture, ethics, politics, and religion, he too goes way beyond the evidence. Here we must distinguish between the empirical and metaphysical aspects of evolution. Dawkins and Dennett are metaphysical Darwinists. Biologist Stephen Jay Gould once termed them "Darwinian fundamentalists."[21] He faulted them, as I do, for using a powerful but quite circumscribed theory to account for phenomena that fall entirely outside its biological reach. Consider three massive features of life that evolution cannot account for.

Evolution cannot explain the beginning of life. Darwin didn't even try. He assumed the first living thing, and then he tried to show how one living thing could be transformed into another. In 1953 there was considerable excitement when Stanley Miller generated amino acids by sending an electrical discharge through a combination of water, hydrogen, methane, and ammonia. This excitement subsided when it was subsequently established that the atmosphere of the early earth was mostly made up of carbon dioxide and ammonia. So Miller's experiment was not relevant to showing how life could have arisen out of non-life through random chemical interactions. Moreover, life involves a lot more than the generation of amino acids. The biggest problem is taking simple chemicals like amino acids and generating proteins and other essential components of life. The origin of life, biologist Franklin Harold confesses, is one of the "unsolved mysteries in science."[22]

The simplest living cell is one of the most complicated structures on earth, containing within it more information than multiple sets of the *Encyclopedia Britannica*. "The genetic code," writes Richard Dawkins, "is truly digital, in exactly the same sense as computer codes."[23] As Dawkins shows, each DNA molecule is an algorithm in biochemical code with a built-in capacity for transcription and replication. Harold remarks that even a bacterial cell "displays levels of regularity and complexity that exceed by orders of magnitude" anything found in the nonliving world. Besides, "A cell constitutes a unitary whole, a unit of life, in another deeper sense: like the legs and leaves of higher organisms, its molecular constituents have functions.... Molecules are parts of an integrated system, and in that capacity can be said to serve the activities of the cell as a whole."[24]

The cell, in other words, shows the marked signature of design. It is crucially important to recognize that this basic template of life, with all its intricate machinery of RNA and DNA, came fully formed with the first appearance of life. Evolution presupposes cells that have these built-in capacities. And scientists have found that the first traces of life go back between 3.5 and 4 billion years, only a short time after the earth itself was formed.[25] Is it even reasonable to speculate that random combinations of chemicals could have produced so marvelously complex and functional a thing as a living cell? That's like positing that chance combinations of atoms could have assembled themselves to produce an airplane. "However improbable the origin of life might be," Dawkins writes, it must have happened this way "because we are here."[26] It takes a lot of faith to believe things like this.

Nor can evolution explain consciousness, which illuminates the whole world for us. We know as human beings that we are conscious. Other creatures, such as dogs, also appear to be conscious, although perhaps not quite in the same way that we are. It does seem incredible that atoms of hydrogen, carbon, oxygen, and so on can somehow produce our capacity to perceive and experience the world around us. So what is the evolutionary explanation for consciousness? What adaptive benefits did it confer? How did unconscious life transform itself into conscious life? Cognitive scientist Steven Pinker admits there is no explanation. In *How the Mind Works*, he writes, "Virtually nothing is known about the functioning microcircuitry of the brain.... The existence of subjective first-person experience is not explainable by science."[27] So baffling is the problem that Daniel Dennett has "solved" it by declaring consciousness to be a cognitive illusion.

Finally, evolution cannot explain human rationality or morality. This was a point first made by Alfred Russel Wallace, who proposed simultaneously with Darwin a theory of evolution by natural selection. Here I don't want to be misunderstood. Evolution can account for how brain size got larger and conferred survival benefits on creatures with larger brains. But rationality is something more than this. Rationality is the power to perceive something as true. We can include in rationality the unique human capacity for language, which is the ability to formulate and articulate ideas that comprehend the world around us. People in the most primitive cultures developed language as a means of rationality, while cats cannot utter a single sentence. Evolution provides an explanation for how creatures develop traits that are useful to their survival. As Steven Pinker puts it, "Our brains were shaped for fitness, not for truth."[28] So where did we humans get this other capacity to figure out not only what helps our genes to make it into the next generation, but also to understand what is going on in the world? To put it another way, what is the survival value of truth itself? Philosopher Michael Ruse, a noted Darwinist, confesses that "no one, certainly not the Darwinian as such, seems to have any answer to this."[29]

Humans have not only a rational but also a moral capacity. In his *Descent of Man*, Darwin admitted that "of all the differences between man and the lower animals, the moral sense or conscience is the most important."[30] Morality speaks to us in a different voice: not what we do but what we ought to do. Frequently morality presses on us to act against our evident self-interest. It urges us not to tell lies even when they benefit us and to help people even when they are strangers to us. In a later chapter, I address how evolutionists seek to account for morality in Darwinian terms. Here let me say something that most of them would agree with: there is much inventive speculation but no good evolutionary explanation for these basic human capacities.

Do you see now why the arrogance of Darwinists like Dennett and Dawkins is entirely misplaced? These fellows seem to think they are armed with some master theory that provides a full explanation for the universe, and for our place in it. Yet their cherished evolutionary theory cannot account for the origin of life, the origin of consciousness, or the origin of human rationality and morality. Any theory that cannot account for these landmark stages can hardly claim to have solved the problem of origins, either of life or of the universe. It can take credit only for elucidating some transitions along the way. Evolution seems right as far as it goes, but it doesn't go very far.

True, one day science may provide us with better answers. I am not making a "God of the Gaps" argument that says because science cannot explain this, therefore God did it. But neither do I want to succumb to the "atheism of the gaps" that holds that even where there is no explanation, we should be confident that a natural explanation is forthcoming. Yes, science has made huge strides in explaining some things but in other areas science has not markedly advanced since the days of the Babylonians. Our best bet is to go with what we know so far and draw conclusions based on that. As of now, evolution is a useful theory but one that falls well short of accounting for the kind of life we have in the world.

Let us now return to the claims by Dawkins and others that Darwin's theory of evolution has decimated Paley's argument from design. Actually, Paley's argument has never been refuted. I am not talking of the specific details that Paley cited, but about his general case for design. That case is actually much stronger today than when Paley made it two centuries ago.

Dawkins is too blinded by anti-religious prejudice to see it, but his argument in *The Blind Watchmaker* actually supports the design argument. To see why, consider the example of a computer. A computer is like Paley's watch: it shows clear evidence of design. No one could seriously contend that the computer somehow "evolved" through the forces of natural selection. Someone made it and someone programmed it. Now let's assume that this is not the case with a certain type of software. Let's assume that this software operates in a kind of "open source" mode. It accepts random changes and somehow the most useful and adaptive programs survive. Let's posit that the process here is evolutionary; it is guided by no one. My question is the following: would the fact of evolution in the case of the software in any way undermine the fact of design in the case of the computer? Obviously not. The software may evolve but someone still had to make the computer and install in it the original programming.

Now apply this analogy to the universe. I have in previous chapters offered strong evidence that the universe is the product of design. The universe could not have evolved through natural selection, as the universe makes up the whole of nature. Someone made the universe and prescribed the laws that govern its operations. Now within the universe there are innumerable life forms that correspond in our analogy to the software programs. These life forms are the product of evolution, and Darwin and his successors have elegantly elucidated the modes of transition. But evolution has no explanation for the origin of the universe or its laws. So how can evolution undercut the argument from design as it applies to the universe itself and the laws that govern it? Clearly it cannot. In this case, as with the computer, the evolution of the part in no way refutes the deliberate design of the whole. The overwhelming evidence is that someone planned the whole thing.

If the laws of physics did not have their finely tuned features in line with the anthropic principle, stars like the sun would not burn in the slow and steady way that they do, giving life in general—and human life in particular—time to evolve. Evolution itself requires a finely tuned designer universe. John Barrow and Frank Tipler argue that physics has supplied a new "design argument remarkably similar to that proposed by Paley."[31] Biologists who insist that evolution operates according to principles of time and chance often forget that it also depends on the laws of a universe that is not the product of time and chance. Even if God did not override the laws of nature in order for mankind to emerge, who programmed the cell with its digital code? Who gave it the capacity to make copies of itself? Who made a universe with the laws that could produce mankind? What is the ultimate explanation for why reality is structured in this way?

Physicist Stephen Barr writes:

When examined carefully, scientific accounts of natural processes are never really about order emerging from mere chaos, or form emerging from mere formlessness. On the contrary, they are always about the unfolding of an order that was already implicit in the nature of things, although often in a secret or hidden way. When we see situations that appear haphazard, or things that appear amorphous, automatically or spontaneously "arranging themselves" into orderly patterns, what we find in every case is that what appeared to be haphazard actually had a great deal of order built into it. . . . What Dawkins does not seem to appreciate is that his blind watchmaker is something even more remarkable than Paley's watches. Paley finds a "watch" and asks how such a thing could have come to be there by chance. Dawkins finds an immense automated factory that blindly constructs watches, and feels that he has completely answered Paley's point. But that is absurd. How can a factory that makes watches be less in need of explanation than the watches themselves?[32]

For one kind of life to evolve into another may be attributed to the blind forces of nature, but the anthropic principle implies that these forces were set in motion deliberately, purposefully, with a view to producing precisely the living beings that biologists superficially presume to have gotten here by accident. It's one thing to say that the finch's beak and the moth's hue and the human eye all evolved by chance. But the universe that lawfully produces finches, moths, and humans is quite clearly the product of intention and creative design. So Dawkins's "refutation" of Paley fails gloriously and completely. Paley was right all along.

It should be clear from all this that the problem is not with evolution. The problem is with Darwinism. Evolution is a scientific theory, Darwinism is a metaphysical stance and a political ideology. In fact, Darwinism is the atheist spin imposed on the theory of evolution. As a theory, evolution is not hostile to religion. Far from disproving design, evolution actually reveals the mode by which design has been executed. But atheists routinely use Darwinism and the fallacy of the blind watchmaker to undermine belief in God. Many scientists have been conned by this atheist tactic. They allow themselves to slide, almost unwittingly, from evolution into Darwinism. Thus they become pawns of the atheist agenda.

Christians should not be afraid of the evolution debate, because there is nothing about it that threatens their faith. The Christian position is that God is the creator of the universe and everything in it, and the evolution debate is about how some of these changes came about. For the Christian, the evolution debate comes down to competing theories about how God did it. My own view is that Christians and other religious believers should embrace evolution while resisting Darwinism. Theists can be champions of science while at the same time exposing the way in which Darwin's ideas are being ideologically manipulated, just as they were by the social Darwinists a century ago. It is this ideological indoctrination masquerading as science that should be fought in the classroom. Evolution should be taught, but it should be taught without the metaphysics of Darwinism. Instead of suing to get theories of creationism and intelligent design into the science classroom, Christians should be suing to get atheist interpretations of Darwin out. Through evolution, rightly understood, Christians can affirm that the book of nature and the book of scripture are in no way contradictory. In fact, both affirm the notion of a universe and its creatures that are the product of supernatural design and divine creation.

CHAPTER FOURTEEN

THE GENESIS PROBLEM:
THE METHODOLOGICAL ATHEISM
OF SCIENCE

"There is no such thing as philosophy-free science. There is only science whose philosophical baggage is taken on board without examination."[1]

—Daniel Dennett, *Darwin's Dangerous Idea*

I**T IS TIME TO HIGHLIGHT** a serious problem with our understanding of modern science. The problem is not with modern science itself, but rather with a faulty view of science: the idea that science is a complete framework for understanding man and the universe, so unscientific claims should be automatically rejected. Although this way of approaching knowledge is put forward as the very epitome of rationality, I want to show that it is profoundly irrational. It would be like trying to understand a murder solely through the laws of physics and chemistry. However indispensable those laws in figuring out which gun was used, and how long the victim was dead when the body was discovered, we have to look elsewhere to discover other crucial elements like why the killer did it. In this chapter we will see why the attempt to explain everything scientifically is inadequate and even unreasonable. Atheists who pursue this approach are ultimately an embarrassment to science.

Scientists like to think of themselves as reasonable people. They fancy themselves ready to follow the path of evidence no matter where it takes them. Indeed in no other field do people go around congratulating themselves so much on how rational they are, how strictly their conclusions conform to testing and experience, and how biases and prejudices are routinely removed through the process of empirical verification and peer criticism. Carl Sagan's boast is typical: "At the heart of science is...an openness to new ideas, no matter how bizarre or counterintuitive."[2] Such is the prestige of science in our culture that these claims are widely accepted.

Yet the actual behavior of some scientists can be manifestly unreasonable. Leading scientists will sometimes embrace a conclusion even when the evidence for it is weak. These savants become indignant when an unsupported conclusion is questioned, and they even accuse their critics of being enemies of science. On other occasions, scientists show their unwillingness to accept conclusions even when a great deal of evidence points to them. In fact, they denounce the reasonable position and prefer to align themselves with unreasonable alternatives that are clearly less plausible.

Several years ago eminent science writer John Maddox published an article in *Nature* titled "Down with the Big Bang."[3] This is strange language for a scientist to use. Clearly the Big Bang happened, but Maddox gives the impression that he wishes it hadn't. He is not alone. In chapter eleven, I quoted astronomer Arthur Eddington's description of the Big Bang as "repugnant." Eddington confessed his desire to find "a genuine loophole" in order to "allow evolution an infinite time to get started."[4] So one reason for resisting the Big Bang is to make room for the theory of evolution.

There are others. Physicist Stephen Hawking explains why a large number of scientists were attracted to the steady state theory of the origin of the universe: "There were therefore a number of attempts to avoid the conclusion that there had been a big bang....Many people do not like the idea that time has a beginning, probably because it smacks of divine intervention."[5] The same point is made by Steven

Weinberg. Some cosmologists endorse theories because they "nicely avoid the problem of Genesis."[6]

What exactly is this problem? Astronomer and physicist Lee Smolin writes that if the universe started at a point in time, this "leaves the door open for a return of religion." This prospect has Smolin aghast. "Must all of our scientific understanding of the world really come down to a mythological story in which nothing exists... save some disembodied intelligence, who, desiring to start a world, chooses the initial conditions and then wills matter into being?" Smolin adds, "It seems to me that the only possible name for such an observer is God, and that the theory is to be criticized as being unlikely on these grounds."[7]

Here we have scientists who do not seem to be acting like scientists. Why is it necessary to object to findings in modern physics in order to give evolution time to get going? Why is it important to avoid the "problem of Genesis" or to shrink away from any theory that suggests a divine hand in the universe? If the evidence points in the direction of a creator, why not go with it?

Douglas Erwin, a paleobiologist at the Smithsonian Institution, gives part of the answer. "One of the rules of science is, no miracles allowed," he told the *New York Times*. "That's a fundamental presumption of what we do."[8] Biologist Barry Palevitz makes the same point. "The supernatural," he writes, "is automatically off-limits as an explanation of the natural world."[9]

Erwin and Palevitz are absolutely correct that there is a ban on miracles and the supernatural in modern scientific exploration of the universe. Yet their statements raise the deeper question: why are miracles and the supernatural ruled out of bounds at the outset? If a space shuttle were to produce photographs of never-before-seen solar bodies that bore the sign YAHWEH MADE THIS, would the scientific community still refuse to acknowledge the existence of a supernatural creator?

Yes, it would. And the reason is both simple and surprising: modern science was designed to exclude a designer. So dogmatic is modern science in its operating procedures that today all evidence of God is a priori rejected by science. Even empirical evidence of the kind normally admissible in science is refused a hearing. It doesn't matter how strong or reliable the evidence is; scientists, acting in their professional capacity, are obliged to ignore it. The position of modern science is not that no miracles are possible but rather that no miracles are allowed.

All of this may seem surprising, in view of how science developed out of the theological premises and institutions of Christianity. Copernicus, Kepler, Boyle, and others all saw a deep compatibility between science and religion. In the past century and a half, however, science seems to have cast aside its earlier presupposition that the universe reflects the rationality of God. Now scientists typically admit the orderliness of nature but refuse to consider the source of that orderliness. One reason for the shift is the increasing secularization of the intelligentsia since the mid-nineteenth century, a process described by Christian Smith in his book *The Secular Revolution*.[10]

Another is the discovery that unexplained mysteries of the universe, once attributed to God, can now be given scientific explanations. "The Darwinian revolution," Ernst Mayr writes, "was not merely the replacement of one scientific theory by another, but rather the replacement of a worldview in which the supernatural was accepted as a normal and relevant explanatory principle by a new worldview in which there was no room for supernatural forces."[11] Consequently, science has become an entirely secular enterprise, and this—oddly enough—creates problems for science. By narrowly focusing on a certain type of explanation, modern science is cutting itself off from truths not amenable to that type of explanation.

We have seen how some leading physicists refuse to admit strong evidence about the origins of the universe to avoid having to consider a creator. Now let us consider how some distinguished biologists are willing to embrace weak evidence to corroborate evolution and eliminate the need for a divine being superintending the process. Biologist Franklin Harold knows how complex are the workings of even the simplest cells, because he wrote a book about it. He also knows evolution presumes the existence of fully formed cells with the power to replicate themselves. So what is the origin of the cell? "Life arose here on earth from inanimate matter, by some kind of evolutionary process." How does Harold know this? "This is not a statement of demonstrable fact," he concedes, "but an assumption." An assumption supported by what? Harold is not afraid to answer, "It is not supported by any direct evidence, nor is it likely to be, but it is consistent with what evidence we do have."[12]

Actually, I've found someone who doesn't share Harold's assumption: Francis Crick, co-discoverer of the structure of DNA. Crick, like Harold, recognizes that the origin of life seems almost a miracle, given the intricate machinery of the cell and given how quickly life appeared on the earth after the planet's formation. Crick cannot agree with Harold, Dawkins, and others who blithely posit that some combination of chemicals must have proved the right one. So Crick offers a different theory: space aliens must have brought life to earth from another planet! This theory is seriously put forth in Crick's book *Life Itself.*[13]

John Maddox recognizes that science knows little about the relationship between brain circuits and human consciousness. Yet he asserts, "An explanation of the mind, like that of the brain, must ultimately be an explanation in terms of the way that neurons function. After all, there is nothing else on which to rest an explanation."[14] Nicholas Humphrey goes even further: "Our starting assumption as scientists ought to be that on some level consciousness has to be an illusion."[15] Most people might find this a remarkable conclusion, but not Humphrey; it is his "starting assumption."

Writing in *The Blind Watchmaker*, Richard Dawkins admits that there are significant "gaps" in the fossil record. Then his argument takes a strange turn. If we take Darwinian evolution seriously, "The gaps, far from being annoying imperfections or awkward embarrassments, turn out to be exactly what we should positively expect." In other words, the absence of evidence is itself proof that the theory is correct. This is so bizarre that it makes one wonder what the presence of evidence might do to this theory. Would a complete fossil record without gaps be evidence against Darwinian evolution, as we hear that

Dawkins and his fellow biologists "exactly" and "positively" expect that such evidence should not be present?

Dawkins finally puts his cards on the table by saying, "The theory of evolution by cumulative natural selection is the only theory we know of that is in principle capable of explaining the existence of organized complexity. Even if the evidence did not favor it, it would still be the best theory available."[16] This is a revealing admission. Steven Pinker makes pretty much the same point: "Because there are no alternatives, we would almost have to accept natural selection as the explanation of life on this planet even if there were no evidence for it."[17] My point is not to deny that there is good evidence for evolution. There is, but it is not as good as you would be led to believe by the champions of Darwinism. That's because the champions of Darwinism are completely blind to weaknesses in the theory. They cannot even imagine that it is not true.

This is a level of dogmatism that would embarrass any theist. Even the strongest religious believer can imagine the possibility that there is no God. So how can these self-styled champions of reason adopt an approach that is so utterly closed-minded? It is the product of a philosophical commitment many of them have without being aware that they have it. Dawkins and the others seem naïvely to think that they are apostles of reason who are merely following the evidence. The reason they are deluded about their philosophical commitment is that it is hidden inside the scientific approach itself.

Modern science seems to be based on an unwavering commitment to naturalism and materialism. Naturalism is the doctrine that nature is all there is. According to naturalism, there are neither miracles nor supernatural forces. Therefore reports of the supernatural can only be interpreted naturalistically. Materialism is the belief that material reality is the only reality. There is no separately existing mental or spiritual reality. Of course, people are conscious and have thoughts and perhaps even spiritual experiences, but this can be understood as only the workings of the neurons in their material brains. The mental and spiritual are presumed to be mere epiphenomena of the material.

Now these philosophical doctrines—naturalism and materialism—have never been proven. In fact, they cannot be proven because it is impossible to demonstrate that immaterial reality does not exist. Naturalism and materialism are not scientific conclusions; rather, they are scientific premises. They are not discovered in nature but imposed upon nature. In short, they are articles of faith.

Here is Harvard biologist Richard Lewontin:

> We take the side of science in spite of the patent absurdity of some of its constructs, in spite of its failure to fulfill many of its extravagant promises of health and life, in spite of the tolerance of the scientific community for unsubstantiated just-so stories, because we have a prior commitment—a commitment to materialism. It is not that the methods and institutions of science somehow compel us to accept a material explanation of the phenomenal world, but, on the contrary, that we are forced by our a priori commitment to material causes to create an apparatus of investigation and a set of concepts that produce material explanations, no matter how counter-intuitive, no matter how mystifying to the uninitiated. Moreover, that materialism is absolute, for we cannot allow a Divine Foot in the door.[18]

And you thought I was making this stuff up!

Is science, then, intrinsically atheistic? Here we must distinguish between two types of atheism. The first kind is procedural or methodological atheism. This means that scientists go about their official business by presuming that we live in a natural, material world. Within this domain, miracles are forbidden, not because they cannot happen, but because science is the search for natural explanations. So, too, the mind and the soul must be studied materially, not because they are purely material phenomena, but because it is the job of science to examine only the material effects of immaterial things.

Science is indeed atheist in this procedural or narrow sense. And this is okay, because we don't want scientists who run into difficult problems to get out of them by saying, "You know, I'm not going to investigate this any longer. I'm just going to put it down as a miracle."

History shows that the search for natural explanations can yield marvelous results. Physicist Paul Davies rightly notes that "however astonishing and inexplicable a particular occurrence may be, we can never be absolutely sure that at some distant time in the future a natural phenomenon will not be discovered to explain it."[19] Of course there is no reason to believe anything based on the expectation of future scientific discoveries that have not yet occurred. Even so, there are very good operational benefits to letting the scientists do their jobs and examine the world in its natural and material dimension.

There are many religious scientists who find no difficulty in working within this domain of procedural atheism and at the same time holding their religious beliefs. Biologist Francis Collins says that as a biologist he investigates natural explanations for the origin of life while as a Christian he believes that there are also supernatural forces at work. "Science," he writes, "is not the only way of knowing."[20] Astronomer Owen Gingerich writes, "Science works within a constrained framework in creating its brilliant picture of nature.... This does not mean that the universe is actually godless, just that science within its own framework has no other way of working." Yet at the same time Gingerich believes that "reality goes much deeper" than the scientific portrait of it. Gingerich argues that the theist view of "a universe where God can play an interactive role" is a valid perspective that goes "unnoticed by science" but at the same time is "not excluded by science."[21]

Some people regard scientific and religious claims as inherently contradictory because they are unwitting captives to a second type of atheism, which we can call philosophical atheism. This is the dogma that material and natural reality is all that exists. Everything else must be illusory. Biologist Francis Crick admits that his commitment to materialism and his hostility to religion motivated him to enter his field. "I went into science because of these religious reasons, there's no doubt about that. I asked myself what were the things that appear inexplicable and are used to support religious beliefs."[22] Then Crick sought to show that those things have a purely material foundation. In the same vein, physicist Steven Weinberg confesses that the hope science will liberate people from religion "is one of the things that in fact has driven me in my life."[23]

The adversaries of religion, like Crick, Weinberg, Dawkins, and Dennett, frequently conflate procedural atheism with philosophical atheism. They pretend that because God cannot be discovered through science, God cannot be discovered at all. Here is a classic statement from biologist Will Provine: "Modern science directly implies that the world is organized strictly in accordance with deterministic principles or chance. There are no purposive principles whatsoever in nature. There are no gods and no designing forces rationally detectable."[24] Provine makes it sound like this is one of modern science's great discoveries, whereas it is modern science's operating premise. Provine assumes without evidence that scientific knowledge is the only kind of knowledge, and that it gives us true and full access to reality.

Are these assumptions valid? I will examine the second one in a subsequent chapter. But consider the first premise, that scientific knowledge is the only kind of knowledge. Physicist John Polkinghorne provides the following example. If you were to ask a scientist, "Why is that water boiling?" he or she would answer in terms of molecules and temperatures. But there is a second explanation: the water is boiling because I want to have a cup of tea. This second explanation is a perfectly valid description of reality, yet it is ignored or avoided by the scientific account.[25] The reason for this, mathematician Roger Penrose writes, is that science is incapable of answering questions about the nature or purpose of reality. Science merely tries to answer the question, "How does it behave?"[26] So science does not even claim to be a full description of reality, only of one aspect of reality.

Philosophical atheism is narrowly dogmatic because it closes itself off from knowledge that does not conform to materialism and naturalism. Only data that fits the theory is allowed into the theory. By contrast, the theist is much more open-minded and reasonable. The theist does not deny the validity of scientific reasoning. On the contrary, the theist is constantly reasoning in this way in work and life. The theist is entirely willing to acknowledge material and natural causes for events, but he also admits the possibility of other types of knowledge. Just because science cannot admit that the evidence of a Big Bang points to the existence of a creator doesn't mean that this is not a valid inference for us to make. Just because science cannot show that human beings have a spiritual dimension that is not present in other living (or nonliving) creatures doesn't mean that such a conclusion, derived from experience, is unreasonable or inadmissible.

Scientific truth is not the whole truth. It cannot make the case for naturalism or materialism because it operates within naturalism and materialism. When we realize this, then philosophical atheism becomes much less plausible. Then we can let science do its admirable job without worrying in the least that its procedural atheism provides any support for atheism generally.

PART V

CHRISTIANITY AND PHILOSOPHY

CHAPTER FIFTEEN

THE WORLD BEYOND OUR SENSES: KANT AND THE LIMITS OF REASON

"We shall be rendering a service to reason should we succeed in discovering the path upon which it can securely travel."[1]

—Immanuel Kant, *Critique of Pure Reason*

SO FAR WE HAVE BEEN CONSIDERING science and the scientific understanding. Now I want to broaden the inquiry to examine the proudest boast of the modern champion of secularism: that he is an apostle of reason itself. What distinguishes the "freethinker," Susan Jacoby writes in her book of that title, is a "rationalist approach to fundamental questions of earthly existence."[2] Taking reason as his star and compass, the atheist fancies himself superior to the rest of the people who rely on faith, superstition, and other forms of irrationality. Sam Harris writes, "Tell a devout Christian that his wife is cheating on him, or that frozen yogurt can make a man invisible, and he is likely to require as much evidence as anyone else, and to be persuaded only to the extent that you give it. Tell him that the book he keeps by his bed was written by an invisible deity who will punish him with fire for eternity if he fails to accept its every incredible claim about the universe, and he seems to require no evidence whatsoever."[3]

But there is one subject on which the atheist requires no evidence: the issue of whether human reason is the best—indeed the only—way to comprehend reality. Writing in *Free Inquiry*, Vern Bullough declares that "humanists at least have reality on their side."[4] Paul Bloom asserts in the *Atlantic Monthly*, "Yes, our intuitions and hypotheses are imperfect and unreliable, but the beauty of science is that these ideas are tested against reality."[5] Steven Weinberg writes that as a scientist he has a "respect for reality as something outside ourselves, that we explore but do not create." In pursuing knowledge, he writes, "the pull of reality is what makes us go the way we go."[6] E. O. Wilson writes that "outside our heads there is a freestanding reality" whereas "inside our heads is a reconstitution of reality based on sensory input and the self-assembly of concepts." By linking the two, Wilson hopes to achieve what he calls "the Enlightenment dream" of "objective truth based on scientific understanding."[7]

Weinberg, Wilson, and other atheists may not recognize it, but there is a huge assumption being made here. These men simply presume that their rational, scientific approach gives them full access to external reality. It is this presumption that gives atheism its characteristic arrogance. Daniel Dennett and Richard Dawkins call themselves "brights" because they think they and their atheist friends are simply smarter than the community of religious believers. In this chapter I intend to show that this arrogance is misplaced.

The atheist or "bright" approach to reality must be measured against a rival approach. Through the centuries the great religions of the world have held that there are two levels of reality. There is the human perspective on reality, which is the experiential perspective— reality as it is experienced by us. Then there is the transcendent view of reality, what may be called the God's-eye view of reality, which is reality itself. Being the kind of creatures that humans are, we see things in a limited and distorted way, "through a glass darkly," as Paul writes in his first letter to the Corinthians 13:12. Indeed we can never, as long as we are alive, acquire the God's-eye view and see things as they really are. Rather, we live in a fleeting and superficial world of appearances, where the best we can do is discern how things seem to be. We can, however, hope that there is a life after death in which we will see everything—including God—as it really is.

Which of these two views—the atheist view or the religious view—is correct? Engaging the argument on the ground chosen by the atheists, the ground of empiricism and reason alone, I intend to show that the religious view is the right one. There is more than one way to do this, but I have chosen the way illuminated by philosopher Immanuel Kant. Kant seems an appropriate choice because he is considered the greatest of modern philosophers. Kant was a leading figure of the Enlightenment, a man of science and philosophy, and he showed what may be termed the Enlightenment fallacy. This is precisely the fallacy that has duped many modern atheists and "brights."

In his book *The World as Will and Idea*, philosopher Arthur Schopenhauer writes, "Kant's teaching produces a fundamental change in every mind that has grasped it. The change is so great that it may be regarded as an intellectual rebirth. . . . In consequence of this, the mind undergoes a fundamental undeceiving, and thereafter looks at things in another light."[8] The greatness of Kant is that he takes our most fundamental assumptions and turns them into questions. We think we are on the ground floor of awareness, but Kant shows us a whole different level beneath it that we can examine.

Before Kant, most people simply assumed that our reason and our senses give us access to external reality—the world out there—and that there is only one limit to what human beings can know. That limit is reality itself. In this view, still widely held by many in our society, human beings can use the tools of reason and science to continually find out more and more until eventually there is nothing else to discover. The Enlightenment fallacy holds that human reason and science can, in principle, gain access to and eventually comprehend the whole of reality.

In his *Critique of Pure Reason*, Kant shows that these assumptions are false. In fact, he argues, there is a much greater limit to what human beings can know. In other words, human reason raises questions that—such is the nature of our reason—it is incapable of answering. And it is of the highest importance that we turn reason on itself and discover what those limits are. It is foolishly dogmatic to go around asserting claims based on reason without examining what kinds of claims reason is capable of adjudicating. Reason, in order to be reasonable, must investigate its own parameters.

Kant begins with a simple premise: all human knowledge is based on experience. We gain access to reality through our five senses. This sensory input is then processed through our brains and central nervous systems. Think about it: every thought, even the wildest products of our imagination, are exclusively based on things that we have seen, heard, touched, smelled, or tasted. If we imagine and draw creatures from outer space, we can give them four eyes and ten legs, but ultimately we have no way to conceive or portray them except in terms of our human experience. It is an empirical fact that our five senses are our only lenses for perceiving reality.

Now Kant asks a startling question: how do we know that our human perception of reality corresponds to reality itself? Most philosophers before Kant had simply taken for granted that it does, and this belief persists today. So powerful is this "common sense" that many people become impatient, even indignant, when Kant's question is put to them. They act as if the question is a kind of skeptical ploy, like asking people to prove that they really exist. But Kant was no skeptic: he saw himself as providing a refutation of skepticism. He knew, however, that to answer skepticism one has to take the skeptical argument seriously. The way to overcome skepticism is by doing justice to the truth embodied in it. Kant's goal was to erect a dependable edifice for knowledge on the foundation of extreme skepticism.

Kant's question about the reliability of human perception has been the central preoccupation of Western philosophy since Descartes. How do we know what we claim to know? Locke had famously pointed out that material objects seem to have two kinds of properties, what he called primary properties and secondary properties. Primary properties are in the thing itself, whereas secondary properties are in us. So when we perceive an apple, for example, its mass and shape are part of the apple itself. But Locke ingeniously pointed out that the redness of the apple, its aroma, and its taste are not in the apple. They are in the person who sees and smells and bites into the apple. What this means is that our knowledge of external reality comes to us from two sources: the external object and our internal apparatus of perception. Reality does not come directly to us but is "filtered" through a lens that we ourselves provide.

Philosopher George Berkeley radicalized this mode of inquiry: "When we do our utmost to conceive the existence of external bodies, we are all the while only contemplating our own ideas."[9] Berkeley's argument was that we have no experience of material objects that exist outside the perceptual apparatus of our mind and senses. Both the primary and the secondary qualities of objects are perceived in this way. We don't experience the ocean, we experience only our image and sound and feel of the ocean. Berkeley famously concluded that we have no warrant for believing in a material reality existing independent of our minds!

The great Samuel Johnson famously "refuted" Berkeley by kicking a rock. There! The rock exists! Alas, this is no refutation. Berkeley's reply to Johnson would be that his entire experience, from perceiving the rock to the sharp pain he felt upon kicking it, occurred entirely within his mind. And Hume completed Berkeley's skeptical argument by applying it to human beings themselves. We have no experience of ourselves other than our sensations and feelings and thoughts. While we know that sensations and feelings and thoughts exist, we have no basis for postulating some "I" behind them that is supposed to be having those reactions.

It was Hume, Kant wrote, who awakened him from his "dogmatic slumber." Kant conceded Berkeley's and Hume's point that it is simply irrational to presume that our experience of reality corresponds to reality itself. There are things in themselves—what Kant called the *noumenon*—and of them we can know nothing. What we can know is our experience of those things, what Kant called the *phenomenon*. If you have a dog at home, you know what it is like to see, hear, smell, and pet it. This is your phenomenal experience of the dog. But what is it like to be a dog? We human beings will never know. The dog as a thing in itself is hermetically concealed from us. Thus from Kant we have the astounding realization that human knowledge is limited not merely by how much reality there is out there, but also by the limited sensory apparatus of perception we bring to that reality.

Consider a tape recorder. A tape recorder, being the kind of instrument it is, can capture only one mode or aspect of reality: sound. Tape recorders, in this sense, can "hear" but they cannot see or touch or smell. Thus all aspects of reality that cannot be captured in sound are beyond the reach of a tape recorder. The same, Kant says, is true of human beings. We can apprehend reality only through our five senses. If a tape recorder apprehends reality in a single mode, human beings can perceive reality in five different modes: sight, hearing, smell, taste, and touch. There is no other way for us to experience reality. We cannot, for example, perceive reality through sonar in the way that a bat does. Our senses place absolute limits on what reality is available to us.

Moreover, the reality we apprehend is not reality in itself. It is merely our experience or "take" on reality. Kant's point has been widely misunderstood. Many people think that Kant is making the pedestrian claim that our senses give us an imperfect facsimile or a rough approximation of reality. Philosophical novelist Ayn Rand once attacked Kant for saying that man has eyes but cannot see, and ears but cannot hear—in short, that man's senses are fundamentally deluded.[10] But Kant's point is not that our senses are unreliable. True, our senses can fool us, as when we see a straight twig as bent because it is partly submerged in water. Human beings have found ways to correct these sensory distortions. Kant is quite aware of this, and it is not what he is after.

Kant's argument is that we have no basis to assume that our perception of reality ever resembles reality itself. Our experience of things can never penetrate to things as they really are. That reality remains permanently hidden to us. To see the force of Kant's point, ask yourself this question: how can you know that your experience of reality is in any way "like" reality itself? Normally we answer this question by considering the two things separately. I can tell if my daughter's portrait of her teacher looks like her teacher by placing the portrait alongside the person and comparing the two. I establish verisimilitude by the degree to which the copy conforms to the original. Kant points out, however, that we can never compare our experience of reality to reality itself. All we have is the experience, and that's all we can ever have. We only have the copies, but we never have the originals. Moreover, the copies come to us through the medium of our senses, while the originals exist independently of our means of perceiving them. So we have no basis for inferring that the two are even comparable, and when we presume that our experience corresponds to reality, we are making an unjustified leap. We have absolutely no way to know this.

It is essential, at this point, to recognize that Kant is not diminishing the importance of experience or of the phenomenal world. That world is very important, if only because it is all we have access to. It constitutes the entirety of our human experience and is, consequently, of vital significance for us. It is entirely rational for us to believe in this phenomenal world, and to use science and reason to discover its operating principles. A recognized scientist and mathematician, Kant did not degrade the value of science. But he believed science should be understood as applying to the world of phenomena rather than to the noumenal or "other" world.

Many critics have also understood Kant to be denying the existence of external reality. This is emphatically not the case. Kant is not a skeptic in that sense. Other philosophers, such as Johann Fichte, went down that road, but Kant did not. For Kant, the noumenon obviously exists because it gives rise to the phenomena we experience. In other words, our experience is an experience of something. Moreover, Kant contends that there are certain facts about the world—such as morality and free will—that cannot be understood without postulating a noumenal realm. Perhaps the best way to understand this is to see Kant as positing two kinds of reality: the reality that we experience and reality itself. The important thing is not to establish which is more real, but to recognize that human reason operates only in the phenomenal domain of experience. We can know that the noumenal realm exists, but beyond that we can know nothing about it. Human reason can never grasp reality itself.

So powerful is Kant's argument here that his critics have been able to answer him only with what may be termed the derision of common sense. When I challenged Daniel Dennett in a *Wall Street Journal* article to debunk Kant's argument, he posted an angry response on his Web site in which he said that several people had adequately refuted Kant. But he didn't provide any refutations, and he didn't name any names.[11] Basically, Dennett was relying on the *argumentum ad ignorantium*, the argument that relies on the ignorance of the audience. He was hoping that his admirers would take it on faith that such refutations exist somewhere in the literature. In fact, there are no such refutations.

Kant's ideas are so counterintuitive that they produce an almost visceral resistance. The notion that reality might be completely different from how it presents itself to us seems absurd, unreal, and impossible to take seriously. We resist Kant emotionally, no matter how compelling his argument. Normally reasonable people like Dennett respond to Kant with evident impatience. They are unable to answer his argument, but they pretend that it is not necessary to answer it. This attitude may be termed the "fundamentalism" of reason. It is reason so sure of itself that it refuses to consider reasonable criticism. Reason has become irrational and now relies entirely on simple intuition or "common sense."

Common sense, however, is not always a reliable guide to the truth. Common sense tells us that the earth is stationary and that the sun goes around it. Common sense tells us that an object is naturally at rest and that a moving object must automatically come to a stop. Common sense tells us that space and time are absolute. All these simple intuitions are false. In fact, the great discoveries of modern science—from Copernicus to Galileo to Newton to Einstein to Bohr to Heisenberg—are all massive violations of common sense. That is why in several cases the geniuses who first put forward those ideas were dismissed as crackpots. We now know that these crackpots were right. So it is a fact, not a matter of opinion, that reality is sometimes very strange and that common sense does not give us an unfailingly accurate picture of the world. To proclaim that it always does is to expose oneself as an ignoramus. Common sense, philosopher Bertrand Russell once said, is the "metaphysics of savages."[12]

Kant recognized that he was producing a revolution in human understanding. Just as Copernicus had turned the world "upside down" and forever altered the way we perceive the earth in relation to the sun, so Kant considered his own philosophy as producing a kind of Copernican revolution in thought. Of course people will still continue to perceive the world pretty much in realist terms—just as we go about our daily lives without worrying about the fact that we live on a planet hurtling through space at many thousands of miles per hour—but even so, this realism has been exposed as an illusion.

The illusion of realism is that it mistakes our experience of reality for reality itself. Realists like Dennett think of themselves as tough-minded empiricists, but they are not empirical enough to realize that all that is available to them are experiences and nothing beyond them. It is Kant, the transcendental idealist, who starts with experience and then proceeds from it by steps that reason can justify. By contrast, the empiricist begins with a presumption that is impossible to validate, and his whole philosophy is constructed on that dubious premise. The empiricist assumes without any evidence or proof that his experiences somehow give him a magical access to reality. So completely does he identify experience and reality that he cannot liberate himself from thinking of the two as one and the same. In equating experience and reality he is making a huge and unwarranted leap, but this breakdown of reason is not easy for him or us to recognize because our human minds have a built-in disposition toward illusion: the illusion that reality must be exactly the way we experience it. The irony is that many of the people who proceed in this irrational way think of themselves as following strictly along the pathways of reason. Their outlook can survive scrutiny only as long as they do not examine its foundations.

To their credit, there are a few "brights" who take Kant seriously and attempt to answer his arguments. Kant cannot be right in saying that we have no access to reality, they say, because you and I and everyone else experience the *same* reality. When we are in a room, we see the same lamps and tables and books on the shelf. Obviously those must exist and we must have direct access to them; otherwise we would not all have the same perception of them. But Kant's answer is that because we are all human beings, we have the same sensory equipment, and it operates in each of us in the same way. Therefore we all have the same experience, but the experience is all we have. Just because we have similar or even identical experiences does not mean that any of us has access to a reality that is beyond that experience.

Biologist E. O. Wilson tries a different tack. Science, he says, is giving us new senses that are enabling us to go beyond our previous perceptual limitations. "With the aid of appropriate instruments we can now view the world with butterfly eyes." With receivers and transformers and night-time photography we can experience the world in pretty much the same way as a bat. "Fish," Wilson tells us, "communicate with one another by means of coded electrical bursts. Zoologists, using generators and detectors, can join the conversation."[13]

If by this point you have grasped Kant's reasoning, you will see right away that Wilson has done nothing to undermine it. Yes, we can use night-time photography, but we are still viewing the images with our human eyes. Yes, we can use generators and detectors, but we are still using our five senses in order to read, hear, and interpret what those instruments say. In other words, our human apparatus of perception conditions the entire field of our experiences, and this has always been so and will continue to be so as long as we are human. Future scientific discoveries cannot alter this limitation because those discoveries too will have to be made and experienced through the constrained perceptual apparatus we possess. Kant's conclusion was that the problem of reason is, in its fullest dimension, insoluble. There are permanent and inescapable limits to human reason, and it is foolish to go on pretending otherwise.

While this conclusion that our reason is confined within the borders of our experience, and that reality in itself in permanently screened off from us by our own sensory limitations, may seem to some to be a very outlandish idea, in fact it is at the very center of Western philosophy. In perhaps the most famous metaphor in Western thought, Plato likened human beings to people living in a cave, shut out from the light of the sun, seeing only shadows and mistaking them for reality. Plato regarded our perceptions as mere images of a deeper and higher reality, the so-called Platonic forms, that he located somewhere outside the realm of human experience. And Plato's teacher, Socrates, regarded himself as the wisest man in Athens because he alone knew how little he knew. For all his breathtaking originality, Kant is squarely in the mainstream of Western thought.

No one who understands the central doctrines of any of the world's leading religions should have any difficulty understanding Kant, because his philosophical vision is congruent with the teachings of Hinduism, Buddhism, Islam, Judaism, and Christianity. It is a shared doctrine of these religions that the empirical world we humans inhabit is not the only world there is. Ours is a world of appearances only, a transient world that is dependent on a higher, timeless reality. That reality is of a completely different order from anything that we know, it constitutes the only permanent reality there is, and it sustains our world and presents it to our senses. Christianity teaches that while reason can point to the existence of this higher domain, this is where reason stops: it cannot on its own investigate or comprehend that domain. But one day, it is promised, when our earthly journey is over, we will know the higher realm and see things as they really are.

Sociologist Peter Berger writes, "The religious impulse, the quest for meaning that transcends the restricted space of empirical existence in this world, has been a perennial feature of humanity."[14] Now Kant has given this religious conviction a completely modern and rational foundation. It is of the highest importance to recognize that Kant's ideas, while they confirm core elements of religious thought, are entirely secular. Kant has arrived at them on the basis of reason alone. He does not employ any religious vocabulary, nor does he rely on any kind of faith. But in showing the limits of reason, Kant said, he did "make room for faith."[15]

Kant is our Virgil, taking us as far as reason can go. From here onward we need a different guide, but Kant has helped to clear the way for us to proceed. Kant's accomplishment was to unmask the intellectual pretension of the Enlightenment: that reason and science are the only routes to reality and truth. This illusion is very much with us today, making Kant's thought, for all its intellectual demands on us, supremely relevant. So the "brights" can do their strutting, but Kant has shown them as intellectually naked. And so, thanks to Kant, the tables have been turned. The atheist is now revealed as dogmatic and arrogant, and the religious believer emerges as modest and reasonable. While the atheist arrogantly persists in the delusion that his reason is fully capable of figuring out all that there is, the religious believer lives in the humble acknowledgment of the limits of human knowledge, knowing that there is a reality greater than, and beyond, that which our senses and minds can ever apprehend.

CHAPTER SIXTEEN

IN THE BELLY OF THE WHALE: WHY MIRACLES ARE POSSIBLE

"To smile in advance at all magic, we have to find the world completely intelligible. But this we can only do when we look into it with an extremely shallow gaze that admits of no inkling that we are plunged into a sea of riddles and incomprehensibilities and have no thorough and direct knowledge and understanding either of things or ourselves."[1]

—Arthur Schopenhauer

HAVING ESTABLISHED THE LIMITS OF REASON as confined to the world of experience, we now take up a very controversial question. In a world of scientific and natural laws, are miracles possible? Is it even credible, in the twenty-first century, to believe in a virgin birth and water being changed into wine and resurrection from the dead? Here I will show that such ideas are completely consistent with modern science, and that the most famous argument against miracles—advanced by the philosopher David Hume—can be shown, on the grounds of Hume's own philosophy, to be invalid.

The issue of miracles is of special importance to Christians, because Christianity is the only major religion in the world that depends on miracles. Other religions, such as Judaism, may report or allow miracles, but only Christianity relies on them. I am thinking specifically of the miracle at the center of the Christian religion. Paul writes in his first letter to the Corinthians 15:14 that without Christ's resurrection, "our preaching is useless and so is your faith." But the resurrection is far from the only miracle reported in the New Testament. While the founder of Islam, the prophet Muhammad, never claimed to have performed a single miracle, Christ performed miracles all the time. He walked on water, quieted the storm, fed the multitudes, healed the blind, and even brought Lazarus back from the dead. Only if miracles are possible is Christianity believable.

Richard Dawkins has shrewdly noticed that miracles represent the common ground on which religion and science seem to make rival claims. Biologist Stephen Jay Gould argues in his book *Rocks of Ages* that science and religion can comfortably coexist as they operate in separate realms: "Science tries to document the factual character of the natural world....Religion on the other hand operates in the equally important, but utterly different, realm of human purposes, meanings, and values."[2] Dawkins correctly observes that this distinction doesn't always work. The reason is that religion too makes claims about nature. The Old Testament reports that Moses parted the Red Sea, and that Jonah lived in the belly of the whale. The New Testament tells of a virgin named Mary who conceived a child, and of a fellow named Jesus who performed innumerable acts that defy human explanation.

"Science is based upon verifiable evidence," Dawkins says. The miracle stories of Christianity, according to Dawkins, are "blatant intrusions into scientific territory. Every one of these miracles amounts to a scientific claim, a violation of the normal running of the natural world." Consequently, "any belief in miracles is flatly contradictory not just to the facts of science but also to the spirit of science." Indeed, in Dawkins's estimation, miracles are nothing other than "bad science." As scientific laws cannot be violated, miracles cannot occur. Reasonable people therefore "have to renounce miracles."[3]

Many liberal Christians are so intimidated by the authority of science that they do their best to banish the miracles. In doing so, they rely on a tradition of biblical scholarship that goes back to David Strauss's *Life of Jesus*, first published in 1835. Strauss treated the miracles as myths. How did Jesus feed thousands of people with a few loaves and fishes? Perhaps he had a secret store of food, or people brought their own packed lunches. How did Jesus walk on water? Maybe there was a platform floating just beneath the surface. How did Jesus raise Lazarus from the dead? Lazarus might simply have been in a trance. How did Jesus come back from the tomb? He probably didn't, but the important thing is that his followers *believed* he did and that belief filled them with joy and hope. These explanations have actually been suggested by theologians.[4] They get rid of miracles by getting rid of Christianity.

I intend to make my case that miracles are possible by refuting the strongest argument against them. I am not trying to defend the veracity of a particular miracle. I am simply saying miracles should not be dismissed in advance as unscientific or incredible. Like all Christians I concede that miracles are improbable—that's why we use the term *miracle*—but improbable events can and do happen, and the same is true with miracles.

The strongest argument against miracles was advanced by philosopher and skeptic David Hume in his book *Enquiry Concerning Human Understanding*. Hume's argument is widely cited by atheists; Dawkins and Christopher Hitchens both invoke it to justify their wholesale rejection of miracles.[5] Hume argued that:

1. A miracle is a violation of the known laws of nature.
2. We know these laws through repeated and constant experience.
3. The testimony of those who report miracles contradicts the operation of known scientific laws.
4. Consequently, no one can rationally believe in miracles.

Hume's case against miracles has been enormously influential, but it can be effectively answered. To answer it, we must turn to the work of Hume himself. His writings show why human knowledge is so limited and unreliable that it can never completely dismiss the possibility of miracles. In formulating his objection to miracles, poor Hume seems to have forgotten to read his own book. My refutation will show that:

1. A miracle is a violation of the known laws of nature.
2. Scientific laws are on Hume's own account empirically unverifiable.
3. Thus, violations of the known laws of nature are quite possible.
4. Therefore, miracles are possible.

To see Hume's influence, we must turn to his modern-day followers, who typically call themselves logical positivists. Atheists and "brights" don't use this term, but if you examine their presuppositions you will see that they are based on logical positivism. A logical positivist thinks that science operates in the verifiable domain of laws and facts, while morality operates in the subjective and unverifiable domain of choices and values. The logical positivist is confident that scientific knowledge is the best kind of knowledge, and whatever contradicts the claims of science must be rejected as irrational. These people are all around us today. Many of them are extremely well educated and speak with an air of certitude, so even people who do not agree with what they say have a hard time answering them.

For the logical positivist, there are two kinds of statements: analytic statements and synthetic statements. An analytic statement is one whose truth or falsity can be established by examining the statement itself. If I say, "My neighbor is a bachelor with a beautiful young wife," you know right away that I am not telling the truth. The term *bachelor* means "unmarried man," so a bachelor cannot have a wife. For Hume, mathematics provides a classic example of analytic truths. Mathematical axioms are true by definition; they are, one may say, inherently true.

A synthetic statement can be verified only by checking the facts. If I say, "My neighbor weighs three hundred pounds and enjoys reading books by Richard Dawkins," you cannot tell from the statement itself whether it is true. You have to visit my neighbor's house and ask him. Hume argued that analytic statements are true a priori, i.e., by definition. Synthetic statements, on the other hand, are true a posteriori, i.e., by looking at the evidence. For Hume, the physical sciences provide the standard model of synthetic truths. Through the scientific method—hypothesis, experimentation, verification, and criticism—we can discover synthetic truths about the world.

On this basis Hume delivered his famous dismissal of metaphysics, which he did not consider any kind of truth at all. Consider the central religious claims that "there is life after death" or "God made the universe." Hume's point is that these statements are neither true by definition, nor can they be verified by checking the facts. Consequently, he argued, these statements are not even untrue—they are meaningless. Hume wrote, "If we take in our hand any volume—of divinity or school metaphysics, for instance—let us ask, does it contain any abstract reasoning concerning quality or number? No. Does it contain any experimental reasoning concerning matters of fact or experience? No. Commit it then to the flames, for it can contain nothing but sophistry and illusion."[6]

This is sometimes known as Hume's principle of empirical verifiability. It allows only two kinds of truths: those that are true by definition and those that are true by empirical confirmation. Right away, however, we see a problem. Let us apply Hume's criteria to Hume's own doctrine: Is the principle of verifiability true by definition? No. Well, is there a way to confirm it empirically? Again, no. Consequently, taking Hume's advice, we should commit his principle to the flames because it is not merely false, it is also incoherent.

There is another problem with Hume's reasoning, less obvious but equally serious. It took the genius of Immanuel Kant to point out an error that had completely escaped Hume's attention. Contrary to Hume's assertions, mathematical truths are not analytic. Consider the famous mathematical proposition in Euclidean geometry that "the shortest distance between two points is a straight line." This seems self-evidently true, and yet it cannot be confirmed simply by examining the sentence. There is nothing in the definition of the terms that makes it true. So how do we know it is true? We have to check. It is only when we make two points on a piece of paper and then draw a line through them that we can observe that the shortest distance between them is a straight line. Kant showed that many other mathematical propositions are of this sort.

I mention Kant's correction of Hume not to suggest that these mathematical axioms are wrong. What I am suggesting is that their veracity can be established only synthetically. We can proceed only by looking at the data. So mathematical laws are, in general, like scientific laws. We can verify them only by examining the world around us. When we examine the world around us, however, we make a disconcerting discovery first noted by Hume himself.

Scientific laws are not verifiable. They cannot be empirically validated. Science is based on the law of cause and effect, and that law cannot be validated in experience either. Hume's argument was a bombshell. So far-reaching were its implications that very few people grasped them, and to this day Hume's ghost continues to haunt the corridors of modern science. It is quite amusing to see educated people, including our community of self-styled "brights," continue to make claims about science that were exploded two centuries ago by Hume.

Why are scientific laws unverifiable? Hume's answer was that no finite number of observations, however large, can be used to derive an unrestricted general conclusion that is logically defensible. If I say all swans are white and posit that as a scientific hypothesis, how would I go about verifying it? By checking out swans. A million swans. Or ten million. Based on this I can say confidently that all swans are white. Hume's point is that I don't really know this. Tomorrow I might see a black swan, and there goes my scientific law.

This is not a frivolous example. For thousands of years before Australia was discovered, the only swans people in the West had seen had been white. Consequently, the entire Western world took it for granted that all swans were white, and expressions like "white as a swan" abound in Western literature. It was only when Europeans landed in Australia that they saw, for the first time, a black swan. What was previously considered a scientifically inviolable truth had to be retired.

At this point one might expect today's champions of science to start patting themselves on the back and saying, "Yes, and this is the wonderful thing about science. It is always open to correction and revision. It learns from its mistakes." Sure enough, Carl Sagan praises scientists like himself for their "tradition of mutually checking out each other's contentions."[7] Sagan's view is echoed by Daniel Dennett, who writes, "The methods of science aren't foolproof, but they are indefinitely perfectible.... There is a tradition of criticism that enforces improvement whenever and wherever flaws are discovered."[8]

To say this is to miss Hume's point, which is that science was not justified in positing these rules in the first place. All scientific laws are empirically unverifiable. How do we know that light travels at the speed of 186,000 miles per second? We measure it. But just because we measure it at that speed one time, or ten times, or a billion times, doesn't mean that light always and everywhere travels at that speed. We are simply assuming this, but we don't know it to be so. Tomorrow we might find a situation in which light travels at a different speed, and then we will be reminded of black swans.

But can't scientific laws be derived from the logical connection between cause and effect? No, Hume argued, because there is no logical connection between cause and effect. We may see event A and then event B, and we may assume that event A caused event B, but we cannot know this for sure. All we have observed is a correlation, and no number of observed correlations can add up to a necessary connection.

Consider a simple illustration. A child drops a ball on the ground for the first time. To his surprise, it bounces. Then the child's uncle, a graduate of the Massachusetts Institute of Technology, explains to the child that dropping a round object like a ball causes it to bounce. He might explain this by employing general terms like *property* and *causation*. If these are not meaningless terms, they must refer to something in experience. But now let us consider a deep question that Hume raises: what experience has the uncle had that the child has not had? The difference, Hume notes, is that the uncle has seen a lot of balls bounce. Every time he has dropped a ball it has bounced. And every time he has seen someone else do it, the result was the same. This is the basis—and the sole basis—of the uncle's superior knowledge.

Hume now draws his arresting conclusion: the uncle has no experience fundamentally different from the child's. He has merely repeated the experiment more times. So it is custom or habit that makes him think, "Because I have seen this happen many times before, therefore it must happen again." But the uncle has not established a necessary connection, merely an expectation derived from past experience. How does he know that past experience will repeat itself every time in the future? In truth, he does not know. In this way Hume concluded that the laws of cause and effect cannot be validated. Hume is not denying that nature has laws, but he is denying that we know what those laws are. When we posit laws, Hume suggests this is simply a grandiose way of saying, "Here is our best guess based on previous tries."

By the way, it is no rebuttal to Hume to say, "Admittedly, scientific laws are not 100 percent true, but at least they are 99.9 percent true. They may not be certain, but they are very likely to be true." How would you go about verifying this statement? How would you establish the likelihood, for instance, of Newton's inverse square law? It says that every physical object in the universe attracts every other physical object with a force directly proportional to their masses and inversely proportional to the square of the distance between them. This law cannot be tested except by actually measuring the relationships between all objects in the universe. And as that is impossible, no finite number of tries can generate any conclusion about how probable Newton's statement is. Ten million tries cannot establish 99.9 percent probability—or even 50 percent probability—because there may be twenty million cases that haven't been tried where Newton's law may be found inadequate.

At this point we should pause to consider astronomer Neil deGrasse Tyson's exasperated outburst. Tyson believes it is simply ridiculous to say that scientific laws are not reliable: "Science's big-time success rests on the fact that it works." If science did not accurately describe the world, then airplanes would not fly and people who undergo medical treatments would not be cured. Airplanes do fly and sick people are healed in the hospital, and on that basis science must be taken as true. Better to fly in an airplane constructed by the laws of physics, Tyson scornfully says, than to board one "constructed by the rules of Vedic astrology."[9]

I agree that science works—and you won't get any argument from me about the limits of Vedic astrology—but it doesn't follow that scientific laws are known to be true in all cases. Consider this dismaying realization. Newton's laws were for nearly two centuries regarded as absolutely true. They worked incredibly well. Indeed, no body of general statements had ever been subjected to so much empirical verification. Every machine incorporated its principles, and the entire Industrial Revolution was based on Newtonian physics and Newtonian mechanics. Newton was vindicated millions of times a day, and his theories led to unprecedented material success. Yet Einstein's theories of relativity contradicted Newton, and despite their incalculable quantity of empirical verification, Newton's laws were proven in important ways to be wrong or at least inadequate. This does not mean that Einstein's laws are absolutely true; in the future they too might be shown to be erroneous in certain respects.

From such examples philosopher Karl Popper concluded that no scientific law can, in a positive sense, claim to prove anything at all. Science cannot verify theories, it can merely falsify them.[10] When we have subjected a theory to expansive testing, and it has not been falsified, we can provisionally believe it to be true. This is not, however, because the theory has been proven, or even because it is likely to be true. Rather, we proceed in this way because, practically speaking, we don't have a better way to proceed. We give a theory the benefit of the doubt until we find out otherwise. There is nothing wrong in all this as long as we realize that scientific laws are not "laws of nature." They are human laws, and they represent a form of best-guessing about the world. What we call laws are nothing more than observed patterns and sequences. We think the world works in this way until future experience proves the contrary.

I am laying out the skeptical case here not because I want to endorse without reservations Hume's (or Popper's) philosophy. Rather, my goal is to overthrow Hume's argument against miracles using his own empirical and skeptical philosophy. Hume insists that miracles violate the known laws of nature, but I say that Hume's own skeptical philosophy has shown that there are no known laws of nature. Miracles can be dismissed only if scientific laws are necessarily true—if they admit of no exceptions. But Hume has demonstrated that for no empirical proposition whatsoever do we know this to be the case. Miracles can be deemed unscientific only if our knowledge of causation is so extensive that we can confidently dismiss divine causation. From Hume we learn how limited is our knowledge of causation, and therefore we cannot write off the possibility of divine causation in exceptional cases.

When we speak of miracles, we could mean either an extremely rare event that is nevertheless scientifically possible, or we could mean an event that somehow contravenes the established laws of nature. Consider the question of whether a dead person can come back to life. We may consider this unlikely in the extreme because no one we know has seen it happen. All medical attempts to revive the dead have failed so far. But it does not follow that for a dead person to return to life is a violation of the laws of nature. Can anyone say with certainty that in the future medical advances will not reach a point at which clinically dead people can be restored to life? Of course not. So the scientific proposition that dead people cannot come back to life is a practical truth—useful for everyday purposes—but it is not a necessary truth.

But if we might see dead people come to life in the future, then it is possible that dead people have, on one or more occasions, been restored to life in the past. I am not making the claim here that this has happened. I am merely saying that if it might happen one day, then it could have happened before. Logical possibility cannot be confined to future events. If it happened in the past, it would be a miracle. If it happens in the future, we'll call it scientific progress. Either way, it's possible, not because nature's laws are necessarily overthrown, but because we have no complete knowledge of what those laws are.

Miracles can also be viewed as actual suspensions of the laws of nature, and here too there is nothing in science or logic that says that these things cannot happen. Who says that these laws are immutable? There is no evidence whatsoever for such a sweeping conclusion. Obviously, if God exists, miracles are possible. For God there are clearly no constraints outside the natural realm. Even modern physics concedes that beyond the natural world the laws of nature do not apply. There is nothing "miraculous" about heaven or hell for the simple reason that there are no laws of nature that operate outside our universe.

But even within nature, God cannot be restricted. Like the author of a novel, God is entirely in charge of the plot. How can He be bound by rules and storylines that He devised? If God abruptly interrupts the "logic" of the story the result will surely be disruption and confusion. But this is the point of miracles, to disrupt the normal course of things and draw attention to something happening outside the narrative. If God made the universe He also made the laws of nature, and He can alter them on occasion if He chooses to.

A SKEPTIC'S WAGER: PASCAL AND THE REASONABLENESS OF FAITH

"God is, or is not. There is an infinite chaos separating us. At the far end of this infinite distance a game is being played and the coin will come down heads or tails. How will you wager?"[1]

—Blaise Pascal, *Pensées*

HAVING SHOWN THE POSSIBILITY of miracles, we can now proceed to examine whether faith is reasonable. At first glance this may seem like a paradoxical quest. How can reason be invoked to justify unreason? I intend to show here that faith is in no way opposed to reason. Rather, faith is the only way to discover truths that are beyond the domain of reason and experience. Drawing on philosopher and mathematician Blaise Pascal, I intend to argue that the atheist's wager against God's existence is manifestly unreasonable. Given what we know and don't know about what is to come after death, there is no alternative but to weigh the odds. When we do this, we discover that from the perspective of reason itself, faith is the smart bet. It makes sense to have faith.

To many these conclusions will seem surprising, because for them faith remains a troubling and even offensive concept. Stephen Jay Gould examines the famous scene in the Gospel of John in which the apostle Thomas refuses to believe that Christ has risen from the dead. Thomas says, "Except I shall see in his hands the print of the nails, and thrust my hand into his side, I will not believe." So Jesus appears to Thomas and allows him to see and touch, and Thomas says, "My Lord and my God." Jesus responds, "Thomas, because you have seen, you have believed. Blessed are they that have not seen, and yet have believed." Gould comments, "I cannot think of a statement more foreign to the norms of science...than Jesus's celebrated chastisement of Thomas. A skeptical attitude toward appeals based only on authority, combined with a demand for direct evidence (especially to support unusual claims), represents the first commandment of proper scientific procedure."[2]

To Daniel Dennett, faith evokes images of Santa Claus and the Easter Bunny, beliefs appropriate for children but certainly not for adults. Carl Sagan writes that while science "asks us to take nothing on faith," religion "frequently asks us to believe without question."[3] From Richard Dawkins's point of view, faith is "a state of mind that leads people to believe something—it doesn't matter what—in the total absence of supporting evidence....Faith seems to me to qualify as a kind of mental illness."[4]

At first glance the atheist hostility to faith seems puzzling. We frequently make decisions based on faith. We routinely trust in authorities and take actions based on their claims that we don't or can't verify. I wasn't present at the Battle of Waterloo, but I am quite convinced that it happened. I have never been to Papua New Guinea, but I am quite sure that it is there. I trust the word of others who have been there, and I trust maps. Similarly, I express a lot of faith in air traffic control and the skill of the pilot every time I board an airplane.

So thoroughly do we rely on faith that modern life would become impossible were we to insist on evidence and verification before proceeding. How do I know my cereal is safe to eat? How can I be sure my car is not going to blow up? Why should I take it for granted that the person whose voice I hear at the other end of the telephone is really there? How do I know my vote for a presidential candidate will be counted as a vote for that candidate?

One answer is that I know because "the system" works. I eat my cereal, and I feel fine. I drive my car, and it gets me to work. And so on.

I can trust technology, banking, maps, and democracy because they deliver the goods. But this is no argument against religious faith because, for the believer, faith also delivers the goods. William James makes this point in his classic book *The Varieties of Religious Experience*. Faith in God, for the millions who have it, is routinely vindicated in everyday life. People come to trust God for His fidelity and love in the same way they come to trust their spouses—through lasting and reliable experience. In fact, religious people trust God more than they trust airlines, maps, and computers, and this too is based on empirical evidence. Computers crash, maps become outdated, and airlines screw up. God does not.

This defense of faith is inadequate, however, because religious faith is not merely about what satisfies human wants and needs, but also about what is true. Faith makes claims of a special kind. The soul is immortal and lives after death. There is a God in heaven who seeks to be eternally united with us. Heaven awaits those who trust in God, while those who reject Him are headed for the other place. And so on. These claims are impossible to verify, and hence they are radically different from claims about Papua New Guinea or Waterloo. I could validate my faith by going to Papua New Guinea or by combing through the historical records pertaining to the Battle of Waterloo. But I have no way to know whether my soul will outlive my body, or whether there is actually a supreme judge in heaven. These things are outside the bounds of experience, and therefore they are outside the power of human beings to check out. As Kant showed, they are beyond the reach of reason itself.

But Kant did not conclude from this that religious faith was unreasonable. On the contrary, he argued that beyond the precincts of reason, it is in no way unreasonable to make decisions based on faith. The important point here is that in the phenomenal or empirical world, we are in a position to formulate opinions based on experience and testing and verification and reason. In that world it is superstitious to make claims on faith that cannot be supported by evidence and reason. Outside the phenomenal world, however, these criteria do not apply, just as the laws of physics apply only to our universe and not to any other universe.

Thus when Christopher Hitchens routinely dismisses religious claims on the grounds that "what can be asserted without evidence can also be dismissed without evidence," he is making what philosophers like to call a category mistake.[5] He is using empirical criteria to judge things that lie outside the empirical realm. He wants evidence from a domain where the normal rules of evidence do not apply. Beyond the reach of reason and experience, the absence of evidence cannot be used as evidence of absence.

Remarkably, there are many people today who wish to conduct their lives on the presumption that there is no God, no afterlife, and no reality beyond the world of experience. These are not only the self-proclaimed atheists but also the agnostics, whose professed ignorance translates into a practical atheism. Often with a self-satisfied smile, they say, "I cannot believe because I simply don't know." This attitude is peculiar for two reasons. First, it is entirely incurious about the most important questions of life: Why are we here? Is this life all there is? What happens when we die? These great mysteries press themselves on all humans who ponder their situation, and yet there are people who refuse even to consider those mysteries. They continue to demand evidence of a kind that is simply not available here. Their attitude is also bizarre because it shows no hint of an awareness of the limits of reason. Empirical evidence is unavailable because the senses cannot penetrate a realm beyond experience.

When reason has reached its limit, there are two possibilities. We can stop, or we can continue onward. Some thinkers, such as philosopher Ludwig Wittgenstein, argued that beyond what we can assert by reason we should assert nothing. "We don't get to the bottom of things," Wittgenstein wrote, "but reach a point where we can go no further, where we cannot ask further questions."[6] To the query, "What lies beyond death?" Wittgenstein refused to answer one way or the other. He certainly didn't, with the misplaced confidence of Richard Dawkins or Sam Harris, answer, "There is nothing." He couldn't say that because he didn't know.

This response—"I don't know"—is an expression of a kind of agnosticism. It involves a suspension of judgment in the face of ignorance that is clearly superior to atheism. Yet curiously this form of agnosticism is shared by the religious believer. The religious believer also does not know. The Bible says in Hebrews 11:1 that faith is "the substance of things hoped for, the evidence of things not seen." If the believer knew, there would be no question of faith. Consider this: I don't have faith that my daughter is in the seventh grade. I know my daughter is in the seventh grade. I haven't been to heaven, and so I cannot say that I know there is such a place. But I believe that there is. Faith is a statement of trust in what we do not know for sure. Faith says that even though I don't know something with certainty, I believe it to be true.

From this we draw a conclusion that will surprise many atheists and even a few Christians: doubt is the proper habit of mind for the religious believer. There is a story in the Gospel of Mark 9:17–24 about a man who came to Christ to cure his son of possession by an evil spirit. Jesus said to him, "If you can believe, all things are possible." And the man replied, "Lord, I believe. Help thou mine unbelief." This is every true believer's prayer. The Christian has faith even though he is not sure, while the unbeliever refuses to believe because he is not sure. But they agree in being unsure. The skeptical habit of mind is as natural to Christianity as it is to unbelief.

Religious faith is not in opposition to reason. The purpose of faith is to discover truths that are of the highest importance to us yet are unavailable to us through purely natural means. Wittgenstein famously said in his *Tractatus* that "even if all possible scientific questions are answered, the problems of life have still not been touched at all."[7] The point is that the game of science is conducted on a field, and the most important questions of life—Why am I here? What should I love? What should I live for?—lie outside that field. Faith is an attempt to reach beyond the empirical realm and illuminate those questions. Both Kant and Wittgenstein say this is impossible, but they mean it is impossible as a project of reason alone. Perhaps there is another way.

Confronted by the supreme questions of human existence, philosopher Brian Magee writes, "We are like soldiers besieging a castle who have sought endlessly and in vain to find a way of penetrating its walls and whose only hope, whether they realize it or not, lies in a different mode of entry, a tunnel that will bring them up inside the fortress without penetrating the walls at all."[8] This account is an excellent description of how faith seeks a route that has been closed to reason. The goal is the same, to find the truth, but faith journeys on when reason has given up the chase. If the agnostic wishes to put down his satchel and quit, he cannot begrudge the believer who is willing to try a new path to reach the summit.

The believer uses faith to gain access to a new domain, that of revelation. There is no other option here because reason has quite frankly run out of steam. The believer hopes that revelation will expose truths otherwise hidden to reason. The believer embraces faith not "blindly" but rather with his "eyes wide open." The Christian relies on faith not to suppress his native powers but to guide them so that they may see more clearly. He expects revelation to reactivate and guide his reason. Augustine's dictum is applicable here: "Believe and you will understand." That is why religious believers are so perplexed when atheists accuse them of jettisoning their intellectual abilities. Social critic Michael Novak says that "using reason is a little like using the naked eye, whereas 'putting on faith' is like putting on perfectly calibrated glasses... to capture otherwise invisible dimensions of reality."[9]

While we have knowledge of an idea or proposition, we have faith in a person. Daniel Dennett should be relieved to learn that this person is not Santa Claus or the Easter Bunny. Religious faith is ultimately a statement of trust in the one monotheistic God, and in His authority and reliability. If there is a divine being who has created the universe with special concern for us as human beings, then it is entirely reasonable to suppose that, absent our ability to find Him, He would find His way to us. The religious believer holds that when man is unable to reach up to God, God can reach down to him. Faith is a kind of gift. It is God's way of disclosing Himself to us through divine revelation. If God did not do this, we have no other way of finding out about Him and He would remain severed from His creation.

Pascal begins with the Kantian postulate that "reason's final step is to recognize that there are an infinite number of things which surpass it."[10] In several of his writings, Pascal contends that it is fortunate for man that the highest truths are accessible through faith rather than reason. In other words, faith is available to everyone. If the only way to find out about God was through reason, then smarter people would have the inside track and the less intelligent would be shut out. Getting into heaven would be like getting into Harvard. Apparently God wants to have people other than PhDs in heaven; He seems to have made room for some fishermen and other humble folk. Reason is aristocratic, but faith is democratic.

Yet why should we choose to have faith in the presence of doubt? This central human conundrum is the subject of Pascal's famous wager. (Pascal did not invent the wager; it was offered by Muslim theologian Abu Hamed al-Ghazali in his medieval work *The Alchemy of Happiness*.[11] Pascal was familiar with al-Ghazali and probably derived the argument from him.) Pascal gave the wager its current classic expression, and in doing so he places an unavoidable choice before all "brights," agnostics, and atheists.

Pascal argues that in life we have to gamble. Let's say you are offered a new job that may take your career to new heights. It looks extremely promising, but of course there are risks. There is no way in advance to know how things will turn out. You have to decide whether to go for it. Or you are in love with a woman. You have been dating for a while, yet you cannot be certain what marriage to her for the next several decades is going to be like. You proceed on the basis of what you know, but what you know is, by the nature of the matter, inadequate. Yet you have to make a decision. You cannot keep saying, "I will remain agnostic until I know for sure." If you wait too long, she will marry someone else, or both of you will be dead.

In the same way, Pascal argues that in making our decision about God, we will never understand everything in advance. No amount of rational investigation can produce definitive answers, as what comes after death remains unknown. Therefore we have to examine the options and make our wager. But what are the alternatives, and how should we weigh the odds? Pascal argues that we have two basic choices, and either way we must consider the risk of being wrong.

If we have faith in God and it turns out that God does not exist, we face a downside risk: metaphysical error. But if we reject God during our lives, and it turns out God does exist, there is much more serious risk: eternal separation from God. Based on these two possible outcomes, Pascal declares that it is much less risky to have faith in God. In the face of an uncertain outcome, no rational person would refuse to give up something that is finite if there is the possibility of gaining an infinite prize. In fact, under these conditions it is unreasonable not to believe. Pascal writes, "Let us weigh up the gain and loss involved in calling heads that God exists. If you win, you win everything. If you lose, you lose nothing. Do not hesitate, then: wager that He does exist."[12]

The ingenuity of Pascal's argument is that it emphasizes the practical necessity of making a choice. This necessity is imposed by death. There comes a day when there are no tomorrows, and then we all have to cast our votes for or against the proposition on the ballot. The unavoidability of the decision exposes the sheer stupidity of "apatheism," the pretense that something doesn't matter when it is quite literally a matter of life and death. The apatheist and the agnostic refuse to choose when there is no option to abstain. So the refusal to choose becomes a choice—a choice against God.

Pascal also exposes the pose of the atheist who fancies himself as a brave and lonely man facing the abyss. We admire a man who is steadfast in the face of unavoidable adversity. If we knew we were alone in the universe and that death was the end, then there is no alternative but to stand tough in our mortal skins and curse the darkness. But what would we think of a man who stands ready to face a horrible fate that he has a chance to avert? If you are trapped in the den with a hungry lion, and there is a door that may offer a way out, what sane person would refuse to jump through the door? Viewed this way, the atheist position becomes a kind of intransigence, a reckless man's decision to play Russian roulette with his soul.

Atheists sometimes express their bafflement over why God would not make His presence more obvious. Carl Sagan helpfully suggests that in order to dispel all doubts about His existence, "God could have engraved the Ten Commandments on the moon."[13] Pascal supplies a plausible reason for what he calls the hiddenness of God. Perhaps, he writes, God wants to hide Himself from those who have no desire to encounter Him while revealing Himself to those whose hearts are open to Him. If God were declare Himself beyond our ability to reject Him, then He would be forcing Himself on us. Pascal remarks that perhaps God wants to be known not by everyone but only by the creatures who seek Him.[14]

Atheists are aware of the power of Pascal's wager. Christopher Hitchens can do no better than to launch an ad hominem attack on Pascal as a "hypocrite" and a "fraud."[15] Richard Dawkins proclaims Pascal's argument "distinctly odd." And why? Because "believing is not something you can decide to do as a matter of policy. At least, it is not something I can decide to do as an act of will."[16] Dawkins is right about this, of course, but the real issue is whether he wants to believe and whether he is open to the call of faith. As we will see in a later chapter, there are powerful psychological motives for resisting this call.

Pascal writes that there are two kinds of reasonable people in the world: "those who serve God with all their heart because they know Him, and those who seek Him with all their heart because they do not know Him."[17] Pascal recognizes that faith is a gift. We cannot demand it but only ask God to give it to us. In the meantime the best thing to do is to live a good and moral life, and to live as if God did indeed exist. And pray the prayer of the skeptic, which I get from philosopher Peter Kreeft:

> God, I don't know whether you even exist. I'm a skeptic. I doubt. I think you may be only a myth. But I'm not certain (at least when I'm completely honest with myself). So if you do exist, and if you really did promise to reward all seekers, you must be hearing me now. So I hereby declare myself a seeker, a seeker of the truth, whatever and wherever it is. I want to know the truth and live the truth. If you are the truth, please help me.[18]

The Bible promises that all who seek God in this way with earnest and open hearts will find Him.

PART VI

CHRISTIANITY AND SUFFERING

CHAPTER EIGHTEEN

RETHINKING THE INQUISITION: THE EXAGGERATED CRIMES OF RELIGION

"Good people will do good things and bad people will do bad things, but for good people to do bad things—that takes religion."[1]

—Steven Weinberg, *Facing Up*

THE PREVIOUS CHAPTERS have sought to answer the intellectual arguments against Christianity as articulated by the best atheist minds of our day. In the next several chapters we turn to their moral arguments and consider the charge that Christianity is worse than irrational—it is evil. For centuries it was God who judged man and Christian clerics who issued charges of heresy and immorality. Now man has perched himself in the judge's seat and points the finger of accusation at God, and Christianity must answer the charge of fostering evil and threatening civil peace. In this chapter I will investigate whether religion is the source of most of the conflict and death in the world, and if so, whether the world would be better off without it.

Prominent atheists have been very successful in convincing millions of people—even religious people—that religion has been the bane of history. In *The End of Faith*, Sam Harris calls it "the most potent source of human conflict, past and present."[2] Steven Pinker writes that "religions have given us stonings, witch-burnings, crusades, inquisitions, jihads, fatwas, suicide bombers, and abortion clinic gun-men."[3] In another book Pinker adds further offenses that he attributes to religion; he says humans believe God has commanded them to "massacre Midianites, stone prostitutes, execute homosexuals, slay heretics and infidels, throw Protestants out of windows, withhold medicine from dying children, and crash airplanes into skyscrapers."[4]

Christianity is typically the focus of the atheist moral critique. In his book *Why I Am Not a Christian*, philosopher Bertrand Russell argues that "the whole contention that Christianity has had an elevat-ing moral influence can only be maintained by wholesale ignoring or falsification of the historical evidence."[5] Columnist Robert Kuttner spells out the case against Christianity: "The Crusades slaughtered millions in the name of Jesus. The Inquisition brought the torture and murder of millions more. After Martin Luther, Christians did bloody battle with other Christians for another three centuries."[6]

Nor have the dangers posed by religion faded with time. Richard Dawkins surveys the Middle East, the Balkans, Northern Ireland, India, and Sri Lanka and contends that "most, if not all, of the violent enmities in the world today" are due to the "divisive force of religion."[7] So parlous is the contemporary influence of religion, notably Islamic extremism and Christian fundamentalism, that Daniel Dennett fears "a toxic religious mania could end human civilization overnight."[8]

The problem with this critique is that it greatly exaggerates the crimes that have been committed by religious fanatics while neglect-ing or rationalizing the vastly greater crimes committed by secular and atheist fanatics. This is the topic of the next two chapters, in which we examine more closely the historical evidence the critics invoke. I intend to show that the widely held view that religion is the primary source of the great killings and conflicts of history is simply wrong—indeed that it can only be held by those who insist on ignor-ing or falsifying the evidence.

Let's begin with the Crusades, which are vividly described by James Carroll as "a set of world historical crimes" whose "trail of violence scars the earth and human memory even to this day."[9] A Catholic, Car-roll is an example of how many liberal Christians have absorbed the secular allegation that the Crusades illustrate the horrors of religion. Moreover, in fairly standard fashion, Carroll reserves his harshest language for the role of Christians in the Crusades. About the horrors perpetrated by the Muslim side, he is notably reticent. Here we have the familiar doctrine: religion is bad but Christianity is worse.

But is it true? Let's remember that before the rise of Islam the region we call the Middle East was predominantly Christian. There were Zoroastrians in Persia and Jews in Palestine, but most of the people in what we now call Iraq, Syria, Jordan, and Egypt were Christians. The sacred places of Christianity—where Christ was born, lived, and died—are in that region. Inspired by Islam's call to jihad, Muhammad's armies conquered Jerusalem and the entire Middle East. They then pushed south into Africa, east into Asia, and north into Europe. They conquered parts of Italy and most of Spain, overran the Balkans, and were preparing for a final incursion that would bring all of Europe, then known as Christendom, under the rule of Islam. So serious was the Muslim threat that Edward Gibbon speculated that if the West had not fought back "perhaps the Koran would now be taught in the schools of Oxford, and her pulpits might demonstrate to a circumcised people the sanctity and truth of the Revelation of Mahomet."[10]

More than two hundred years after Islamic armies conquered the Middle East and forced their way into Europe, the Christians finally did strike back. Rallied by the pope and the ruling dynasties of Europe, in the eleventh century the Christians attempted to recover the heartland of Christianity and defend it against militant Islam. These efforts are now called the Crusades. (The term is a later invention; it was not used by the Christians and Muslims who fought in those battles.)

Who were the Crusaders? Historian Jonathan Riley-Smith disputes the idea that they were rapacious conquerors or murderers. Rather, he says, they were pilgrims. They were responding to Christ's call to Christians to "deny yourself and take up your cross and follow me." Many of them put their fortunes and their lives at risk. Their rulers provided nothing—the Crusaders were expected to bring their own horses, pack animals, and equipment. The proof that they were not in this for gain is that virtually all of them returned poorer than they left.

Yes, there was looting and foraging on the way, but Riley-Smith says this is because the Crusaders had to make provision for their own survival.[11]

The First Crusade was a success. The Christians captured Jerusalem in 1099 and held it for several decades. Eventually the Muslims regrouped and routed the Crusaders. Saladin reconquered Jerusalem in 1187. Subsequent Crusades were failures, and Jerusalem remained under Muslim rule. So the Crusades can be seen as a belated, clumsy, and unsuccessful effort to defeat Islamic imperialism. Yet the Crusades were important because they represented a fight for the survival of Europe. Without the Crusades Western civilization might have been completely overrun by the forces of Islam. The Crusades are also seen as a precursor to Europe's voyages of exploration, which inaugurated the modern era. Certainly one can dispute the worthiness of these objectives, and there were expeditions of rape and murder committed during the Crusades, including the wanton killing of many Jews, that no one can justify. Even so, these rampages do not define the Crusades as a whole. In the context of the history of warfare, there is no warrant for considering the Crusades a world historical crime of any sort. The Christians fought to defend themselves from foreign conquest, while the Muslims fought to continue conquering Christian lands.

And the Inquisition? Contemporary historians have now established that the horrific images of the Inquisition are largely a myth concocted first by the political enemies of Spain—mainly English writers who shaped our American understanding of that event—and later by the political enemies of religion. Henry Kamen's book *The Spanish Inquisition* is subtitled "A Historical Revision," and it is a long book, because Kamen has a lot of revising to do. One of his chapters is called "Inventing the Inquisition." He means that much of the modern stereotype of the Inquisition is essentially made up.

The Inquisition, Kamen points out, "only had authority over Christians." The idea that the Inquisition targeted Jews is a fantasy. The only Jews who came under the purview of the Inquisition were Jews who had converted to Christianity. There were quite a few of these, as King Ferdinand and Queen Isabella had issued an ordinance in 1492 expelling Jews from Spain. The only way to stay was to convert. Of course, many Christians suspected that some of these *conversos* or "new Christians" were not Christians at all. They were Jews pretending to be Christians. Interestingly the main source of allegations against the "new Christians" came from other Jews who were angry about their fellow Jews relinquishing their Judaism. These Jews had no qualms about testifying before the Inquisition courts because as Jews they were exempt from its jurisdiction. Kamen points out that the grand inquisitor himself, Tomás de Torquemada, had known Jewish ancestry.

Inquisition trials, according to Kamen, were fairer and more lenient than their secular counterparts, not only in Spain but also across Europe. Frequently the only penalty given was some form of penance, such as fasting or what we would today call "community service." How many people were executed for heresy by the Inquisition? Kamen estimates that it was around 2,000. Other contemporary historians make estimates of between 1,500 and 4,000. These deaths are all tragic, but we must remember that they occurred over a period of 350 years.[12]

The best example of religiously motivated violence in America is the Salem witch trials. How many people were killed in those trials? Thousands? Hundreds? Actually, fewer than twenty-five. Nineteen were sentenced to death, and a few others died in captivity. Yet the witch trials have been memorialized in books, movies, and plays like Arthur Miller's *The Crucible*. Miller tried to use the Salem trials as a historical precedent to show the extensive harms of McCarthyism, but little did he realize that his historical example actually proved the opposite. Wrong though the trials were, they harmed a relatively small number of people. Few casualties, big brouhaha.

It's interesting to see the way in which atheist writers try to magnify the horror of the witch trials. In *The Demon-Haunted World*, Carl Sagan writes of the witch trials in Europe, "No one knows how many were killed altogether—perhaps hundreds of thousands, perhaps millions." That's one big "perhaps." Sagan cites no sources, and the most reasonable conclusion is that he has no idea. His fellow atheist Sam Harris, who has actually done some reading on the subject, cites contemporary historical sources that put the number of witches burned much lower, at 100,000. That's a substantial figure, but it's a far cry from Sagan's demon-haunted estimate, and twenty times lower, Harris notes, than some previous absurd estimates.

Still, Harris argues, "Such a revaluation of numbers does little to mitigate the horror and injustice of this period."[13] Why not? Let's apply his logic to other historical events and the absurdity will become apparent. The two atomic bombs at Hiroshima and Nagasaki caused an estimated 100,000 civilian deaths, and the debate continues over President Truman's decision to end the war in this way. But let's reduce the casualty figures by a factor of twenty, in the manner of Harris, and we are down to 5,000 deaths for both bombs. Would this, in Harris's words, "do little to mitigate the horror and injustice" of the bombs? On the contrary, it would dispel much of the horror and virtually eliminate any moral debate over the legitimacy of Truman's action.

When the numbers aren't on your side, it's time to try some hypothetical reasoning. Putting on his biggest philosophical hat, Carl Sagan asks how the civilized people of Europe could possibly have condoned witch-burning. His answer: "If we're absolutely sure that our beliefs are right, and those of others wrong…then the witch mania will recur in its infinite variations."[14] In other words, it could happen again, and right here in America. But how plausible is this? Carl Sagan believed in evolution, the Big Bang, and lots of other things. I'm sure he was convinced he was absolutely right, and that his enemies the creationists and fundamentalists were absolutely wrong. Even so, Sagan didn't burn anyone. I believe certain things to be absolutely true, and yet my personal record on witch-burning is exemplary. If you go to Salem today, you'll see that the witches are thriving. They don't even bother to employ security when they perform their rituals—indeed, they have become tourist attractions. Clearly Sagan was engaging in a little paranoia.

How about the Thirty Years' War? This conflict involving the Holy Roman Empire and the Protestant states in Germany lasted from 1618 to 1648. While religious motives were present initially, historians today emphasize that these wars were mainly fueled by political contests of power. The emerging nation-states of Europe were clashing with each other over territory and influence. We can see how political motives overrode religious ones in the role played by Catholic France in the latter phases of the war: concerned about the strength of the greatest Catholic power in the world, the Holy Roman Empire, French statesman Cardinal Richelieu organized a force made up of Swedes and Frenchmen to help the Protestant side.

Just as in the Thirty Years' War, many current conflicts that are counted today as "religious wars" are not being fought over religion. This is a point that never seems to get through to atheists like Dawkins and Harris. Dawkins complains about the media's insistence on describing the conflicts in Northern Ireland, the Balkans, and Iraq as "ethnic" rather than religious. But the media is right and Dawkins is wrong. These are ethnic rivalries. Dawkins terms the clash between the Shiites and Sunni in Iraq as "religious cleansing."[15] Nonsense. Aside from the radicals of al Qaeda, the fight in Iraq is between one group that, in league with the secular despot Saddam Hussein, ruled Iraq for a quarter century, and another group—the Shiite majority— that is now in power. Religion has very little to do with this internecine conflict.

Dawkins gives several other examples, and they all work against him. The Israeli-Palestinian conflict is not, at its core, a religious one. Rather, it arises from disputes over self-determination and land. Hamas and the extreme orthodox parties in Israel may advance theological claims—"God gave us this land" and so forth—but even without these religious motives the conflict would remain essentially the same. But aren't the Jews fighting for this land because it is holy? No, they are fighting because this is their ancestral land and, after the Holocaust, many Jews have become convinced that they can feel secure only in a country of their own. The people who founded the state of Israel were secular, not religious, Jews. The Palestinian Liberation Organization was from its origin a secular nationalist group.

Ethnic rivalry, not religion, is the source of the tension in the Balkans. Christopher Hitchens gratuitously proposes that the "ethnic cleansing" of the Balkans be called "religious cleansing" even though he admits that "xenophobic nationalism" and territorial aggrandize-ment rather than religion are the primary motivations for the vio-lence. Moving on to Northern Ireland, Hitchens tells a joke without realizing that it undermines his own argument. A man is walking down a street in Belfast when a gunman leaps out of a doorway, points a gun, and says, "Protestant or Catholic?" The man exclaims, "Neither. I'm an atheist." To which the gunman replies, "Catholic atheist or Protestant atheist?"[16] The real point of the joke is that it doesn't mat-ter because religion is not really the issue. In the same vein, the Protes-tants and Catholics in Northern Ireland aren't fighting about transubstantiation or some point of religious doctrine. They are fight-ing over issues of autonomy and over which group gets to rule the country.

Even when religion is clearly not the issue, modern atheist writers insist on twisting evidence to make it the culprit. Consider Sam Har-ris's analysis of the conflict in Sri Lanka. Harris is trying to blame sui-cide bombing on religious people. Yet he has a problem. The inventors of the modern form of suicide bombing are the Tamil Tigers. So Har-ris gets to work. "While the motivations of the Tamil Tigers are not explicitly religious, they are Hindus who undoubtedly believe many improbable things about the nature of life and death. The cult of mar-tyr worship that they have nurtured for decades has many of the fea-tures of religiosity that one would expect in people who give their lives so easily for a cause."[17] In other words, while the Tigers see themselves as combatants in a secular political struggle over land and self-deter-mination, Harris detects a religious motive because these people hap-pen to be Hindu and surely there must be some underlying religious craziness that explains their fanaticism.

I do not for a moment deny that religion can be a source of self-righteousness, and that this tendency can lead to persecution and vio-lence. In the past, it has indeed been so. In the Muslim world, violence in the name of religion is still a serious problem. But for Christians the tragedy of violence in the name of religion is thankfully in the ancient past.

I'll conclude this chapter by suggesting why this is so. In Dosto-evsky's novel *The Brothers Karamazov,* one of the brothers tells the story of the grand inquisitor, in which Christ himself appears before the tribunal. He is immediately recognized and thrown into prison. That night, the inquisitor comes to visit him. He asks him to "go and never return again." The reason is clear. Christ's teachings are those of a peacemaker. They are the very opposite of the persecutions and vio-lence that have sometimes been perpetrated in the name of Christian-ity. Jesus says in Matthew 7:1–5, "Judge not that you be not judged. For with what judgment you judge, you shall be judged, and with what measure you mete, it shall be measured to you again. . . . Thou hyp-ocrite, first cast out the beam from your eye, and then you shall see clearly how to cast the mote out of your brother's eye." This may not always have been the spirit of Christians, and it is not always the spirit of every Christian today. But it is the spirit of the founder and guiding light of Christianity, and it continues to supply a noble standard for a war-weary and violent world.

CHAPTER NINETEEN

A LICENSE TO KILL: ATHEISM AND THE MASS MURDERS OF HISTORY

"Without God and the future life? How will man be after
that? It means everything is permitted now."[1]

—Fyodor Dostoevsky, *The Brothers Karamazov*

WHILE THEY REGULARLY FAULT RELIGION for its role in promoting conflict and violence, secular writers rarely examine the role of atheism in producing wars and killing. It's interesting that we routinely hear about how much historical suffering religion has caused, but we seldom hear about how much suffering atheism has caused. Five hundred years after the Inquisition, we are still talking about it, but less than two decades after the collapse of "godless Communism," there is an eerie silence about the mass graves of the Soviet Gulag. Why the absence of accountability? Does atheism mean never having to say you are sorry?

Atheist writers who take up the question concede that atheists, like religious people, sometimes do terrible things. According to Richard Dawkins, "What matters is...whether atheism systematically influences people to do bad things. There is not the smallest evidence that it does." In other words, "Individual atheists may do evil things but they don't do evil things *in the name of atheism*."[2] Physicist Steven

Weinberg concedes that scientific atheism "has made its own contributions to the world's sorrows" but "where the authority of science has been invoked to justify horrors, it really has been in terms of *perversions* of science."[3]

In this chapter, I want to focus on the really big crimes that have been committed by atheist groups and governments. In the past hundred years or so, the most powerful atheist regimes—Communist Russia, Communist China, and Nazi Germany—have wiped out people in astronomical numbers. Stalin was responsible for around twenty million deaths, produced through mass slayings, forced labor camps, show trials followed by firing squads, population relocation and starvation, and so on. Jung Chang and Jon Halliday's authoritative recent study *Mao: The Unknown Story* attributes to Mao Zedong's regime a staggering seventy million deaths.[4] Some China scholars think Chang and Halliday's numbers are a bit high, but the authors present convincing evidence that Mao's atheist regime was the most murderous in world history. Stalin's and Mao's killings—unlike those of, say, the Crusades or the Thirty Years' War—were done in peacetime and were performed on their fellow countrymen. Hitler comes in a distant third with around ten million murders, six million of them Jews.

So far, I haven't even counted the assassinations and slayings ordered by other Soviet dictators like Lenin, Khrushchev, Brezhnev, and so on. Nor have I included a host of "lesser" atheist tyrants: Pol Pot, Enver Hoxha, Nicolae Ceaușescu, Fidel Castro, Kim Jong-il. Even these "minor league" despots killed a lot of people. Consider Pol Pot, who was the leader of the Khmer Rouge, the Communist Party faction that ruled Cambodia from 1975 to 1979. Within this four-year period Pol Pot and his revolutionary ideologues engaged in systematic mass relocations and killings that eliminated approximately one-fifth of the Cambodian population, an estimated 1.5 million to 2 million people. In fact, Pol Pot killed a larger percentage of his countrymen than Stalin and Mao killed of theirs.[5] Even so, focusing only on the big three—Stalin, Hitler, and Mao—we have to recognize that atheist regimes have in a single century murdered more than one hundred million people.

Religion inspired killing simply cannot compete with the murders perpetrated by atheist regimes. I recognize that population levels were much lower in the past, and that it's much easier to kill people today with sophisticated weapons than it was in previous centuries with swords and arrows. Even taking higher population levels into account, atheist violence surpasses religious violence by staggering proportions. Here is a rough calculation. The world's population rose from around 500 million in 1450 AD to 2.5 billion in 1950, a fivefold increase. Taken together, the Crusades, the Inquisition, and the witch burnings killed approximately 200,000 people. Adjusting for the increase in population, that's the equivalent of one million deaths today. Even so, these deaths caused by Christian rulers over a five-hundred-year period amount to only 1 percent of the deaths caused by Stalin, Hitler and Mao in the space of a few decades.

Dawkins seems to have deluded himself into thinking that these horrors were not produced on atheism's behalf. But can anyone seriously deny that Communism was an atheist ideology? Communism calls for the elimination of the exploiting class, it extols violence as a way to social progress, and it calls for using any means necessary to achieve the atheist utopia. Not only was Marx an atheist, but atheism was also a central part of the Marxist doctrine. Atheism became a central component of the Soviet Union's official ideology, it is still the official doctrine of China, and Stalin and Mao enforced atheist policies by systematically closing churches and murdering priests and religious believers. All Communist regimes have been strongly anti-religious, suggesting that their atheism is intrinsic rather than incidental to their ideology.

Similarly, Nazism was a secular, anti-religious philosophy that, strangely enough, had a lot in common with Communism. While the Communists wanted to empower the proletariat, the Nazis wanted to empower a master race. For the Communists the enemy was the capitalist class; for the Nazis the enemy was the Jews and other races deemed inferior. The Communists and the Nazis treated the Christian churches as obstacles and enemies. Both groups proclaimed that they were engaging in revolutionary action in order to create a new type of human being and a new social order freed from the shackles of traditional religion and traditional morality.[6]

In comparing the crimes of religion and the crimes of atheism, it's important for us to apply a consistent standard. Philosopher Daniel Dennett supplies such a standard in his book *Breaking the Spell*. He proposes that religion be judged by its consequences, or, as the biblical expression has it, "by their fruits ye shall know them." Dennett doesn't particularly care whether these consequences were intended by the founders of the religion or if they represent its highest values. He's not especially interested in separating the true teachings of religion from its distortions. "It is true that religious fanatics are rarely if ever inspired by, or guided by, the deepest and best tenets in those religious traditions. So what? Al Qaeda and Hamas terrorism is still Islam's responsibility, and abortion clinic bombing is still Christianity's responsibility."[7] This is all very fine. Let's accept Dennett's standard. But then by this very same criterion the millions of murders committed by Stalin, Hitler, and Mao—not to mention those of a range of lesser tyrants—are all atheism's responsibility.

Alas, Steven Weinberg wants to have it both ways. Weinberg apparently believes that the crimes of religious regimes reflect the true face of religion, while the crimes of atheist regimes represent a distortion of the atheist spirit of rational and scientific inquiry. By Dennett's standards, this is an evasion. If Christianity has to answer for Torquemada, atheism has to answer for Stalin. By the same token, if the ordinary Christian who has never burned anyone at the stake must bear some responsibility for what other self-styled Christians have done on behalf of religion, then atheists who think of themselves as the kinder, gentler type do not get to absolve themselves for the horrible suffering that their beliefs have caused in recent history. Weinberg is employing a transparent sleight-of-hand that holds Christianity responsible for the evils done in its name, while seeking to exculpate secularism and atheism for the greater crimes perpetrated in theirs.

Along the same lines, Sam Harris attempts to exonerate atheism by alleging that Stalinism and Maoism were each "little more than a political religion." Christopher Hitchens advances a similar line of argument, suggesting that as the Stalinists and Maoists sought to replace religion those ideologies should be considered substitute religions. Should religion now be responsible not only for its crimes but also for the crimes committed by atheists on behalf of atheist ideologies?

As for Nazism, Harris writes that "the hatred of Jews in Germany... was a direct inheritance from medieval Christianity." Indeed, "the Holocaust marked the culmination of...two hundred years of Christian fulminating against the Jews." Therefore, "knowingly or not, the Nazis were agents of religion."[8] Atheist Web sites routinely claim that Hitler was a Christian because he was born Catholic, never publicly renounced his Catholicism, and wrote in *Mein Kampf,* "By defending myself against the Jew, I am fighting for the work of the Lord."[9]

How persuasive are these claims? Hitler was born Catholic just as Stalin was born into the Russian Orthodox Church and Mao was raised as a Buddhist. These facts prove nothing, as many people reject their religious upbringing as these three men did. From an early age, historian Allan Bullock writes, Hitler "had no time at all for Catholic teaching, regarding it as a religion fit only for slaves and detesting its ethics."[10] How then do we account for Hitler's claim that in carrying out his anti-Semitic program he was an instrument of divine providence? During his ascent to power, Hitler needed the support of the German people—both the Bavarian Catholics and the Prussian Lutherans—and to secure this he occasionally used rhetoric such as "I am doing the Lord's work." To claim that this rhetoric makes Hitler a Christian is to confuse political opportunism with personal conviction. Hitler himself says in *Mein Kampf* that his public statements should be understood as propaganda that bear no relation to the truth but are designed to sway the masses.[11]

The Nazi idea of an Aryan Christ who uses the sword to cleanse the earth of the Jews—what Hitler once called "Positive Christianity"— was obviously a radical departure from traditional Christian understanding, and was condemned as such by Pope Pius XI at the time. Moreover, Hitler's anti-Semitism was not religious, it was racial. Jews were targeted not because of their religion—indeed many German

Jews were completely secular in their way of life—but because of their racial identity. This was an ethnic and not a religious designation.

We can see the difference by looking at attitudes toward Jews in medieval Europe. In fifteenth-century Spain, a Jew could escape Christian persecution simply by converting to Christianity. Ferdinand and Isabella did not object to having ethnic Jews in Spain; they objected to the practice of Judaism in what they wanted to be a completely Catholic country. Hitler's objection to Jews, on the other hand, was not religious. A Jew could not escape Auschwitz by pleading, "I no longer practice Judaism," "I am an atheist," or "I have converted to Christianity." This mattered nothing to Hitler because he believed the Jews were inferior racial stock. His anti-Semitism was secular.

Hitler's Table Talk, a revealing collection of the Führer's private opinions assembled by a close aide during the war years, shows Hitler to be rabidly anti-religious.[12] He called Christianity one of the great "scourges" of history, and said of the Germans, "Let's be the only people who are immunized against this disease." He promised that "through the peasantry we shall be able to destroy Christianity." In fact, he blamed the Jews for inventing Christianity. He also condemned Christianity for its opposition to evolution. Hitler reserved special scorn for the Christian values of equality and compassion, which he identified with weakness. Hitler's leading advisers—Goebbels, Himmler, Heydrich and Bormann—were atheists who hated religion and sought to eradicate its influence in Germany.

Some atheist writers like Christopher Hitchens have sought to push Hitler into the religious camp by pointing to Nazism as a "quasi-pagan phenomenon."[13] Hitler may have been a polytheist who worshipped the pagan gods, these writers say, but polytheism is still theism. This argument fails to distinguish between ancient paganism and modern paganism. It's true that Hitler and the Nazis drew heavily on ancient archetypes—mainly Nordic and Teutonic legends—to give their vision a mystical aura. But this was secular mysticism, not religious mysticism. The ancient Germanic peoples truly believed in their pagan gods. Hitler and the Nazis, however, relied on ancient myths in the modern form given to them by Nietzsche and Wagner. For Nietzsche and Wagner, there was no question of the ancient myths being true. Wagner no more believed in the Norse god Wotan than Nietzsche believed in Apollo. For Hitler and the Nazis, the ancient myths were valuable because they could give depth and significance to a secular racial conception of the world.

Historian Richard Evans writes that "the Nazis regarded the churches as the strongest and toughest reservoirs of ideological opposition to the principles they believed in."[14] Once Hitler and the Nazis came to power, they launched a ruthless drive to subdue and weaken Christian churches in Germany. Evans points out that after 1937 the policies of Hitler's government became increasingly anti-religious. The Nazis stopped celebrating Christmas, and the Hitler Youth recited a prayer thanking the Führer rather than God for their blessings. Clergy regarded as "troublemakers" were ordered not to preach, hundreds of them were imprisoned, and many were simply murdered. Churches were under constant Gestapo surveillance. The Nazis closed religious schools, forced Christian organizations to disband, dismissed civil servants who were practicing Christians, confiscated church property, and censored religious newspapers.[15] Harris cannot explain how an ideology that Hitler and his associates perceived as a repudiation of Christianity can be portrayed as a "culmination" of Christianity.

If Nazism represented the culmination of anything, it was that of the nineteenth-century and early twentieth-century ideology of social Darwinism. As historian Richard Weikart documents, both Hitler and Himmler were admirers of Darwin and often spoke of their role as enacting a "law of nature" that guaranteed the "elimination of the unfit." Weikart argues that Hitler himself "drew upon a bountiful fund of social Darwinist thought to construct his own racist philosophy" and concludes that while Darwinism is not a "sufficient" intellectual explanation for Nazism, it is a "necessary" one. Without Darwinism, there might not have been Nazism.[16]

The Nazis also drew on philosopher Friedrich Nietzsche, adapting his atheist philosophy to their crude purposes. Nietzsche's vision of the *übermensch* and his elevation of a new ethic "beyond good and evil" were avidly embraced by Nazi propagandists. Nietzsche's "will to power" almost became a Nazi recruitment slogan. I am not for a moment suggesting that Darwin or Nietzsche would have approved of Hitler's ideas. But Hitler and his henchmen approved of Darwin's and Nietzsche's ideas. Sam Harris simply ignores the evidence of the Nazis' sympathies for Darwin, Nietzsche, and atheism. So what sense can we make of his claim that the leading Nazis were "knowingly or unknowingly" agents of religion? Clearly, it is nonsense.

Some people have expressed bafflement that atheist regimes have produced bloodbaths that no other force in history has matched. Dawkins himself raises the question of how an absence of belief can possibly cause social harm. Little does Dawkins realize that his own deepest beliefs provide a clue to the "final solution." The atheist killers regarded their cause as so grand and noble that nothing should be allowed to stand in its way. They viewed themselves as acting on behalf of inexorable and incontrovertible forces like science, reason, and progress.

Science? Yes, the Nazis saw themselves promoting the survival of the fittest, in precisely the way evolution has always done. Reason? The Communists saw their project as an institutionalization of the age of reason. Marx was in the Enlightenment tradition of the French Jacobins, who enthroned a goddess of reason in the Cathedral of Notre Dame and then unleashed the Reign of Terror, in which "unreasonable" people—noblemen, priests, and other representatives of the old order—were sent to the guillotine. And progress? As the Communists and the Nazis always stressed, history was on their side, and therefore their opponents were religious or bourgeois reactionaries who should be eliminated because they were retarding the forward march of society. This secular apotheosis of science, reason, and progress—a doctrine that is very much with us today—is precisely what licensed men to do things to other people in a manner and on a scale that were previously unthinkable.

A second reason for the horrors of atheist regimes is that they operated without any of the moral restraints that are the product of religion and that, however slightly, held back the bloodthirsty tyrants of the past. Nietzsche saw this coming. Writing in the nineteenth century, he predicted that the next two centuries would be cataclysmic, with wars and violence beyond all imagining.[17] The death of God, Nietzsche wrote, would result in the total eclipse of all values. Since values no longer came from God, they would now be made up by man. And since man is descended from the animal kingdom—an idea Nietzsche adopted from Darwin—man was likely to embrace the value of the *libido dominandi* (the lust to dominate) that we see everywhere in nature. Superior humans would eliminate inferior ones for the same reason that lions eat antelopes. "Master morality" prevails over "slave morality." It becomes useless to appeal to pity and compassion and decency any more. That would be like telling lions that they should stop being lions.

In other words, the atheist bloodbath is the product of a hubristic modern ideology that sees man, not God, as the creator of values. In rejecting God, man becomes scornful of the doctrine of human sinfulness and convinced of the perfectibility of his nature. Man now seeks to displace God and create a secular utopia here on earth. In order to achieve this, the atheist rulers establish total control of society. They invent a form of totalitarianism far more comprehensive than anything that previous rulers attempted: every aspect of life comes under political supervision. Of course if some people—the Jews, the landowners, the unfit, the handicapped, the religious dissidents, and so on—have to be relocated, incarcerated, or liquidated in order to achieve this utopia, this is a price the atheist tyrants have shown themselves quite willing to pay. The old moral codes do not apply, and ordinary atheist functionaries carry out behavior that would make a church inquisitor quake. The atheist regimes, by their actions, confirm the truth of Dostoevsky's dictum: if God is not, everything is permitted.

Whatever the cause for why atheist regimes do what they do, the indisputable fact is that all the religions of the world put together have in three thousand years not managed to kill anywhere near the number of people killed in the name of atheism in the past few decades. It's time to abandon the mindlessly repeated mantra that religious belief has been the main source of human conflict and violence. Atheism, not religion, is responsible for the worst mass murders of history.

PART VII

CHRISTIANITY AND MORALITY

CHAPTER TWENTY

NATURAL LAW AND DIVINE LAW: THE OBJECTIVE FOUNDATIONS OF MORALITY

"When Gentiles, who do not have the law, do by nature things required by the law, they show that the requirements of the law are written on their hearts."

—St. Paul, Letter to the Romans, 2:14

RELIGION AND MORALITY SEEM TO BE TWO SEPARATE THINGS, and yet many people's objections to Christianity seem to derive mainly from their resistance to Christian morality. To many, this morality seems arbitrary, authoritarian, and even cruel. Richard Dawkins puts it this way: "The God of the Old Testament is arguably the most unpleasant character in all fiction: jealous and proud of it, a petty, unjust, unforgiving control freak; a vindictive, bloodthirsty ethnic cleanser; a misogynistic, homophobic, racist, infanticidal, genocidal, filicidal, pestilential, megalomaniacal, sadomasochistic, capriciously malevolent bully."[1] Gone is the measured scientific tone, and Dawkins shows that he doesn't just disbelieve in the Christian God, he detests Him. Is morality, then, the universal set of rules issued by a divine scarecrow with a long beard and a wagging finger? Or is morality better understood in natural and secular terms, as adaptable rules that we make up as we go along in order to serve human objectives like peace and coexistence?

In this chapter I will show that this is a false choice. Morality is both natural and universal. It is discoverable without religion, yet its source is ultimately divine. Darwinist attempts to give a purely secular explanation of morality are a failure, and each of us knows—however disingenuously we deny it—that there are absolute standards of right and wrong, and these are precisely the standards we use to judge how other people treat us. It is not Christian morality that is the obstacle to our moral freedom; it is conscience itself, the judge within.

Leading atheists fault religion—and specifically Christianity—for imposing stern morality on people and thus constraining their freedom. Typical is Christopher Hitchens, who condemns Christianity as a "creepy movement to impose orthodoxy on a free and pluralist and secular republic."[2] At the same time Hitchens and other atheists insist they are not against morality. They assure us that they are as moral, if not more so, than religious people, and that morality is quite possible without the presumption of God or religion. Daniel Dennett observes that "there are many wise, engaged, morally committed atheists and agnostics" and that unbelievers don't seem to act any better or worse than Christians.[3] Richard Dawkins writes that it "requires quite a low self-regard to think that, should belief in God suddenly vanish from the world, we would all become callous and selfish hedonists, with no kindness, no charity, no generosity, nothing that would deserve the name of goodness."[4] The atheist objection is not to morality but to absolute morality. Rather than deriving morality from an external code of divine commandments, atheists think of morality as man-made, something forged through individual and group experience.

I think there is a lot to what the atheists are saying here, but in the end I'm afraid they miss the point. For starters, I am not sure how to assess Dawkins's argument for the morality of atheism, because a religious society suddenly deprived of God would presumably still retain many Christian ways of thinking and acting. Even so, I have known quite a few atheists, and I am happy to testify that they can be good and admirable people. Both Hume and Darwin were famous for their decency and moral rectitude, and I believe E. O. Wilson when he writes that although he is not a Christian, he shares most of the Christian virtues.[5] I have also known a few religious believers who could match any atheist in breaking the commandments. Novelist Evelyn Waugh once responded to the question, "How can a Catholic like you be so debauched and spiteful?" with the classic rejoinder, "Think how much worse I would be if I were not a Catholic!"

There are three central issues here: Is there a universal or objective morality? Does it have a religious foundation? How can it be known? We are accustomed to speaking of the scientific laws of nature. It's worth asking if there are moral laws of human nature. Many of us are the unwitting heirs to a philosophy that denies objective morality. We hold that science is objective, but values are subjective. We believe we can know scientific things but morality is a matter of mere opinion. On this basis we say things like "don't impose your beliefs on me" while it would never occur to us to say "don't impose your algebra on me." Yet have we considered the possibility that there are moral laws in nature that are no less reliable and comprehensible than scientific laws?

Humans are unique in many ways, but mostly in the fact that we are moral beings. More than language, more than rationality, it is our moral nature that distinguishes humanity from even our closest animal relatives. Primatologist Frans de Waal, who studies chimpanzees and has done much to emphasize their close kinship with humans, admits that morality is something chimps don't have. "It is hard to believe that animals weigh their own interests against the rights of others, that they develop a vision of the greater good of society, or that they feel lifelong guilt about something that they should not have done."[6] We can say to Bonzo, "You shouldn't have done that" and "Bad chimpanzee!" but those are our own ways of speaking. We have no grounds to believe that chimps feel that way.

This distinction between chimps and humans points to a deeper chasm that separates human beings from the rest of the universe. All other objects, living and nonliving, function according to physical or scientific laws. Dangle a meaty bone in front of a dog and, no matter how much it has just eaten, it goes for the bone. Its response is a product of seemingly uncontrollable instinct. Place a large stone on a slanted hillside, and it will automatically roll down. It has no choice in the matter. It is simply obeying physical laws.

But human beings are not like this. Human beings live in two worlds, the physical domain and the moral domain. If a person insults your mother, you respond, "You shouldn't have done that." When a friend tells you he deceived his business partners or family, you tell him he shouldn't have lied. These normative statements are fundamentally different from physical laws. It makes no sense to say that the earth ought to revolve around the sun or that it would be unfair if it didn't. A law of nature may be true or false, but it cannot be broken. As Carl Sagan puts it, "Nature...arranges things so that its prohibitions are impossible to transgress."[7]

There are parts of our human nature that operate according to these descriptive natural laws. If you tickle me, I will laugh. If either of us eats contaminated food, it will upset our stomachs. If we are dropped from a tall tower, we will plummet to the ground. These are the laws of physics and chemistry working on us, and we have no choice in the matter. On the other hand, there is a part of our human nature that is not descriptive but prescriptive. The simple proof of this is that moral norms and precepts, unlike natural laws, can be violated.

Honor thy father and mother. Thou shalt not murder. Thou shalt not covet thy neighbor's goods. None of these commandments would make any sense if we had no option. But there is more. When we humans invoke the language of morals—praising and blaming, approving and disapproving, applauding and scorning—we appeal to a shared standard of judgment external to ourselves. Let us call this standard the natural law or the moral law. It differs from the scientific laws of nature in that it tells us not what we do but what we ought to do. Consequently we are free to break these laws in a way that we are not free to violate the laws of gravity.

By their very nature, moral laws are both universal and objective. This may not seem obvious upon first consideration. Don't the moral practices of the different cultures of the world vary widely? Isn't there moral diversity within our own society? It seems there is no universal, objective morality. Such a conclusion, however, arises from an error of fact and an error of logic. It is certainly true that the moral behavior of the world's cultures shows enormous variation. Carl Sagan writes that there are cultures like the Ik of Uganda, "where all the Ten Commandments seem to be systematically, institutionally ignored."[8] My own anthropological work on the Ik is incomplete, so I cannot say whether he is right. But let's assume that he is. What does this show? That the Ik are radically different from us? But we too live in a culture where the Ten Commandments are systematically and institutionally ignored. Sagan's example seems to establish not diversity but unity of practice.

But even better examples fail to establish Sagan's point. Let's say that anthropological investigation reveals that the Ik routinely beat their wives. Would this prove that beating your wife is the right thing to do? Of course not. The presence of moral disagreement does not indicate the absence of universal morality. How can the fact of behavior, however eccentric and diverse, invalidate the norm of what is right?

It would be interesting to conduct a global survey to see if all the cultures of the world accept the heliocentric theory. Let's say that such a study shows there are people in South America and Southeast Asia who, even when shown the reasoning of Copernicus, supplemented by photographs taken by modern spacecraft, emphatically reject the idea that the earth goes around the sun. These people are delighted to discover that a fellow named Ptolemy held a rival view, and they decide to go with Ptolemy. Would anyone conclude from this that the heliocentric theory had been refuted? The suggestion is absurd. I am highly confident that there are many cultures in the world, even today, that would emphatically reject Darwin's theory of evolution and Einstein's theory of relativity. None of this would show that scientific laws are relative, only that the people who reject them happen to be wrong. Thus the testimony of a hundred quarreling tribes and widespread differences of opinion about morality do nothing to undermine the notion of universal morality.

Over the last several decades, anthropologists have been comparing the norms and practices of the various cultures of the world. Two of their findings are relevant for our purpose. First, morality is universal.

Scholars know of no culture, past or present, that does not have a system of morality. Even though moral standards may vary from one culture to another, or even within a particular culture, every culture distinguishes "what is" from "what ought to be." It is impossible for a culture either to rise above morality or to get out from under it.

Second, the moral diversity we have all heard so much about is in fact vastly exaggerated. In particular, the major religions of the world, which represent the vast majority of humans on the planet, disagree quite a bit about God but agree quite a bit about morality. All the major religions have some form of the Golden Rule: do unto others as you would have them to do unto you. In 1993 theologian Hans Küng assembled a "parliament" of leading representatives of the world's religions, including Jews, Christians, Muslims, Hindus, and Buddhists. The group issued a declaration of common beliefs, including a wide range of moral values that are held across religious boundaries.[9]

This moral unanimity is not confined to monotheistic or even religious cultures. The Greeks and Romans shared many of the moral teachings of Judaism and Christianity, even though Athens and Rome were once polytheistic empires. Confucius in his *Analects* articulates precepts of the same kind, even though his was a moral code devoid of any substantial theology. Anthropologists have discovered many of the same moral principles even among cultures that are animistic or have no formal religious beliefs at all. In the early twentieth century, scholars like Margaret Mead and others went to faraway places and breathlessly reported, "Gee, they don't do things the same way over here." But this scholarship has been substantially revised in the light of later, more careful studies.

Yes, there is diversity of moral practice, but there is much less diversity of moral standards. One group may permit one wife and another group four or more wives, but all groups agree on the indispensability of the family and its moral obligation to provide for the young. James Q. Wilson's book *The Moral Sense* makes the case for a universal grammar of morality rooted in our human instincts.[10] Donald Brown's study *Human Universals* reveals more than three hundred unvarying patterns of behavior, including a host of moral beliefs that are shared by all known cultures.[11] To take two of his examples, various cultures may specify situations in which it is morally permissible to lie or act in a cowardly manner, but in no culture are dishonesty and cowardice upheld as virtues.

What, then, are we to make of relativism—the influential doctrine that says that morality is relative? I agree that relativism has something going for it, in that people even within our own society disagree about the content of morality. There are also debates about the priority of one moral principle over another. Different individuals and even societies disagree over how a moral principle should be applied in a given situation. But on the existence of moral standards there is no disagreement. Consequently relativism of moral belief and practice in no way invalidates the claim that morality is absolute. Indeed I submit that not only is morality absolute, but everyone, including self-proclaimed relativists, knows that it is absolute. Relativism in its pure sense simply does not exist.

If you are confronted by a relativist who insists that all morality is relative, go ahead and punch him in the face. If he does not respond, punch him again. At some point he will protest, "That's not right. You shouldn't have done that." Then you can explain to him that your actions were purely educational. You were simply demonstrating to him that even he does not believe his relativist doctrine. His objection was not "I don't like being punched" but rather "you should not have done it." He was appealing to an unwavering standard, which he expected you to share, that what you did was wrong.

Another way to make the point, when you hear people solemnize about the relativism of values, is to find a value they cherish and excoriate it. This is a useful approach because most of the time, when people deny absolute morality, they are engaging in a rhetorical strategy in order to undermine some particular moral belief you hold and they don't. Social liberals, for example, often discuss topics like drugs, pornography, and prostitution by saying, "How can you impose your beliefs on me? Who is to say what's right?" They seem to be denying absolute morality. If they are not self-aware, they might even believe this.

So the way to call their bluff and expose their relativism as purely tactical is to insult the moral values they cherish. For example, you could say, "I don't know why we have laws outlawing racial discrimination and gay-bashing. How can people presume to legislate morality?" Or "I am surprised people object so strongly to the Confederate flag. I don't have a strong view one way or the other, but since morality is relative, can anyone really say that the South's cause was wrong?" Or how about "What's the big deal about the environment? Why should I preserve the planet for the sake of future generations? What have future generations ever done for me?" Say these things as if you believe them, even if you don't.

Before you are finished, I think you will find your relativist up in arms, insisting that prejudice and racism are immoral and unjust, and that we ought to have laws restricting them and protecting the environment. The person who affirms these doctrines is not saying that his views on bigotry and environmentalism are simply a matter of personal preference. He is implying that everyone should feel this way, and no decent person should behave in a manner contrary to his principles. He may ignore the moral law in the way he acts toward you, but he is quick to invoke it as a standard for how he expects you to act toward him. In short, his actions confess that despite his loud denials, he too espouses morality as an absolute.

The concept of absolute morality fits very well with religion because the afterlife becomes the venue in which rewards and punishments are finally handed out. Without heaven and hell, life on earth becomes very unjust. Many people violate the moral law and prosper, and many who abide by the moral law come to grief. Is this really the end of the story? In Hinduism you get your comeuppance through reincarnation. If you act badly in this life, you may be a cockroach in the next one. In Judaism, Christianity, and Islam there is no reincarnation but there is a Last Judgment in which all earthly accounts are settled and cosmic justice is achieved. Within the religious framework, violations of the universal moral law are also held to be violations of God's law, and they are given a new name: sin.

Not only are moral laws easily integrated into a religious scheme, but the existence of a universal, absolute morality is also a powerful argument for the existence of God. If there are moral laws that operate beyond the realm of natural laws, where do these laws come from? Moral laws presume a moral lawgiver. In other words, God is the ultimate standard of good. He is responsible for the distinction between good and evil that we universally perceive as binding on human action. The fact that these standards are distinctive to human beings implies that there is something special about us, and that God has a special interest in how we live.

So the existence of absolute morality poses a supreme challenge for atheism. Leading Darwinians like Daniel Dennett, Steven Pinker, and Richard Dawkins have sought to meet this challenge. They do so by attempting to explain morality as a product of evolution and natural selection. Human beings do good and act altruistically, and on the face of it, this altruism seems counter to the evolutionary principle that creatures act self-interestedly to survive and reproduce. Dennett and Dawkins draw on the work of evolutionary pioneers like R. A. Fisher, W. D. Hamilton, and Robert Trivers to show that what appears to be altruism is actually a long-term strategy of survival and reproduction that has been programmed into our genes.

Two terms are critical here: "kin selection" and "reciprocal altruism." Kin selection means self-help by way of natural selection. But in this paradigm natural selection operates not at the level of individuals but at the level of genes. It is the genes that are programmed to perpetuate themselves, even if we—their survival machines—perish in the process. Richard Dawkins masterfully develops this argument in his book *The Selfish Gene*.[12]

By this logic, a mother who dives into a burning car to save her two children trapped inside is not acting out of pure altruism. Her children share her genes, and her actions are best explained as an effort to ensure that her genes make it into the next generation. Even if she dies, her genes live on through her children. The power of "kin selection" is that it helps to explain why we take big risks and make big sacrifices for our immediate family: they are genetically closest to us. We take smaller risks and make smaller sacrifices for cousins and other relatives: they too are genetically tied to us, but more distantly. Biologist J. B. S. Haldane once quipped that he would be willing to sacrifice his life for "two brothers or eight cousins."[13]

What about strangers? Darwinian theory says we should be indifferent to them because they are genetically alien to us. Even so, we do trade with strangers and coexist with them and generally treat them decently and fairly. The Darwinians explain this as a consequence of "reciprocal altruism," which is the moral equivalent of "I'll be nice to you, so that you will be nice to me." This strategy can take various forms—"first be nice to me, and then I'll be nice to you" or "I'll continue to be nice to you as long as you are nice to me"—but the general idea is that morality is a strategy we employ for our own long-term benefit. Darwinians go to elaborate lengths to establish these strategies, resorting to game theory and obscure analogies from the behavior of ants and vampire bats, but I don't need to reproduce those arguments; the underlying logic is clear and persuasive enough.

The problem is that this entire framework of Darwinian analysis does not even come close to explaining morality. It confines itself to explaining altruism, but it only succeeds in explaining what may be termed "low altruism." But humans also engage in "high altruism," which may be defined as behavior that confers no reciprocal or genetic advantage. A man stands up to give his seat on a bus to an old lady. She is nothing to him, and he is certainly not thinking that there may be a future occasion when she or someone else will give him a seat. He gives up his seat because he is a nice guy. There is no Darwinian rationale that can account for his behavior.

Richard Dawkins concedes that the Darwinian thesis cannot explain why people give blood, a fact that he puts down to "pure disinterested altruism" that confers no benefit to the genes.[14] Nor can the Darwinian model account for Christ's maxim "love your enemies." Or for Patrick Henry's *cri de coeur*, "Give me liberty or give me death!" Or for Mother Teresa's lifelong dedication to the sick and dying on the streets of Calcutta. Or for the biblical story of the Good Samaritan who went out of his way to assist a stranger from a reviled community.

Some time ago, I read the true account of a Catholic priest, Maximilian Kolbe, who was imprisoned in a Nazi concentration camp for his anti-Nazi activities. Each day the Nazis would choose one person from the group for execution. One of the first persons they selected was a man who pleaded for his life, saying he had a wife and children who were dependent on him and he needed to live in order to look after them. Just as the Nazis were about to drag him from the room, the priest stood up and said, "Take me in his place." The Nazis were uncomprehending and refused, but the priest insisted. The man was equally uncomprehending, so the priest told him, "I don't have a family. I am old, and won't be missed like you will." The Nazis finally agreed, and the priest went to his death. The man whose place he took survived the war and returned to his family.

Now where is the Darwinian explanation for Kolbe's sacrifice? It does not exist. Ernst Mayr, a leading evolutionary biologist, admits that "altruism toward strangers is a behavior not supported by natural selection."[15] I have great respect for the work of Fisher, Trivers, and others in their field, and I do think that in time the evolutionists will produce more satisfactory accounts of human cultural and moral behavior. But I predict their project to comprehensively account for morality in Darwinian terms will fail. The Darwinian project is necessarily confined to the domain of self-interest, and it is the essence of morality to operate against self-interest. The whole point of morality is that you are doing what you ought to do, not what you are inclined to do or what is in your interest to do. Morality is described in the language of duty, and duty is something that we are obliged to do whether we want to or not, whether it benefits us or not.

C. S. Lewis demonstrates this point with a beautiful example that I am modifying for my own purpose.[16] You are walking on the river bank, and you hear the screams of someone who is drowning. You are a very poor swimmer and the fellow is nothing to you. If two of your brothers were drowning you might jump in, because each of them has half your genes. If a bunch of your relatives were in a boat that was sinking you might jump in, because this might be a reasonable strategy for your genes to live on through your aunts, uncles, and cousins. In this case, however, the drowning man is unrelated to you. Kin selection is not involved, and neither is reciprocal altruism, as there is no reason to think that there will be an occasion when he will risk his life to save yours. And yet, Lewis points out, there is a little voice in your head that says you should jump into the water and try to save the man's life. Darwinian thinkers like Dawkins realize that this cannot be explained as "acting for the good of society" because why should self-interested people care what's good for society except when it benefits them? For you to worry about the good of society, you have to be unselfish in the first place, and this is what we are trying to explain.

A better answer is that human beings have a "herd instinct" or an instinctive natural sympathy for members of our own species, and perhaps this can account for rival inclinations: one saying "go ahead and help," the other saying "leave and don't help." Lewis notes that even when there are competing inclinations like this, a third voice, distinct from the other two, enters the picture. This is the voice that says you ought to help. Speaking gently but with unmistakable firmness, the voice urges you to listen to the good inclination that says "help" and ignore the selfish inclination that says "don't help." That is the hidden call of conscience.

Many people think of conscience as a mere feeling or inclination. But conscience is not itself an inclination but rather an arbiter of inclinations, what Adam Smith once called the "impartial spectator" that gives us our highest sense of ourselves.[17] When there is a strong inclination like the instinct for survival and a weak inclination like the instinct to help a stranger, conscience typically intervenes on the side of the weaker instinct. Except in pathological people, its voice is clear and incontrovertible. It uses no compulsion in urging us to follow its edicts, yet it exercises both a critical and even a kind of judicial authority: you are obliged to do this, no matter how you feel about it.

There is no other voice in our experience that speaks to us in this way. Conscience is our perennial guide and personal moral tutor. It seemingly requires nothing besides itself, and it provides individualized instruction tailored to each specific situation. Conscience is unconcerned with convenience or reputation, and it seems to operate most strongly when no one is looking. We can, of course, reject the appeal of conscience, but if we do, we cannot help but pass judgment on ourselves using the very criteria supplied by conscience. Conscience has the ability to impose self-reproach, remorse, and shame, and at the same time to make us feel that such consequences are deserved. It is truly one of the most mysterious and powerful aspects of our humanity.

For Kant, conscience is a kind of noumenal voice that speaks to us directly from within ourselves, giving us a certainty that is unavailable to us from outer or phenomenal experience. This is a philosophical way to describe morality, but Lewis puts it more simply: conscience is nothing other than the voice of God within our souls. It is the bridge that links the creature to the creator. Even the atheist hears this internal clarion call because even the atheist has morality at the core of his being, and while the atheist may have rejected God, God has not rejected him.

THE GHOST IN THE MACHINE: WHY MAN IS MORE THAN MATTER

"This idea of immaterial souls ... has outlived its credibility thanks to the advance of the natural sciences."[1]

—Daniel Dennett, *Freedom Evolves*

IT IS POSSIBLE TO ASSERT A STRONG OBJECTION to our discussion of conscience, morality, and the traditional notions of right and wrong. We might think we experience the call of conscience, but how do we know that this is not an illusion? Religion tells us that these transactions of good and evil take place in the "soul," but where can this soul be located? There is a powerful strain of atheism that teaches that human beings are nothing more than matter. In this materialistic view, the soul is a fiction, a "ghost in the machine" that has been invented by religion for its own purposes. After all, we never encounter this ghost within the material frame of human beings. What we do encounter is brains, arteries, blood, and organs. These are all made up of the same atoms and molecules as trees and stones, and are assembled by a process of evolution and natural selection into this intricate machine we call *Homo sapiens*. From this perspective, man is a kind of intelligent robot, a carbon-based computer. Consequently, man should be understood in the same material terms in which we understand software programs.

"If we do indeed possess an immaterial soul," physicist Victor Stenger writes in *God: The Failed Hypothesis*, "then we should expect to find some evidence for it."[2] But science has found none, which leads Stenger to conclude that the soul is a myth. Philosopher Daniel Dennett writes, "Our brains are made of neurons, and nothing else. Nerve cells are very complicated mechanical systems. You take enough of those, and you put them together, and you get a soul."[3] Dennett is not suggesting that the soul is itself a material object. Rather, he is implying that the soul is simply the name for the brain's ability to do certain kinds of mechanical processing.

Physicist Jerome Elbert writes that souls cannot exist, because "if souls exist and are essential for thinking and decision making, our mental processes involve frequent communications from the brain to the soul and from the soul to the brain." As a scientist, Elbert confesses, "I find the idea of such interactions very disturbing." The reason he is troubled is that he cannot possibly see how an immaterial entity like the soul can move or influence a material object like the brain. He also raises a deeper issue. "If such interactions exist, the human brain is an interface to another, nonphysical world. Such interactions suggest that the rules of science apply to all of the universe—except for human beings....This picture gives humans a unique position in the universe. This anthropocentric picture seems very unacceptable to the scientific worldview."[4] For Elbert, the existence of the soul jeopardizes the very nature of modern science.

Yet there are equally profound consequences to insisting that man is nothing more than matter operating according to physical laws. If that is so, then we live in a deterministic universe and free will is an illusion. Some, like Francis Crick and E. O. Wilson, unhesitatingly assert that human beings do not have free will. "It seems free to you," Crick says, "but it's the result of things you are not aware of."[5] Wilson writes that "the hidden preparation of mental activity gives the illusion of free will."[6]

But Richard Dawkins argues that although we are the product of our selfish genes, "we have the power to turn against our creators. We, alone on earth, can rebel against the tyranny of the selfish replicators." Thus, if we "understand what our own selfish genes are up to...we may then at least have the chance to upset their designs."[7] If this is true, then by Dawkins's own admission we humans occupy a unique position in the universe, because our minds can control our biological destiny. But how is it possible for us to rebel against our genes? How are we different from computers, who cannot rebel against their programming, or cheetahs, who unquestioningly obey the mandate to hunt and survive, or meteors, which travel in placid obedience to the laws of force and gravity? Dawkins has no explanation for this and doesn't seem to think he needs one.

Steven Pinker is even more cavalier. In his various books, he insists that the human brain is nothing more than an ingeniously assembled computer whose programming has been done by chance and natural selection. "The self...is just another network of brain systems....The evidence is overwhelming that every aspect of our mental lives depends entirely on physiological events in the tissues of the brain."[8] Yet Pinker does not see why this view of man should threaten free will or purpose or morality in any way: "I can't imagine how anything coming out of the laboratory...could possibly subtract from the meaning of life." In another book, he says that "happiness and virtue have nothing to do with what natural selection designed us to accomplish.... They are for us to determine." Pinker writes that just because his genes are programmed for survival and reproduction doesn't mean he has to act in this way. "Well into my procreating years I am, so far, voluntarily childless...ignoring the solemn imperative to spread my genes.... If my genes don't like it, they can go jump in the lake."[9]

Notwithstanding Pinker's rhetorical flourish, for him to say that we can declare ourselves independent of our selfish genes makes no sense. Pinker, like a lot of other people, has chosen not to have children. The key word here is "chosen," which presumes free choice. Pinker has not explained where this free choice has come from.

Moreover, he has not faced the Darwinian objection to the content of his choice. If our genes have built us to survive and reproduce, how has the human inclination to avoid having children survived the process of natural selection? It is not enough to say, "My genes say reproduce, but I say go to hell." This kind of reasoning would destroy all Darwinian explanations of human behavior. Moreover, how can happiness and virtue be something "for us to determine"? Where is this "us" that emerges apart from the designs of our genetic programming? How do we get the ingenuity and strength to battle a foe as formidable as our own nature? Having disposed of the ghost in the machine, Pinker seems to be surreptitiously bringing it back.

Let us confront the central materialist doctrine that man, like the rest of nature, is made up of matter and nothing more. The best evidence going for this theory is that matter is all we can see, touch, and measure. Moreover, matter seems "responsible" for our thoughts, emotions, and perhaps even our moral intuitions. A powerful blow to the head can cause unconsciousness. Alcohol and fatigue interfere with concentration. Electrical stimulation of certain parts of the brain can produce a desired emotional response. Patients who suffer certain kinds of brain damage lose the capacity to sympathize with others or to recognize shapes. Alzheimer's disease produces physical deterioration that leads to mental lapse and a complete disappearance of moral awareness.

As consciousness, perception, and thinking all occur in the brain, Francis Crick describes the brain as a conscious, perceptive, and thinking organ. Crick writes, "Both hemispheres can hear what is being said.... What you see is not what is really there; it is what your brain believes is there.... Your brain makes the best interpretation it can.... The brain combines the information...and settles on the most plausible interpretation.... This allows the brain to guess a complete picture."[10]

In Crick's view, the brain "sees," "hears," "believes," "guesses," and even makes "interpretations." But as philosopher Peter Hacker and neuroscientist Max Bennett point out, it is a conceptual fallacy to attribute qualities to the brain that are possessed only by persons.[11]

My brain isn't conscious; I am conscious. My brain doesn't perceive or hear things; I do. My brain isn't thinking; I am thinking. Crick is guilty of something called the pathetic fallacy, which is the fallacy of ascribing human qualities to inanimate objects. Certainly we use our brains to perceive and reason, just as we use our hands and feet to play tennis. But it is just as crazy to say my hands and feet are playing tennis as it is to say my racket is playing tennis. By the same token it is wrong to portray the brain as perceiving, feeling, thinking, or even being aware of anything.

There is a deeper problem with extending the materialistic understanding of nature to human beings. For starters, we experience the outside world—the world described by the laws of physics and chemistry—very differently than we experience ourselves. This is a point emphasized by philosopher Arthur Schopenhauer. All other things we experience indirectly, from the outside, through the apparatus of our senses, but ourselves we experience directly, from the inside, without the involvement of our senses. Only about ourselves do we have this kind of "inside information," which is the clearest, most fundamental knowledge we can have. Based on this privileged and unique access, we know that the external account of reality, however accurate it may be in describing raindrops and cheetahs, is not the full story when it comes to describing ourselves.

We are sure, for example, that we exist. David Hume said that we can't really even know this: "When I enter most intimately into what I call *myself*, I always stumble on some particular perception or other, of heat or cold, light or shade, love or hate, pain or pleasure. I never can catch *myself* at any time without a perception and never can observe any thing but the perception."[12] Consequently, for Hume, the self is a fiction because it cannot be empirically located. But the remarkable thing is that we are conscious of our own existence prior to having any feelings and thoughts. Besides, our feelings and thoughts are experienced as "possessions" somehow distinct from the self, while the self is experienced directly. Schopenhauer writes that as we are the subjects of our own inquiry, the materialist mistake is that of "the subject that forgets to take account of itself."[13] Hume is observing sensations while ignoring the fact that he is the one who is doing the observing. He is allowing his indirect knowledge of external phenomena to trump his direct knowledge of the "I" that is having these experiences.

We not only exist, but we are also conscious. This consciousness seems utterly basic: we cannot get "behind" it, and it is our entire mode of access to the world of experience. We seem to share consciousness with at least some other animals, but not with plants or nonliving things. Moreover, human consciousness seems to be of a different order than animal consciousness. For instance, consider the way that we experience music. From the materialist point of view, music is nothing but vibrations that collide with eardrums and provoke neural reactions in the brain. But we experience music in an entirely different way. Even our most mundane thoughts and experiences seem inexplicable when described in terms of physical and chemical transactions alone. A doctor, for example, may know more about my cerebral cortex than I do, but of my inner thoughts he knows nothing, and he will never be able to see or weigh or touch them, no matter how good his instruments.

In an earlier chapter on evolution we saw that there is no good scientific or Darwinian account of consciousness. The best that cognitive scientists like Steven Pinker can offer is promissory materialism: we believe consciousness is an epiphenomenon of material reality, but we'll explain later how atoms and molecules can produce something as radical and original as subjective consciousness. But an explanation yet to come is no explanation at all. Until it arrives it makes far more sense to take consciousness for the irreducible reality we experience it as. Why let conjecture and unpaid intellectual IOUs make us abandon something as fundamental as our self-awareness? Why accept the mental as a projection of the physical when, as far as we are concerned, it is our indispensable window to all the physical reality we can ever experience?

In addition to consciousness, we also experience intention and purpose. We experience these within ourselves, and we can effectively interpret the actions of others by presuming that they too embody the same qualities. Philosopher Bryan Magee gives an example. If the human body sitting across the room from me raises itself out of its chair into an erect position, transports itself across the room to a table, locates a silver box, removes a cigarette, and places it into its mouth, I know that these events are occurring because the embodied object that I call a person wants a cigarette. I know what the other person is doing even if I have never smoked a cigarette in my life. Magee observes that if we were to try to give a purely scientific account of this event in terms of atomic motion and molecular transactions, it would be totally incomprehensible.[14] We simply cannot understand other people as consisting of matter alone. Pinker admits that "human behavior makes the most sense when it is explained in terms of beliefs and desires, not in terms of volts and grams."[15]

The materialist or "objective" understanding of human experience seems inadequate because we experience our lives as a unity. I have a multitude of different feelings and thoughts and experiences, but I experience them all within a single unified field, what Kant somewhat grandiosely calls the "transcendental unity of apperception." The matter that makes up my body changes constantly, and yet I remain the same person. First I was young, now I am middle-aged, and one day I will be old, but through all these transformations I remain "Dinesh." If I meet my college roommate, whom I haven't seen for twenty-five years, at the airport, I might be surprised to see that he now has gray hair and weighs a lot more than he used to, but I don't react to this by saying, "Who on earth are you?" I recognize that he is still my old roommate, no matter how much his physical constitution may have deteriorated over the years.

Our self-conception is strongly rooted in memory of past experiences, without which it is not clear that the "self" would retain any meaning at all. Imagine if I could not remember the experiences that I had yesterday, or five minutes ago, or if I wasn't sure that those experiences were had by the same person. In such a case I could not meaningfully speak of "my" past or "my" future, and my sense of identity would completely collapse. Through our memories of the past and our expectations for the future we maintain both continuity and singularity through our lives. Our lives have an a priori unity that we have no reason to disregard in our self-understanding. Therefore the idea that we are merely an assembly of changing chemical interactions is both unbelievable and absurd.

The materialist understanding seems to be guilty of a crude form of reductionism. Physicist Paul Davies explains this by way of an analogy: "An electrical engineer could give a complete and accurate description of an advertising display in terms of electric circuit theory, explaining exactly why and how each light is flashing. Yet the claim that the advertising display is therefore nothing but electrical pulses in a complex circuit is absurd."[16] Davies's point here is that a human being is a collection of atoms in the same way that Shakespeare's plays are collections of words or Beethoven's symphonies are collections of notes. It hardly follows from this, however, that *Othello* is nothing more than words or that the Fifth Symphony is no more than an assembly of notes. There is a holistic unity to *Othello* and the Fifth Symphony that seems ignored in describing them in this way. So too are human beings made up of atoms and molecules, but that does not even begin to describe the unity we experience in our everyday lives.

The longer you ponder materialism, the graver the difficulties that present themselves. How can materialism account for the fact that we consider our accounts of the world to be not merely chemically generated reactions but true beliefs? British biologist J. B. S. Haldane sums up the problem: "If my mental processes are determined wholly by the motions of atoms in my brain, I have no reason to suppose my beliefs are true...and hence I have no reason for supposing my brain to be composed of atoms."[17] Physicist Stephen Hawking takes up the horns of this dilemma and finds himself impaled:

> Now if you believe that the universe is not arbitrary, but is governed by definite laws, you ultimately have to combine the partial theories in science into a complete unified theory that will describe everything in the universe. But there is a fundamental paradox in the search for such a complete unified theory. Our ideas about scientific theories...assume we are rational beings who are free to observe the universe as we want and to draw logical deductions from what

we see. In such a scheme it is reasonable to suppose that we might progress ever closer toward the laws that govern our universe. Yet if there really is a complete unified theory, it would also presumably determine our actions. And so the theory itself would determine the outcome of our search for it! And why should it determine that we come to the right conclusions from the evidence? Might it not equally well determine that we draw the wrong conclusion?

Here is Hawking's solution:

> The only answer I can give to this problem is based on Darwin's principle of natural selection. The idea is that in any population of self-reproducing organisms, there will be variations in the genetic material and upbringing that different individuals have. These differences will mean that some individuals are better able than others to draw the right conclusions about the world around them and act accordingly. These individuals will be more likely to survive and reproduce and so their pattern of behavior and thought will come to dominate.[18]

Hawking's solution is based on a non sequitur. Biologists invoke evolution to explain the challenges primitive man faced in prehistoric environments. But evolution cannot explain more than this. There were no survival pressures that required man to develop the capacity to understand the rotation of the planets or the microscopic content of matter. Moreover, evolution selects only for reproduction and survival, not for truth. Based on evolution, our ideas may be considered useful to us, but there are no grounds for presuming that they correspond with truth. Indeed, a useful lie is preferable to a truth that plays no role in genetic self-perpetuation. In reducing everything to the laws of nature we risk denying that there is any rationality or truth behind nature's laws.

Perhaps the strongest argument against materialism is the argument from free will. Let me illustrate. I am sitting at my computer with a cup of coffee on my desk. I can reach over and take a sip if I choose;

I can knock the coffee mug onto the carpet if I choose; I can just leave the cup alone and let the coffee get cold. Now I ask: is there anything in the laws of physics that forces me do any of these things? Obviously not. In Milton Friedman's phrase, I am "free to choose." This freedom characterizes many, although not all, of the actions in my life. I am not free to stop breathing while I am asleep, nor am I free to control the passage of food through my intestines. I am, however, free to knock my coffee mug onto the floor. Now once I decide to do this, and actually do it, then the trajectory of the coffee cup's descent is entirely determined by the laws of physics. My choice to send it on that trajectory, however, is determined by no scientific law but rather by my free decision.

Kant deepens this argument in characteristic fashion by steering it into the domain of morality. We are moral beings. We have moral concepts like "right" and "wrong" and "good" and "evil." We "ought" to do this and "ought not" to do that. Try as we can, we cannot avoid this way of thinking and acting. Morality is an empirical fact no less real than any other experience in the world. Kant argues that for these concepts to have any meaning or applicability whatsoever, it must be the case that we have a choice whether to do something. *Ought* implies *can*. This is not to deny that factors both material and unconscious might influence our decision. But even so, we are at least sometimes at liberty to say yes to this option and no to that option. If we never have such a choice, then it is simply false to say I "should" do this and "shouldn't" do that because there is no possibility of deciding one way or the other. For anyone to recommend one course or action instead of another is completely pointless. If determinism is true, then no one in the world can ever refrain from anything that he or she does. The whole of morality—not just this morality or that morality but morality itself—becomes an illusion.

Our whole vocabulary of praise and blame, admiration and contempt, approval and disapproval would have to be eradicated. If someone murdered his neighbor, or exterminated an entire population, we would have no warrant to punish or even criticize that person because, after all, he was simply acting in the manner of a computer program malfunctioning or a stone involuntarily rolling down a hill.

But Kant says that this way of thinking is not only unacceptable, but is also impossible for human beings. People who operate outside the sphere of morality we call psychopaths, and rather than assign them to teach philosophy we put them in straightjackets. We are, by our nature, moral. And it follows from this that we are free, at least to a certain degree, to choose between alternative courses of action because this is the only way we can think and act morally.

Kant follows this train of reasoning to its remarkable conclusion: we enjoy at least some measure of freedom in the operation of our will. This freedom means doing what we want to do or what we ought to do, as opposed to what we have to do. Freedom implies autonomy, which Kant distinguishes from subservience to natural inclination. So at least some of what we think and do is not governed by the necessity imposed by the laws of science. If I give a dollar to a man on the street, the movements of our bodies are determined by nature, but my choice to give and his choice to take are free decisions that we both make.

It follows that there is an aspect of our humanity that belongs to the world of science, and there is an aspect of our humanity that is outside the reach of scientific laws. Simultaneously, we inhabit the realm of the phenomenal, which is the material realm, and also the realm of the noumenal, which is the realm of freedom. It is the noumenal realm, the realm outside space and time, that makes possible free choices, which are implemented within the realm of space and time. Materialism tries to understand us in two dimensions, whereas in reality we inhabit three.

To some, it may seem fantastic that all nature should obey fixed laws but a single type of animal, hairy, omnivorous, and bipedal, should be able to act in violation of these laws. But there is, and we are that animal. Moreover, we have discovered with the help of Kant that the material world is not the only world there is, and that there is a higher domain we rely on in every free choice we make. We have shown, in other words, that materialism is wrong, and contrary to its dogmatic assertion, there *is* a ghost in the machine, which we may for convenience term the soul.

THE IMPERIAL "I": WHEN THE SELF BECOMES THE ARBITER OF MORALITY

"To thine own self be true."[1]

—William Shakespeare, *Hamlet*

WHILE THERE ARE SOME IN OUR CULTURE who will deny the soul, there are others who will at least admit that human beings have a "higher self." This self, they insist, is not identical with the soul, nor does it follow the dictates of traditional morality or an external moral code. Rather, this is a self that forges a morality all its own. This morality, however, is no less binding for its adherents than traditional morality is for religious believers. What we have here is not a denial of morality, as many religious people suspect. Nor do we have a slide from morality. Rather, we have before us a new morality that may be called liberal morality or secular morality.

This secular morality has already overtaken much of Europe, Canada, and Australia, and it has made impressive headway in the United States. It is now being exported to other cultures, where it is gaining recruits—especially among young people. While traditional morality held sway in the past, secular morality has staked its claim as the ethic of the future. The "culture wars" in America, involving issues like abortion, divorce, and homosexual marriage, can be largely understood as a clash between traditional morality and secular morality.

Traditional morality is based on the idea that there is a moral order in the universe that is external to us and makes claims on us. In ancient times this moral order was believed inherent in nature itself. Shakespeare conveys this in *Macbeth*: on the Tuesday before Duncan's murder his horses turn wild in the night, "contending against obedience" and almost seeking to "make war with mankind." The night of the murder is disturbed by "lamenting heard in the air, strange screams of death," and the sky remains dark long after the day should have begun. Similarly in *Julius Caesar*, the night preceding Caesar's death is convulsed by reports of frightful horrors of nature. In the Shakespearean universe, the physical order itself is disrupted prior to some terrible moral crime.

Today we no longer make a direct link between the natural world and the moral realm. We don't see the order in the cosmos as related to the order in the soul. Such a link lives only in fairy tales, where good and evil come embodied in witches, spying ravens, poisoned apples, fairy godmothers, and princes named "Charming." The great scientific habit of mind has made it impossible for us to take such ideas seriously as descriptions of the real world. But the idea of an eternal moral order has persisted. It remains a powerful idea in Western culture, and it is the predominant code of morality for the rest of the world.

Traditional morality is objective morality. It is based on the idea that certain things are right or wrong no matter who says differently. In various religions, traditional morality is contained in some form of a written code. The best example is the Ten Commandments, the most famous list of dos and don'ts (mostly don'ts) in history. God is usually considered the author of traditional morality. In living up to His edicts, we are presenting ourselves to Him for His favor. This is important because everyone knows that good people sometimes come to grief while bad people flourish. God's role in traditional morality is to guarantee that, in the next life, these injustices will be corrected and everyone will get his "just deserts."

Secular morality emerged in resistance to traditional morality. In the traditional view morality is "out there," whereas for many people today morality is "in here." The new source of morality is no longer the external code but the inner heart. When facing a moral dilemma, we resolve it not by consulting a commandment, nor do we follow the instructions of a parent or teacher or preacher. Instead we are guided by the advice Polonius gave to Laertes: "to thine own self be true." As beings with inner depths, we plumb within ourselves and look to that internal rudder inside us. We grant to this secret inhabitant of our internal selves the authority to guide us infallibly in our actions. Thus we seek to create a harmony between our inner self and our external life. Secular morality is a quest for our best or truest self, which is believed to reside within.

In some respects the new morality is quite close to Christianity. Traditionally Christians have held that there are two ways of following the will of God: abiding by His commandments and harkening to His voice within us. In Luke 17:21 Jesus recommends the latter: "the kingdom of God is within you." So did the church father Augustine: "I entered into the depths of my soul, and with the eye of my soul I saw the Light that never changes casting its rays over me."[2] In Augustine's view, God is the interior light that powers our souls. The Reformation, too, developed the idea of the priesthood of the individual believer, in which each person looks within himself to discover God's will. Outward behavior is not enough, because there is an inner self that only God perceives.

Secular morality breaks with Christianity in its counsel of inwardness as an autonomous moral source. Augustine and Luther presumed that the inward journey is merely the mode of access to the Creator, and through this relationship man finds joy and completeness. The secular innovation is to cut off the interior quest from any external source of authority, including God's. Philosopher Charles Taylor explains this point of view: "I am free when I decide for myself what concerns me, rather than being shaped by external influences. Our moral salvation comes from recovering authentic moral contact with ourselves. Self-determining freedom demands that I break the hold of external impositions, and decide for myself alone."[3] So the inner light is now the final arbiter of how I should live my life. The self defines what is good and becomes the exclusive source of unity and wholeness.

Today's secular morality is rooted in the romantic philosophy of Jean-Jacques Rousseau. In Rousseau's thought we discover a deeper schism between liberal morality and Christianity. In the Christian view, human nature is corrupted by original sin. Original sin does not refer only to the sin of Adam and Eve; it also refers to the idea that our natures are, from the start, sinful. Augustine asks us to look at the infant, how thoroughly self-absorbed it is, how petulantly it strikes its little arms out at the nurse. If babies do not do harm, Augustine wryly notes, it is not for lack of will but only for lack of strength.[4] In the Christian understanding, the inner self is corrupt, so we need God's grace to enter from the outside and transform our fallen human nature. Christianity is a religion of self-overcoming.

In Rousseau's understanding, by contrast, human beings were originally good but society has corrupted them. We are not to blame for our failings because "society made us do it." Consequently, in order to discover what is good and true, we must dig deep within ourselves and recover the voice of nature in us. Rousseau never counseled a return to the primitive state. It is not a matter, he wrote in *Emile*, of moving back among the apes and the bears.[5] But man's original state can to some extent be recovered as a state of mind. Within us dwells an original being that is our true self, uncorrupted by the pressures of society. The problem is that the voice of this inner self has been rendered inaudible by the din of convention and artificially generated desires. By connecting with the inner self and giving its voice an authoritative role in our lives, we can avoid "selling out" to a mercenary society and recover our essential goodness. In the secular ethic, James Byrne reminds us, it is not God but we who are "the dispensers of our own saving grace."[6]

It should not be thought the secular ethic is a complete repudiation of morality. It preserves the distinction between the "is" and the "ought." Nature is the way we are, and it also provides the model for the way we ought to be. We *should* follow the call of our inner selves; if we don't, we are not being true to ourselves and are missing out on the goal of self-fulfillment. This is subjectivism—because each of us has a distinctive way of being ourselves—but it is not relativism, because there is no suggestion here that "anything goes." In the secular ethic, the inner self speaks definitively and we are obliged to follow it. Secular morality differs from Christianity not in rejecting the notion of the good but in positing a self-sufficient inner source for what is good.

Perhaps surprisingly, secular morality retains some of the most distinctive features of traditional Christianity. For example, many Christians habitually engage in rituals of self-disclosure and confession. The confessional style is not limited to Catholics, who at least confine the narrative of their sins to a single confessor. Many born-again Christians will at the slightest provocation uncork astonishing details of what drunks, drug addicts, and moral reprobates they used to be until they fell into the arms of Christ. Our secular culture continues this tradition. Turn on Oprah or another talk show, and you will hear people discussing without inhibition the intimate details of their sex lives, what Peeping Toms they used to be as teenagers, how they still fantasize about making love to the Peabody twins who live down the street, or how they have come to suspect that their partner's sex organs are not functioning entirely well. In the Oprah case, the purpose of all this titillating detail is not, however, to surrender these anxieties and turn to Christ. It is to advance the process of self-discovery, aided by audience participation.

Oprah's popularity reveals some of the appealing elements of the secular ethic. It promotes individuality, because each of us now has our own moral script and our own way of being human. It eschews hypocrisy. Nothing could be worse under this ethic than to pretend to be the kind of person you are not. Why put on airs and live a lie? It's better to live naturally, even if this raises a few eyebrows, and to encourage people to accept you as you are. It promotes independence. When you become your own person you are no longer subservient to the will of others, or to the artificial appeal of "society."

Under the secular code, art assumes a central role as a means of self-realization and self-expression. The artist is no longer copying nature, in the manner of conforming to an external code, but rather employing sculpture and painting and poetry to reveal his own (sometimes incomprehensible) inner self. No wonder that art has largely replaced religion as the institution to which secular people pay homage: it is much more fashionable to serve on the local museum's board than on the parish committee's.

The deepest appeal of secular morality is its role in the formation and preservation of "love relationships." How do we know that we love? There is no other way but to reach deep into ourselves and consult the inner voice, which is not the voice of reason but the voice of feeling. We succumb to that inward self so completely that we feel that we have lost control. We don't love, but are "in love," and we are now not entirely responsible for what we do.

Love is the sin for which we find it almost impossible to repent. That is why Paolo and Francesca, the two adulterers who inhabit the outer ring of Dante's inferno, still cling together like doves, appealing to the law of love, "which absolves no one from loving."[7] Love has transported them into an almost transcendental state outside the real world, and yet more real than the world. Love of this kind is, quite literally, "beyond good and evil," and that is why the new morality has become such a powerful justification for adultery. When the inner self commands love, it does so authoritatively, defiantly, and without regard to risk or cost or all other commitments. As C. S. Lewis once observed, erotic love of this kind tends to "claim for itself a divine authority."[8]

High rates of divorce in the West can be accounted for by the moral force generated by the secular ethic. Today the woman who leaves her husband says, "I felt called to leave. My life would have been a waste if I stayed. My marriage had become a kind of prison. I just had to follow my heart and go with Ted." So divorce has become, as it never was before, a form of personal liberation, what Barbara Dafoe Whitehead terms "expressive divorce."[9]

Here we have the first hint of a serious problem with secular morality. In its central domain, that of love, it is notoriously fickle. It starts out very sure of itself, promising not just "I love you" but "I will always love you." This is stated not hypocritically or cunningly but sincerely. Each time actress Elizabeth Taylor got married she could be heard on television saying something like, "This time I've got it right. This time it's the real thing." Love's permanence gives it moral power, the power to lift us above the narrow confines of ourselves and join with another person to become a higher unity. But, as I say, the inner self has repeatedly proven itself a liar. Even Rousseau, that great champion of the inner self, admits in *Emile* that in love "everything is only illusion."[10] Or as Lewis puts it, "Eros is driven to promise what Eros of himself cannot perform."[11] So the West has paid an enormous social price—evident in the ineffable sadness of the children of divorce—for its adoption of secular morality.

Moreover, there is a deeper and more fundamental problem with secular morality. This morality is based on the assumption that the inner self is good. Is this assumption correct? If we consult the great works of Western literature, the answer would seem to be a resounding no. Read Shakespeare's plays or take in Wagner's *Ring* trilogy. As great artists, Shakespeare and Wagner draw us into the inner depths of human nature, and what do we find there? We find gentleness and tenderness and sweetness and pity, to be sure, but we also find cruelty, brutality, lust, hatred, and envy. We find also *schadenfreude*, a word the Germans use to describe the pleasure we take in another person's misery. Humans are, in their inner depths, cauldrons of good and evil mixed together.

Quite possibly evil predominates in this mixture, but that may not be apparent to us. A whole body of scientific and psychological scholarship shows that beneath the motives that we admit to ourselves, there are often less admirable motives at work. Even our good motives, such as pity and compassion, may be derived from feelings of superiority and condescension we are reluctant to acknowledge. Evolutionary psychology shows that apparent acts of generosity may in fact be propelled by selfish motives of self-aggrandizement and self-perpetuation. I am not saying that human nature is bereft of virtue. The propensity for good is certainly there, but so is the propensity for vice and evil. The question for secular morality is, in seeking the inner self, which self are you seeking? What principle do you have that distinguishes the good inner self from the bad inner self?

To these questions secular morality has no answer. It refuses to admit the ancient truth of Christianity: there is corruption at the core of human nature. Human nature is, in Christian terms, "fallen." I am not making a religious argument here, nor am I appealing to the Adam and Eve story in Genesis. I am simply making an observation about human motivation, derived both from experience and from art. However morality is defined, there seems to be a universal human tendency to fall short of it. So there is a natural propensity in human beings to evil, and that is the significance of the events that transpired in the Garden of Eden. In this sense "original sin" is not a theological proposition but one to which all rational people can give assent. A realistic assessment of human malevolence should convince even secular people that secular morality is based on an inadequate anthropology.

I am not advocating the wholesale repudiation of the new morality, which would be an impractical suggestion in any case. The secular ethic is now deeply rooted in Western society, and there is no easy way to root it out. Sociologist Alan Wolfe points out that even some Christians today use the language of authenticity and self-realization to describe what God accomplishes in their lives.[12] Even so, secular morality in most prevalent forms is irresponsible. It offers no check on those who invoke "self-discovery" as an excuse to engage in behavior traditionally considered improper and immoral. "Love made me do it" provides an ideal banner for anyone who seeks to act self-indulgently without regard to the consequences for others. But the problem is not necessarily with self-fulfillment or authenticity. Those are valid moral ideals, but by themselves they are incomplete. I should pursue my self-fulfillment, but only in ways that are good. I will be happier as a genuine, authentic person, but only if this authenticity and candor is allied with goodness. Hitler, let us remember, did not lack commitment or authenticity.

The Christian solution to this problem is, oddly enough, not a religious one. It is not to embrace Christ and become a born-again believer. Rather, it is to follow the examined path of the "impartial spectator," which is to take conscience as your guide. For religious people conscience is the divine taskmaster within us—what John Henry Newman once termed "the connecting principle between the creature and its creator"—but secular people don't have to believe this in order to recognize that they too have an impartial spectator they can turn to. This impartial spectator frequently directs us to act against our inclination and self-interest. Yes, I know that you feel for this woman, but remember that you have a wife and children. Conscience can be an enemy of love, and a real spoilsport to boot, but conscience is what enables man to rise above being a prisoner of his inclinations. Conscience enables us to go beyond what feels good and to do what is right.

OPIATE OF THE MORALLY CORRUPT: WHY UNBELIEF IS SO APPEALING

"It is wonderful not to have to cower before a vengeful deity, who threatens us with eternal damnation if we do not abide by his rules."[1]

—Karen Armstrong, *A History of God*

IN THE PREVIOUS CHAPTER we have seen how secular morality, while marching behind the banner of autonomy and self-fulfillment, can provide a cover for selfish and irresponsible behavior. Now it's time to ask a deeper question: is unbelief itself driven by similar motives? To listen to prominent atheists, you get the idea that their sole cause for rejecting God is that He does not meet the requirements of reason. Philosopher Bertrand Russell was once asked what he would say if he discovered, after death, that there is an afterlife. Russell pompously said he would tell God, "Sir, you did not give me enough evidence." I have throughout this book taken the rational objections of Russell and others seriously, but it should be obvious by now that atheism is far from the only reasonable alternative. Unbelief, especially when it comes in the belligerent tone of a Russell, Dawkins, or Hitchens, is not merely a function of following the evidence where it leads. Rather, unbelief of this sort requires a fuller psychological explanation.

Let's remember that atheists frequently attempt to give psychological reasons for the religious commitment of believers. In his commentary on the works of Hegel, Karl Marx famously said that religion is the "opium of the people,"[2] meaning that religion is a kind of escapism or mode of wish fulfillment. In Marx's view, people imbibe religion as a drug, to numb themselves to the pain and grief around them and to give themselves the illusion that the injustices of this world will be corrected in the next one. Sigmund Freud saw religion as providing a cowardly refuge from the harsh realities of life and the inevitability of death.[3] We console ourselves by thinking that there is another world insulated from the hardship, injustice, and confusion of this one. As French atheist Michel Onfray recently put it, "God is a fiction invented by men so as not to confront the reality of their condition."[4] Another explanation for the popularity of religion, recently expressed by James Haught in *Free Inquiry*, is in terms of the wish fulfillment of its self-serving leaders. In this view, which seems quite popular today, religion persists because "churches and holy men reap earnings and exalted status from the supernaturalism they administer to their followers."[5]

I'm not convinced by any of these explanations. I agree that there are priests and mullahs who are self-aggrandizing salesmen, but why do people go along with their schemes? Yes, there is an element of wish fulfillment in religion, but not of the kind that the atheists presume. Theologian R. C. Sproul makes a telling point: why would the disciples invent a God "whose holiness was more terrifying than the forces of nature that provoked them to invent a God in the first place?"[6] The God of the three Abrahamic religions—Judaism, Christianity, and Islam—is a pretty exacting fellow, demanding of us purity rather than indulgence, virtue rather than convenience, charity rather than self-gratification. There are serious penalties attached to ultimate failure: for the religious believer, death is a scary thing, but eternal damnation is scarier. So wish fulfillment would most likely give rise to a very different God than the one described in the Bible. Wish fulfillment can explain heaven, but it cannot explain hell. Even so, my purpose here is not to dispute the atheist explanation for the appeal of religion. I intend to turn things around and instead pose the issue of the appeal of atheism. Who benefits from it? Why do so many influential people in the West today find it attractive? If Christianity is so great, why aren't more people rushing to embrace it?

Some atheists even acknowledge that they would prefer a universe in which there were no God, no immortal soul, and no afterlife. Nietzsche writes that "if one were to prove this God of the Christians to us, we should be even less able to believe in him."[7] On the possibility of life after death, H. L. Mencken wrote, "My private inclination is to hope that it is not so."[8] In *God: The Failed Hypothesis*, physicist Victor Stenger confesses that not only does he disbelieve in God, he doesn't like the Christian God: "If he does exist, I personally want nothing to do with him."[9] And philosopher Thomas Nagel recently confessed to a "fear of religion itself." As he put it, "I want atheism to be true....It isn't just that I don't believe in God....I don't want there to be a God; I don't want the universe to be like that."[10]

The aversion to religion and the embrace of atheism becomes especially baffling when you consider that, on the face of it, atheism is a dismal ideology. Many atheists like to portray themselves as noble figures venturing into the cold night, raging against the dying of the light, and facing the pointlessness of it all. This strikes me as a bit of a pose, and an inauthentic and slightly comic one at that. As Michael Novak observes, if there is no God, what is there to rage at? Is it brave to spit in the face of a volcano or a tidal wave? Natural forces are neither good nor evil; they just are. So where does heroism come in if atheists are merely taking the world as it is?[11]

Other atheist writers—and I would place Sam Harris and Richard Dawkins in this camp—seem serene and almost gleeful about living in a world whose defining feature seems to be nature red in tooth and claw. This is an odd reaction, because as a number of evolutionary biologists, like George Williams, have admitted, Darwinism would seem to be a repulsive doctrine. Williams expresses open disgust at the ethical implications of a system that assigns no higher purpose to life than selfish bargains and conspiracies to propagate one's genes into future generations. According to Williams, a moral person can respond to this only with condemnation, yet Dawkins and others embrace Darwinism without ambivalence and indeed with genuine enthusiasm.[12] Why are they drawn to such a philosophy and where, in its grim hallways, do they find room for such evident good cheer?

Biologist Stephen Jay Gould provides a clue. Pondering the meaning of life, Gould concludes that "we may yearn for a higher answer— but none exists." Then he says something very revealing. "This explanation, though superficially troubling if not terrifying, is ultimately liberating and exhilarating."[13] In other words, the bad news is good news. Doctrines that might ordinarily seem to be horrifying— death is the end, there is no cosmic purpose or divine justice, free will is an illusion—can from another vantage point be viewed as emancipating.

Emancipation from what? To listen to some atheists, they want to free themselves from the shackles of religion in order to practice virtue. "In a world where God is no longer present," Santiago Zabala writes in *The Future of Religion*, man is now free "to actively practice solidarity, charity, and irony."[14] What admirable motives! The only problem is that you don't have to get rid of religion to be charitable in the name of human brotherhood. As Francis of Assisi or Mother Teresa could have told Zabala, charity and human kinship are two of Christianity's central themes.

It is time to look more honestly and critically at the real motives behind modern atheism. These are often different and more interesting than the surface motives usually given by or ascribed to atheist figures. It is widely believed, for example, that Darwin lost his faith when he discovered that natural selection, not God, was responsible for the evolution of life forms. But Darwin himself says he lost his faith because he could not endure the Christian notion of eternal damnation.[15] We also learn from his writings that Darwin suffered terribly from the loss of his ten-year-old daughter, Annie.[16] One gets the powerful sense that he could not forgive God. Atheism, in some cases, is a form of revenge.

These are powerful motives for unbelief, but they are not the main motive. We have to probe deeper, and one way to do it is to go back in history, all the way back to the ancient philosophers Epicurus, Democritus, and Lucretius. My account of this is indebted to Ben Wiker's marvelous book *Moral Darwinism*.[17] Epicurus is mainly known today as a hedonist, and he was. But like Lucretius and Democritus, he was also a materialist. All three of these pre-Socratic thinkers believed that material reality is all there is. Lucretius and Democritus even suggested that man is made up wholly of atoms, an uncanny foreshadowing of modern physics. At the time that the pre-Socratics wrote, however, there was no scientific evidence to back up any of their mechanistic claims about the natural world. Why then were they so attracted to teachings that were completely without empirical basis?

Epicurus confesses that his goal is to get rid of the gods. He also wants to eliminate the idea of immortal souls and to "remove the longing for immortality." Lucretius too writes of the heavy yoke of religion, imposing on man such burdens as duty and responsibility. The problem with gods, Epicurus says, is that they seek to enforce their rules and thereby create "anxiety" in human beings. They threaten to punish us for our misdeeds, both in this life and in the next. The problem with immortality, according to Epicurus, is that there may be suffering in the afterlife. By positing a purely material reality, he hopes to free man from such worries and allow him to focus on the pleasures of this life.

Not that Epicurus was a hedonist in our modern sense. He counseled that people control their sexual impulses and subsist on barley cakes and water. He was less concerned with wild pleasure than with minimizing suffering, what he termed "freedom from disturbance." Even death, he said, is a kind of relief, because our atoms dissipate and there is no soul to experience the lack of life or to endure the consequences of a life to come. In sum, Epicurus advocated a philosophy and a cosmology that was purely naturalistic in order to liberate man from the tyranny of the gods. And so did Lucretius, who sought through his philosophy to "unloose the soul from the tight knot of religion." For these men, their physics was the ground of their ethics. As Wiker puts it, "a materialist cosmos must necessarily yield a materialistic morality."[18]

Here is a clue to the moral attractiveness of Darwinism. Darwin himself wrote that "he who understands baboon would do more towards metaphysics than Locke."[19] He was implying that a better understanding of our animal nature might radically change the way we view morality. So the appeal of Darwinism for many is that it eliminates the concept of a "higher" human nature and places man on a continuum with the animals. The distinctive feature of animals, of course, is that they have no developed sense of morality. A gorilla cannot be expected to distinguish between what is and what ought to be. Consequently Darwinism becomes a way to break free of the confines of traditional morality. We can set aside the old restraints and simply act in the way that comes naturally.

From Darwin's own day, many people were drawn to his ideas not merely because they were well supported but also because they could be interpreted to undermine the traditional understanding of God. As biologist Julian Huxley, the grandson of Darwin's friend and ally Thomas Henry Huxley, put it, "The sense of spiritual relief which comes from rejecting the idea of God as a supernatural being is enormous."[20] And from Julian's brother Aldous Huxley, also a noted atheist, we have this revealing admission: "I had motives for not wanting the world to have a meaning; consequently I assumed that it had none, and was able without any difficulty to find satisfying reasons for this assumption....For myself, as no doubt for most of my contemporaries, the philosophy of meaninglessness was essentially an instrument of liberation. The liberation we desired was...liberation from a certain system of morality. We objected to the morality because it interfered with our sexual freedom."[21]

As the statements of the two Huxleys suggest, the reason many atheists are drawn to deny God, and especially the Christian God, is to avoid having to answer in the next life for their lack of moral restraint in this one. They know that Christianity places human action under the shadow of divine scrutiny and accountability. Paul writes in his letter to the Romans 2:6–8, "For he will render to every man according to his works: to those who by patience in well-doing seek for glory and honor and immortality, he will give eternal life; but to those who are factious and do not obey the truth, but obey wickedness, there will be wrath and fury." We read in the book of Revelation 21:8: "As for the cowardly, the faithless, the polluted, as for murderers, fornicators, sorcerers, idolaters, and all liars, their lot shall be the lake that burns with fire and brimstone, which is the second death." The implication of these passages—and there are many more like them—is that death does not bring extinction but accountability.

Here I must pause to note a feature of Christianity that has not escaped the attention of most atheists. Christianity is a religion of love and forgiveness, but this love and forgiveness are temporal and, in a sense, conditional. Christian forgiveness stops at the gates of hell, and hell is an essential part of the Christian scheme. While the term *gospels* means "good news," these books also contain warning messages to prepare us for ultimate judgment. This is a reckoning that scripture says many people are extremely eager to avoid. As John 3:20 puts it, "everyone who does evil hates the light, and will not come into the light for fear that his deeds will be exposed." The point here is not that atheists do more evil than others, but rather that atheism provides a hiding place for those who do not want to acknowledge and repent of their sins.

In a powerful essay, "The Discreet Charm of Nihilism," Nobel laureate Czeslaw Milosz argues that in order to escape from an eternal fate in which our sins are punished, man seeks to free himself from religion. "A true opium of the people is a belief in nothingness after death—the huge solace of thinking that for our betrayals, greed, cowardice, murders, we are not going to be judged."[22] So the Marxist doctrine needs to be revised. It is not religion that is the opiate of the people, but atheism that is the opiate of the morally corrupt.

If you want to live a degenerate life, God is your mortal enemy. He represents a lethal danger to your selfishness, greed, lechery, and hatred. It is in your interest to despise Him and do whatever you can to rid the universe of His presence. So there are powerful attractions to life in a God-free world. In such a world we can model our lives on one of the junior devils in Milton's *Paradise Lost*, Belial, who was "to vice industrious, but to nobler deeds timorous and slothful." If God does not exist, the seven deadly sins are not terrors to be overcome but temptations to be enjoyed. Death, previously the justification for morality, now becomes a justification for immorality.

The philosopher who best understood this "liberation" was Nietzsche. Contrary to modern atheists, who assure us that the death of
God need not mean an end to morality, Nietzsche insisted that it did.
As God is the source of the moral law, His death means that the
ground has been swept out from under us. We have become, in a
sense, ethically groundless, and there is no more refuge to be taken in
appeals to dignity and equality and compassion and all the rest. What
confronts us, if we are honest, is the abyss.

Yet unlike Matthew Arnold, who saw the faith of the age retreating
like an ocean current and was terrified by it, Nietzsche in a sense wel-
comes the abyss. He is, as he puts it, an "immoralist." In his view, the
abyss enables us for the first time to escape guilt. It vanquishes the
dragon of obligation. It enables us to live "beyond good and evil."
Morality is no longer given to us from above; it now becomes something that we devise for ourselves. Morality requires a comprehensive
remaking, what Nietzsche terms a "transvaluation." The old codes of
"thou shalt not" are now replaced by "I will."

Therefore, in Nietzsche's scheme it is not strictly accurate to say
that God has died. Rather, man has killed God in order to win for himself the freedom to make his own morality. And the morality that Nietzsche celebrates is the morality of striving and self-assertion, "the
deification of passion," "splendid animality," or in Nietzsche's famous
phrase, "the will to power." Any goal, even one that imposes massive
hardship or suffering on the human race, is legitimate if we pursue it
with energy, resolution, and commitment.[23]

There is a recklessness and savagery in Nietzsche's rhetoric that
thrills the heart of many modern atheists. We see it in the French exis-
tentialists like Jean-Paul Sartre, who used Nietzsche as their foundation
for a philosophy based on moral freedom. I also hear a Nietzschean
strain in Christopher Hitchens when he protests against the moral
supervision of God, whom he portrays as a jealous tyrant. But most
contemporary atheists—Hitchens included—aren't willing to go as far
as Nietzsche does in reviling the traditional norms of pity and Christian
charity. Their rebellion is more confined. It is, one may say, a pelvic
revolt against God.

It is chiefly because of sex that most contemporary atheists have chosen to break with Christianity. "The worst feature of the Christian religion," Bertrand Russell wrote in *Why I Am Not a Christian*, "is its attitude toward sex."[24] Hitchens writes that "the divorce between the sexual life and fear…can now at last be attempted on the sole condition that we banish all religions from the discourse."[25] When an atheist gives elaborate justifications for why God does not exist and why traditional morality is an illusion, he is very likely thinking of his sex organs. It may well be that if it weren't for that single commandment against adultery, Western man would still be Christian!

Malcolm Muggeridge, the noted commentator and convert to Catholicism, pointed out that eroticism is the mysticism of materialism. Oddly enough, this doctrine is set forth most clearly in the work of that apostle of sexual deviancy, the Marquis de Sade. His *Dialogue Between a Priest and a Dying Man* features the dying man's confession that abandoning a belief in God is the first step to unleashing the genitals and enjoying life. In *Philosophy in the Bedroom*, de Sade features a fifteen-year-old nun who has shed her faith in God and discovered in its place the delights of incest, sodomy, and sexual flagellation.

Most modern atheists find de Sade as excessive as Nietzsche, and they confine themselves to promiscuity, adultery, and other forms of illicit sex. I am not objecting to their passions here. These are completely understandable to every religious believer. Recall the newly converted Augustine, praying to God to make him chaste, "but not yet."[26] Augustine would not find it puzzling or mysterious that a whole generation of young people today rebel against Christianity because of its teachings on premarital sex, contraception, abortion, homosexuality, and divorce.

The orgasm has become today's secular sacrament. This is not because we are living in an age of sensuality but because, in a world of material things that perish, it gives people a momentary taste of eternity. In this context I cannot resist a personal story. I once met a monk who admitted to me that he fasts regularly and sometimes even beats his legs with a small whip to "mortify my body for the love of Christ." I was quite shocked to hear this, but the fellow had an interesting response. The same people who laugh at monks for mortifying their bodies for spiritual purposes think nothing of undergoing painful surgeries to produce cosmetic improvements. Nor do they shrink from the most punishing physical regimens in order to lose weight and tone their bodies for sex.

If sex is unhooked from the old moral restraints, there are going to be unwanted pregnancies. Here we get to atheism's second sacrament, which is abortion. The real horror of abortion is not that a woman kills an unborn child but that a woman kills her own unborn child. The guilt in doing this, for all morally healthy persons, can only be tremendous. So it is necessary for atheism to pave the way for abortion with a clear conscience. The first step is to get rid of God, because then there is no spirit of the dead child to disturb the conscience, no hell to pay for violating the commandment against the deliberate taking of life. The second step is to define the fetus as not really human. As Sam Harris puts it in *The End of Faith*, "Many of us consider human fetuses in the first trimester to be more or less like rabbits" who do not deserve "full status in our moral community."[27]

Bioethicist Peter Singer invokes Darwinism to make the point that there is a continuum, not a clear separation, between humans and animals. Therefore animals should be given some of the rights that are now given only to humans. Singer also argues that humans should be denied some of the protections they now have on the grounds that they are not fundamentally different from animals. If man is the product of evolution rather than special creation, Singer contends, then the whole structure of Judeo-Christian morality has been discredited. Indeed we cannot continue to speak in hushed tones about the sanctity of life. Therefore abortion, euthanasia, and infanticide all become permissible and in some situations even desirable.[28] In Singer's work we see echoes of both Darwin and Nietzsche; indeed, Darwin becomes the weapon with which to strike down Christian belief and clear the ground for Nietzschean immoralism.

In a now famous article in the *New York Times*, Steven Pinker invoked the logic of evolution to explain why it's really not such a big deal for mothers to kill their newborn children, even after they are out

of the womb. Pinker's article was written in the wake of some disturbing news reports, including one about a teenage girl who gave birth to
a baby at a school dance and then dumped the newborn in the trash.
Pinker sought to reassure the American public, noting that "a capacity for neonaticide is built into the biological design of our parental
emotions," thus encouraging parents, if a "newborn is sickly or if its
survival is not promising," to "cut their losses and favor the healthiest
in the litter or try again later on." Pinker added that many cultural
practices are "designed to distance people's emotions from a newborn"
precisely so that the child may be killed without too many qualms.[29]
"The problem with *Homo sapiens* may not be that we have too little
morality," Pinker writes in *The Blank Slate*. "The problem may be that
we have too much."[30]

Pinker is right that abortion and infanticide are quite common in
world history. The reason that they have been forbidden for centuries
in the West is because Western values were shaped by Christianity.
Ben Wiker makes the point that "the laws against abortion and infanticide in the West are only intelligible as a result of its Christianiza-
tion, and the repeal of those same laws is only intelligible in light of its
de-Christianization."[31] If America were a purely secular society, there
would be no moral debate about child killing. So one reason that
Pinker and so many others attack Christianity so bitterly is precisely
to remove its moral influence and make society hospitable for abortion, infanticide, and euthanasia.

It may seem strange to see all this callousness toward human life in
a society whose primary social value is compassion. But the paradox
is resolved when you see that it is precisely because we are so awful in
our private lives that we need to pretend to be virtuous in our public
lives. People who do things that are morally disgusting, like cheating
on their spouses and killing their offspring, cannot escape the pang of
conscience. Thus it is of the highest importance to deflect that conscience, not only to give other people the impression that we are kind
and wonderful, but also to convince ourselves of the same. For the person who has just slept with his business associate, it is morally imperative that he make a sizable contribution to the United Way.

My conclusion is that contrary to popular belief, atheism is not primarily an intellectual revolt, it is a moral revolt. Atheists don't find God invisible so much as objectionable. They aren't adjusting their desires to the truth, but rather the truth to fit their desires. This is something we can all identify with. It is a temptation even for believers. We want to be saved as long as we are not saved from our sins. We are quite willing to be saved from a whole host of social evils, from poverty to disease to war. But we want to leave untouched the personal evils, such as selfishness and lechery and pride. We need spiritual healing, but we do not want it. Like a supervisory parent, God gets in our way. This is the perennial appeal of atheism: it gets rid of the stern fellow with the long beard and liberates us for the pleasures of sin and depravity. The atheist seeks to get rid of moral judgment by getting rid of the judge.

THE PROBLEM OF EVIL: WHERE IS ATHEISM WHEN BAD THINGS HAPPEN?

"If Jesus could heal a blind person he happened to meet, then why not heal blindness?"[1]

—Christopher Hitchens, *God Is Not Great*

IN SUGGESTING THAT ATHEISM is often driven by base motives, I do not mean to imply that there is not sincere unbelief. In this chapter I consider a problem that has baffled believers no less than unbelievers, one that poses a serious obstacle to belief in the Christian God. Horrible things happen in this world. Millions are put to death in concentration camps. Hurricanes and tsunamis unleash their murderous fury on unsuspecting populations. A psychopath opens fire on a university campus, killing innocent students. My friend Bruce Schooley, to whom I've dedicated this book, is battling to survive cancer. None of this seems to have any explanation. Voltaire railed against a divine being who would permit the 1755 Lisbon earthquake and all its devastation. Darwin was struck by nature's cruel capriciousness, a theme Richard Dawkins stresses in his more recent anti-religious polemics. "The God of birds and trees," Steven Weinberg writes, "would also have to be the God of birth defects and cancer." He adds that for himself as a Jew, "Remembrance of the Holocaust leaves me unsympathetic to attempts to justify the ways of God to man."[2] Steven Pinker poses the dilemma in its classic form, "If the world unfolds according to a wise and merciful plan, why does it contain so much suffering?"[3] Weinberg and Pinker raise the good question: if God exists, why does He allow any of it?

The problem of evil and suffering is considered by many people to be the strongest argument against the existence of God. The reasoning goes like this: If God exists, He is all-powerful. If He is all-powerful, He is in a position to stop evil and suffering. But we know from experience that evil and suffering go on, scandalously, mercilessly, without even a hint of proportion or justice. Thus there cannot be an omnipotent being capable of preventing all this from happening, because if there were, He surely would. Therefore God does not exist.

I agree that evil and suffering pose a serious intellectual and moral challenge for Christians. (Interestingly, in Hinduism and Buddhism there is no such problem. Hindus believe your suffering in this life is the consequence of your actions in a previous life. Buddhism holds that suffering is the product of egocentric desire and can be overcome through a dissolution of the self that has those desires.) When terrible things happen they seem more easily explained by God's absence in the world than by His presence. But what few have noticed is that evil and suffering also pose a formidable challenge for atheists. The reason is that suffering is not merely an intellectual and moral problem; it is also an emotional problem. Suffering doesn't wreck minds; it wrecks hearts. When I get sick, I don't want a theory to explain it; I want something that will make me feel better. Atheism may have a better explanation for evil and suffering, but it provides no consolation for them. Theism, which doesn't have a good explanation, nevertheless offers a better way for people to cope with the consequences of evil and suffering.

I noticed this in April 2007 when the deranged student at Virginia Tech went on a homicidal rampage, perpetrating one of the worst mass killings in American history. In the aftermath of the carnage, even on the secular campus, atheism was nowhere to be found. Every time there was a memorial ceremony or a public gathering, there was talk of God, divine mercy, and spiritual healing. Even people who were not personally religious began to use language that was drenched with Christian symbolism and meaning.

The problem is not with atheists, but with atheism. Of course, atheists were present among the victims and the mourners. I am not implying that they suffered less than anyone else. What I am saying is that atheism seems to have little to offer at a time like this. Consider this manifesto by Richard Dawkins in his book *River Out of Eden*: "The universe we observe has precisely the properties we should expect if there is, at bottom, no design, no purpose, no evil and no good, nothing but blind pitiless indifference."[4] Jacques Monod writes that to ascribe meaning or purpose to life is a kind of "animism," like the primitive tribes who found spirits in stones. We are here, according to Monod, purely as a result of chance: "Our number came up in the Monte Carlo game."[5] In the same vein, Steven Weinberg notes that "the more the universe seems comprehensible, the more it also seems pointless."[6]

Here we see the underlying horror of materialism: everything becomes dark and meaningless. We also see the materialist solution to the problem of evil: evil is not a problem, because evil does not exist. Life in this view is indeed a tale told by an idiot, full of sound and fury, signifying nothing. And if a crying mother asks what the purpose of it all is, Dawkins and Weinberg have no better answer than, "Sorry, there is no purpose for any of it. Life happens, and then it stops. That's all there is to it." I can see why my friend Bruce cannot bring himself to embrace atheism. Only God offers Bruce the promise of a life to come, of a soul that outlasts death. Atheism offers only extinction.

When I wrote an article noting the absence of atheist sermons at the Virginia Tech ceremonies, I received a torrent of abusive e-mails from atheists. I was a jerk. I was a cretin. I should seek mental counseling. I was exploiting the tragedy in a deeply cynical way. Interestingly, few questioned my point that atheism provides neither consolation nor understanding in the face of evil or tragedy. One atheist conceded atheism's limitations in this respect, but then angrily asked me if I preferred consoling lies and fairy tales to hard truths that we must learn to face.

No, I don't. But this presumes that the existence of evil and suffering has established that God does not exist. In reality, all it has shown is that evil and suffering have no explanation that we can figure out. Still, it's possible that they serve a higher purpose not evident to us. Consequently we cannot treat atheism as an established truth. Not even modern science can claim such a secure status. One of the best arguments for modern science is that it works, which is to say that it delivers the goods and meets our wants and needs. But this is precisely what I am claiming for religion in a time of evil and suffering. Religion works, which is to say it speaks to human longings and needs in a way that no secular language can. Just as science seems indispensable to make modern life go well, God seems indispensable when life goes badly or when we are staring death in the face.

Pragmatist William James put the matter with characteristic realism: Atheists are like people who live on a frozen lake surrounded by cliffs that offer no means of escape. They know that the ice is melting and the inevitable day is coming when they must plunge ignominiously into the water. This prospect is as meaningless as it is horrifying. The Christian too must endure the chill and the inevitability of death, but his faith enables him to endure them much better. When it comes to suffering, James writes, "Religion makes easy and felicitous what is in any case necessary." When it comes to death, he adds, Christianity offers at least the prospect of the afterlife and the chance of salvation. "No fact in human nature is more characteristic than its willingness to live on a chance. The existence of chance makes the difference . . . between a life of which the keynote is resignation and a life of which the keynote is hope."[7]

While the argument from evil is often used to challenge God's existence, in a strange way the same argument can be used as evidence for that existence. Consider this: why do we experience suffering and evil as unjust? If we are purely material beings, then we should no more object to mass murder than a river objects to drying up in a drought. Nevertheless we are not like rivers. We know that evil is real, and we know that it is wrong. But if evil is real, then good must be real as well. How else would we know the difference between the two? Our ability to distinguish between good and evil, and to recognize these as real, means that there is a moral standard in the universe that provides the basis for this distinction. And what is the source of that moral standard if not God?

Even so, evil remains rationally inexplicable on any human account. Believers can appeal to the consolations of religion, but they are not spared the conundrum of why God permits evil and suffering to occur at all. In the Bible, this is the question that Job boldly, angrily, and eloquently poses to God. Job's point is that he is a good man, so why should he suffer? Why are his possessions taken from him? Why would God treat anyone this way, let alone one of His devoted servants?

Rather than reply directly to Job, God asks what gives the creature the right to question its creator. Did Job make the universe? Did he give himself life? God seems to be pulling rank on Job here, and Job finally acquiesces, surrendering to God without having his questions fully answered. Thus Job becomes a biblical hero not of understanding, but of faith.

We must press on, however, because Job's question remains a valid one: why do evil things happen to good people? One answer is free will. God does not want to reign over an empire of automatons. Freedom of choice means that we are free to do good and we are also free to do evil. Man can be a saint only in a world where he can also be a devil. Thus the existence of evil in the world is entirely consistent with a God who despises evil but values freedom.

God didn't kill all those people at Virginia Tech, the shooter did. Why, however, didn't God intervene and stop it? This is a deep question about God's role in the world. Why doesn't God make Himself manifest, especially when there are tragedies to be averted? Here's one possible reason. Imagine if God had intervened to prevent the homicidal maniac from doing what he did. Leave aside the violation of free will. Just focus on the consequences. The shooter would be—by miraculous intrusion—disarmed, the shootings would have been prevented, and life would go on.

In other words, life would proceed as if God had not intervened in the first place. So God in this view becomes a kind of cosmic errand boy, who is supposed to do our chores and clean up our messes and we then wish Him a very good day and return to our everyday lives. But perhaps God's purpose in the world is to draw His creatures to Him, and the empirical evidence is that tragedies like the one at Virginia Tech help to do that.

At this point I can imagine the indignant outburst, "Are you saying that God causes horrible massacres to occur just so that people can turn to Him?" To repeat: God didn't cause this to happen. Blame guns, blame the school's security system, most of all blame the killer himself. But don't blame God. As C. S. Lewis points out, most of the evil and suffering in the world has been produced by human beings with whips, guns, bayonets, gas chambers, and bombs.[8] These crimes are not divinely inflicted but man-made. Even so, it is not unreasonable to suppose that there is a providential purpose behind history, and if human horrors show us our dependence on God's love and restorative powers, that's not such a bad thing. In no way is God responsible for evil; He is responsible only for using evil to bring forth good.

Christians can point to the example of Christ to show that their God, far from being indifferent to evil and suffering, became man precisely for the purpose of enduring and overcoming it. In Christian theology God became man in order to take upon himself the sins of the world. Christ suffered unjustly in the same way that humans suffer unjustly, but to a much higher degree. For the Christian, therefore, to endure evil and suffering is somehow to share the passion of Christ. Ultimately Christ prevailed over evil and this is what the Christian also seeks to do, at least in his own life.

So far this account has largely focused on moral evil. It does not account for "natural evil," which is evil produced not by human beings but by nature itself. Here I am thinking of such things as hurricanes and cancer. So we must ask one more time: why do bad things happen to good people? The Christian answer is that there are no good people. None of us deserves the life that we have, which is a gratuitous gift from God. Bruce is dying, and in the process he is returning to God the life God gave to him. In this Bruce is not alone. As philosopher Peter Kreeft points out in his book *Making Sense Out of Suffering*, we are all dying, relinquishing little bits of life every day, and while medical technologies can win us a short delay, they cannot prevent us from moving steadily, inexorably to our graves.[9]

I pray every day that God will cure Bruce. I realize, however, that even if this happens Bruce will not be spared death. He will live longer, but death will still catch up with him eventually, as it will with me and you and all of us. For this reason we all need a deeper kind of healing, which is the healing of the soul. The unbeliever will say that we must learn to face death, and in a natural sense that's true. Death is the one certainty of life, and Bruce and you and I must all learn to accept that. The real question is whether death is the final chapter. The unbeliever insists that the promise of eternal life is a false one, but he does not know that.

All I am trying to show here is that the only way for us to really triumph over evil and suffering is to live forever in a place where those things do not exist. It is the claim of Christianity that there is such a place and that it is available to all who seek it. No one can deny that, if this claim is true, then evil and suffering are exposed as temporary hardships and injustices. They are as transient as our brief, mortal lives. In that case God has shown us a way to prevail over evil and suffering, which are finally overcome in the life to come.

PART VIII

✝

CHRISTIANITY AND YOU

JESUS AMONG OTHER GODS: THE UNIQUENESS OF CHRISTIANITY

*"In the course of justice, none of us
Should see salvation."*[1]

—William Shakespeare, *The Merchant of Venice*

S O FAR THIS BOOK HAS EXAMINED CHRISTIANITY largely from a secular viewpoint. I have shown how Christianity has shaped our culture and our world. I have also sought to demonstrate that the central premises of theism in general, and Christianity in particular, are completely supported by modern science and modern thought. In the concluding section of this book I will delineate what makes Christianity different from other religions. Finally I will show how our lives change when we become Christians.

There are two types of people who allege that all religions are the same. The first group is made up of religious believers, although not of the very fervent kind. These well-meaning folks insist that all religions are equal pathways to heaven—a position that only one major religion, Hinduism, actually endorses. But there is a widespread sentiment in the West that religions are similar in that they are all human pathways to the divine. By this measure it doesn't really matter very much which religion you subscribe to, and to go around trying to persuade others to adopt your religion is a mark of impoliteness, if not fanaticism.

The second group that considers all religions to be the same is atheists. This group views all religions as equally false, and some unbelievers also hold them to be equally pernicious. When I write about Christianity I often hear contemptuous responses to this effect: "Why are you so down on atheism? You too are an atheist as far as Allah is concerned." Richard Dawkins himself makes this point in *A Devil's Chaplain*: "When it comes to Baal and the Golden Calf, Thor and Wotan, Poseidon and Apollo, Mithras and Ammon Ra," all modern theists are "actually atheists.... Some of us just go one god further."[2] Arguments that refute one religion are held by Dawkins to be equally telling against other religions. Revelation, from this point of view, is all a bunch of nonsense, so it becomes a matter of hair-splitting whether we are dealing with Christian nonsense, Jewish nonsense, or Zoroastrian nonsense.

But contrary to what these people say, all religions are not the same. At some level, we all know this. Most religions make exclusive and uncompromising claims about God and the human condition. As these claims are often incompatible, there is no way that all religions can be true. Certainly it is possible for several to contain elements of the truth. If one is comprehensively true, however, it follows that the rest must be false.

Even so, well-meaning people eager to avoid controversy commonly insist that all religions are different ways of comprehending the same truth. This is an erroneous view, although it contains an element of truth. As we have seen, there is a common morality that the great religions of the world share. Also, the monotheistic religions are attempts to worship the one God and therefore the same God. They differ, however, in their understanding of why man needs God and how man can find Him.

We can see that religions are not the same by looking at the way in which basic concepts are differently interpreted. *Martyr* is a term common to Christianity and Islam but largely alien to Judaism, Hinduism, and Buddhism. It comes from a Greek word meaning "witness."

In Christianity, the martyr voluntarily gives up his life rather than his God. The Christian martyr was the man the Romans placed in the lion's den to be devoured for his refusal to renounce his faith. In Islam, a martyr takes up the cause of jihad and loses his life fighting for Allah.[3] This is the sense in which Khomeini and bin Laden have called on Muslims to be true Muslim "witnesses." One term, but two different meanings.

In his comparative study of major religions, Huston Smith lists some crucial differences among them. Buddhism does not have a concept of the afterlife or God. There is only one other religion that Christianity entirely embraces as divine revelation: Judaism. Christianity views itself as superseding Judaism, Islam views itself as superseding both Judaism and Christianity. Islam considers Moses and Jesus prophets, and Muslims even endorse the concept of Christ's virgin birth, but they do not regard Christ as the messiah, and they do not believe he was crucified or resurrected into heaven.[4]

In this chapter, I am not trying to prove that Christianity is the best religion, but I am trying to show in what respect Christianity differs from all other religions and is, in this sense, unique. All religions are an attempt to solve the dilemma Pascal outlined in the *Pensées*.[5] Pascal notes that for thousands of years man employed great intelligence and effort to solve certain basic problems. We want to have peace in the world. We want to live in harmony with one another. We want to raise our children well. We want our lives to matter. Pascal says we have been at this for a very long time, so why haven't we solved any of these problems? Why does the pursuit of happiness remain largely a pursuit? For leading atheists like Dawkins and Harris, the simple answer is that man is ignorant, and science is the way to dispel that ignorance. The religious person knows that this is a half-truth. Ignorance is only half the problem; the other half is the problem of good and evil. Moreover, science is only one way to achieve knowledge, and it is a certain kind of knowledge. Science provides no answer to the questions raised above. To reduce all knowledge to scientific knowledge is to condemn man to ignorance about the things that matter most in life.

How, then, can we understand the problem of good and evil that is such an obstacle to our happiness? Pascal noted that man is simultaneously heroic and wretched. He is capable of noble and wonderful thoughts and deeds, yet he also plots and performs horrible actions that are unworthy of even the lowest animals. Indeed, part of man's greatness is that he can use his faculty of reason to recognize his baseness.

The situation can be described another way. Man has very high standards, but he is constantly falling short of them. He knows what is good, but he will not do it. He is captive to selfish and evil desires, and he gives in to those desires because his will is weak. All religions seem to agree in diagnosing the problem in this manner. And just about every religion agrees that the solution is to give man codes, commandments, and instructions for how to raise himself above his inclinations so that he can come within the reach of God. Religion in general is man's strategic manual for how to reach God.

But Christianity is not a religion in this sense. Christianity holds that man, no matter how hard he tries, cannot reach God. Man cannot ascend to God's level because God's level is too high. Therefore there is only one remedy: God must come down to man's level. Scandalous though it may seem, God must, quite literally, become man and assume the burden of man's sins. Christians believe that this was the great sacrifice performed by Christ. If we accept Christ's sacrifice on the basis of faith, we will inherit God's gift of salvation. That's it. That is the essence of Christianity. To some it may seem ridiculously simple. In this simplicity, however, there is considerable depth and richness. We can appreciate all this better if we put it into slow motion, so to speak, and examine each of its central tenets more closely.

The first premise is that the propensity to sin is in man's nature. In other words, selfishness, acquisitiveness, lust, and greed are part of who we are as humans. I think Darwin would have agreed with this. Indeed the Darwinian portrait of man is a remarkable corroboration of the Christian doctrine of original sin. Darwin's unflattering view of man is much more realistic and accurate than Rousseau's naïve view that man is by nature good and society is responsible for his problems.

Darwin understood that man is closer to the beasts than to the angels. In some ways man is worse than the animals because they simply do what comes naturally, while man sins willfully and deliberately.

So man must pay the wages of sin, and the wages of sin is death. This is the second premise of Christianity. The Bible equates death in the biological realm with sin in the moral realm. Some people will find this unduly harsh, but let me show why it is duly harsh. Sin structures our personalities and defines our thoughts and behavior. Sin is built into our habits so that we sin routinely, almost unthinkingly. Sin is not peripheral to humans, something we occasionally do, but is much more intrinsic to our identities. So does sin deserve a heavenly reward? Should God, who is eternally just and holy, compromise that justice and holiness and offer us salvation despite our hatred for Him and our desecration of His laws? It seems only fair that we who sin both against God and man should pay for our sins. This means that sinners cannot enter the kingdom of God.

How, then, are we to have salvation? For most religions, man must take the active role. Hinduism and Buddhism offer solutions that are remarkably similar: Through meditation we confront our selfish desires and recognize that the "self" is the core of the problem. So we strive, in various ways, to eliminate this self and achieve its extinction. In effect, we seek to become nothing. We can advance toward this goal not merely through meditation but also through disciplined self-renunciation: renunciation of possessions, renunciation of sensual pleasure, and so on. This is a supremely difficult project. Among Buddhists only the monks claim to even approach nirvana. I believe the awareness of the chasm separating holiness from human weakness has produced, in Hindu and Buddhist cultures, their distinctive fatalism. Many Hindus believe fate will decree whether they reappear as a prince, a dog, or a flea in the next life.[6]

Judaism and Islam offer a different formula, although they lead their adherents down the same path. Judaism and Islam are religions of law. Both have elaborate rituals and codes: Pray five times a day. Pack up and go to Mecca. Sacrifice a lamb or a goat. Wear a long beard. Keep kosher. The great Jewish jurist Maimonides even argues that circumcision is essential for salvation: "Whoever neglects the covenant of our ancestor Abraham and retains the foreskin...will have no portion in the world to come."[7] The rigor of these rules has caused many Jews and Muslims to ignore many of them and simply follow a select few prescriptions they can live with. These are the "reformed" Jews and Muslims, who seem to have given up trying to live up to the full rigor of their legal codes. They are basically living in hope that God is not a stickler for details.

But God is not a lenient tradesman willing to accept 30 percent payment; His justice demands full reimbursement. Still, it is hard not to sympathize with the slackers. They are actually correct that it is too difficult to render adequate recompense to God. I even sympathize with Christopher Hitchens, who complains that if God wanted man to live up to these high standards, "he should have taken more care to invent a different species."[8] Christianity agrees with Hitchens that the standards are difficult. Indeed Christianity says they are more than difficult; they are impossible. Not only is it impossible to stop sinning—even the most devout Christians cannot stop sinning—but it is also impossible to atone for one's past sins. How would you go about atoning for them? Can you locate everyone you have wronged and make them whole? Yes, you can resolve to live a subsequent life of goodness, but this is no atonement; you should be doing this anyway.

Christianity raises the bar even higher than other religions by insisting that in order to enter God's kingdom we must be perfect. Not good, but perfect. Being good is not good enough.[9] As no one is perfect, Christians have the saying that "the ground is level at the foot of the cross." My brother may be a better man than I am, and you may be a better man than he is, but ultimately none of this matters because none of us will make it under our own steam. The only solution is for us to "die to ourselves" and become totally different people, morally pure in the eyes of God: "for unless the grain of wheat die to itself, it shall not produce fruit."[10] So Christianity agrees with Hinduism and Buddhism on the need to extinguish the old self. It disagrees by declaring in advance that this project is impossible.

So how can a salvation be reconciled with divine holiness and justice? This is posing the question in the right way. The Christian answer is that God decided to pay the price himself for human sin. Not just this sin or that sin but all sin. God did this by becoming man and dying on the cross. I want to reflect for a moment on God's incredible sacrifice. I am not referring to Christ's crucifixion. I am referring to God's decision to become man. No other religion can even conceive this. The Greek and Roman gods of antiquity often disguised themselves as mortals, but they would not actually become mortal. Mexican author Carlos Fuentes writes that when the Christian missionaries first presented their doctrines to the Aztecs, the Aztecs were totally uncomprehending. Fuentes writes, "In a universe accustomed to seeing men sacrificed to the gods, nothing amazed the Indians more than the sight of a god who had sacrificed himself to men."[11] Yet what other religions hold to be absurd and scandalous, Christianity holds to be true.

Richard Dawkins writes that "atonement, the central doctrine of Christianity, is vicious, sadomasochistic, and repellent."[12] This criticism makes sense only if you presume that the Christians made the whole thing up, which would be horrible of them to do to their God. Christians view the atonement of Christ as a beautiful sacrifice. Somehow God not only became man but took on all his sins and burdens in order to make him eligible for the heavenly kingdom. As San Diego pastor Bob Botsford puts it, "Christ paid a debt he didn't owe because we owe a debt we cannot pay." Christ on his cross literally assumed all the darkness, loneliness, and sin of the world. Thus, through the extremity of Golgotha, Christ reconciles divine justice and divine mercy and provides man with a passport to heaven. The bridge man was unable to build to God, God has built for man.

"Christ offers us something for nothing," C. S. Lewis writes. "He even offers everything for nothing. In a sense, the whole Christian life consists in accepting that very remarkable offer."[13] So what is the difficulty? The difficulty is in realizing that we are sinful and that there is nothing we can do to solve this problem. A related obstacle is accepting God's authority and His plan for our life. The obstacles, in other words, are those of human pride. Better hard liberty, one of Milton's devils truculently asserts, than "the easy yoke of servile pomp." The serpent's temptation in the Garden of Eden was also lethally directed at human pride: Why should you serve? Why not choose your own future, which will perhaps be a better future than the one God has planned for you? Why obey God when you can be as a god, a law unto yourself?

The hubristic resistance that many people feel to God's authority is eloquently conveyed by Hitchens: "It would be horrible if it were true that we were designed and then created and then continuously super- vised throughout all our lives waking and sleeping and then continue to be supervised after our deaths—if that were true, it would be horri- ble.... It would be like living in celestial North Korea. You can't defect from North Korea but at least you can die. With monotheism they won't let you die and get away from them. Who wants that to be true?"[14] Hitchens helps us understand the psychology of atheism, which is often based not on inability to believe but unwillingness to believe. That is why the atheist embraces the scientific way of knowl- edge as the only way, not because this is necessary to operate his cell phone or iPod, but because this is how he can deny the supernatural, on the basis that it doesn't show up in any laboratory experiments.

The atheist basically wants to shut himself off from God, and this helps us see why heaven is not closed to atheists. Nor is hell the fiery pit into which atheists are flung for their misdeeds. Heaven is God's domain, where He is eternally present. Hell is where God is eternally absent. God doesn't reject the atheist; the atheist rejects God. God doesn't dispatch the atheist to hell; the atheist wishes to close his eyes and heart to God and God reluctantly grants him his wish. In a sense, the gates of hell are locked from the inside.

The Bible says that salvation is the gift of God. Many people—even many Christians—understand this to mean that God is offering us sal- vation as a gift. But the Bible doesn't say that salvation is the gift from God. Rather, it says that salvation is the gift of God. God Himself is the gift. Heaven is best understood not as a place but as a description of what it is like to be with God. To be with God requires that we want to be with Him, that we accept His present of Himself. In a lovely book on faith, J. Gresham Machen writes that we become Christians not by accepting that Christ died to save others or that he died to save mankind but that he died to save me.[15] This is what it means to be a "born again" Christian.

For some, the Christian concept of a "second sailing" or a "new life" will continue to sound absurd and offensive. Whatever the rewards promised by Christianity, it is humiliating to have to admit that we are sinners helpless to solve our human problem through our own efforts. Aristotle would have found it incomprehensible that a totally degenerate person could have his life transformed. Yet Christianity not only says that this can happen, but that it must happen to each and every one of us, if we are to be with God. Evangelist D. James Kennedy says it is significant that Christ specifies the requirement of being born again to Nicodemus, who is neither a thief nor a prostitute but rather a learned and righteous man. Kennedy's point is that even righteousness is not enough.[16] The only person who we know made it to heaven is the penitent thief hanging on the cross by Christ's side. "Lord, help me," he said, "for I am a sinner." And Christ replied, "This day you will be with me in paradise."

What an encouragement this is for us, because once we have confronted our pride we realize that we don't have to do anything to earn our heavenly reward. In fact, there is nothing that we can do to earn it. What is denied to us by effort is supplied to us through grace. So when around us we see the decay of our life, when every earthly hope of redemption has failed us, when those whom we love cannot help us, when we have tried everything and there is nothing else to try, when we have tossed our last log on the fire and all the embers have flickered out, it is at this point that God's hand reaches out to us, steady and sure. All we have to do is take it. This is the uniqueness of the Christian message.

A FORETASTE OF ETERNITY: HOW CHRISTIANITY CAN CHANGE YOUR LIFE

"Finally it is not a matter of obedience. Finally it is a matter of love."

—Thomas More, *A Man for All Seasons*

NOW THAT WE KNOW WHAT MAKES **C**HRISTIANITY UNIQUE, we need to ask ourselves whether we should adopt it. In this book I have tried to meet the strongest critiques and objections to Christianity, but that is not always enough. Scholar and preacher John Stott tells the story of a man who was full of questions. Every time Stott answered his question, he had another question. One day Stott asked him, "If I were to answer your problems to your complete intellectual satisfaction, would you be willing to alter your manner of life?" The man blushed and smiled slightly, and Stott realized that his resistance to Christianity was not intellectual. The man didn't want Christianity because he feared it would mess up his plans and disrupt his life.[1] For many people, the reluctance to embrace Christianity is as practical as it is intellectual. They want to know what Christianity's benefits are, and how their lives will change if they become Christians. I conclude this book by addressing these concerns.

Christianity is an embrace not merely of a teaching but also of a person. So let's look at Christianity's central figure, Jesus Christ. Our secular culture cannot get enough of Christ. Two thousand years after his death, he continues to be a big story, as well as the focus of never-ending controversies. *The Da Vinci Code* seems to have inspired a whole host of spinoffs, all alleging in some way that the Christ of the Gospels was not the real Christ. Oscar-winning director James Cameron released a documentary denying Christ's resurrection on the basis that the tomb containing his remains has now been located. Cameron's film also suggests that Christ married Mary Magdalene and had a son. On a trip to India I encountered the headline "Jesus Faked Death on Cross." According to the story, Jesus staged the whole thing to escape from his enemies.[2] Christopher Hitchens goes further, suggesting that Christ may be a mythical rather than a historical figure, alluding to the "highly questionable existence of Jesus."[3]

Even some biblical scholars—a group that can be quite hostile to Christianity—engage in massive attempts at revisionism. Among their conclusions: the real Christ did not claim to be divine, he didn't want to found a church, and his simple message of love was subsequently distorted by Christians into an elaborate theology. Typical of this debunking theology is the Jesus Seminar, a group whose members vote on whether central events in the Bible actually happened. So far, the group has decided that Christ's divinity is a myth, the virgin birth is a myth, Christ's resurrection is a myth, and that fewer than 20 percent of the sayings attributed to Christ were really said by him.[4] These "discoveries" are regularly trumpeted in the media.

Put aside the credibility of these claims for a minute and ask a different question: Why are these issues such a big deal? If you are not a Christian, why would you care? There are three important reasons.

The first answer is that Christ remains the most influential figure in history. Any list of world-transforming individuals would no doubt include Moses, Buddha, and Muhammad. Moses, Buddha, and Muhammad, however, occupy totally different places in Judaism, Buddhism, and Islam than Christ occupies in Christianity. Moses, Buddha, and Muhammad never professed to perform miracles; indeed, they never claimed to be anything more than men. They viewed themselves simply as God's messengers. Christ is the only person in history who has defined a whole religion around his person.

Even people who are not Christian or even religious are influenced in big and small ways by Christ. They divide history into the time before and after his birth, BC and AD. Sunday is a worldwide holiday, not, as many believe, because it is the day of the Sabbath (which is Saturday) but because it was traditionally held to be the day of Christ's resurrection. The history of the West, indeed of the world, is incomprehensible without Christ, and would be unimaginably different had he not lived.

The Christ we encounter in the New Testament is so extraordinary that it's hard to imagine the Gospel writers inventing such a person. C. S. Lewis once noted that, along with Socrates and Samuel Johnson, Christ is one of the few historical figures we would recognize instantly if he walked into the room. Yet we know Christ, as we know Socrates, through the reports of others. Neither ever wrote a single word. The Bible gives a single instance where Christ wrote with his finger on the ground, but we don't know what he wrote. But when we hear Christ's voice in the four Gospels, it is unmistakable.

Shakespeare is our greatest dramatist, but there is no single character in Shakespeare who can match Christ's eloquence. "By their fruits you shall know them." "For where your treasure is, there will your heart be also." "Forgive us our trespasses as we forgive those who trespass against us." "Turn the other cheek." "Man does not live by bread alone." "Blessed are the meek, for they will inherit the earth." "Whoever finds his life will lose it, and whoever loses his life for my sake will find it."

While there is much about his early life that we don't know, we do know that Christ existed. This is the second reason Christ is such a big deal. He's a historical figure, and the great events that defined his life really happened. Historians debate whether some other figures of ancient times, like Homer, existed at all, but there is general unanimity among historians that Christ was a real person. Do you believe in the existence of Socrates? Alexander the Great? Julius Caesar? If historicity is established by written records in multiple copies that date originally from near contemporaneous sources, there is far more proof for Christ's existence than for any of theirs. The historicity of Christ is attested not only by Christian but also by Greek, Roman, and Jewish sources. Apart from the Gospels, we find references to him in Suetonius, Pliny the Younger, and Josephus. Tacitus in his *Annals* deplores "the detestable superstition" of "Christus," the founder of a new sect called Christianity. These sources testify not only that Christ lived but also that he had a big following, that he alienated the Jewish and Roman authorities, and that he died by crucifixion.

While the Gospel accounts individually provide different angles and emphases, together they offer a remarkably coherent account of Christ's life. The earliest Gospels were composed only thirty or so years after Christ's death, and the last was written before 100 AD. Moreover, historians have innumerable early manuscripts of scripture, a vastly greater body of material than they possess of many ancient and classical texts, and so they are in a good position to confirm that the biblical writings are authentic.[5] Finally, in recent decades archaeologists have been compelled to reconsider people and events long regarded as legendary. They have located the tomb of Caiaphas, the high priest who interrogated Jesus, and have unearthed an ancient plaque honoring Pilate, the Roman prefect who decreed Christ's crucifixion. Skeletal remains exist showing that Roman crucifixions were performed in precisely the manner outlined in the Bible. Summarizing the evidence, writer Jeff Sheler notes that "the picture that has emerged overall closely matches the historical backdrop of the Gospels."[6]

Let us now consider the historicity of Christ's resurrection. "If Christ had not been raised," Paul writes in 1 Corinthians 15:17, "our preaching is useless and so is your faith." The resurrection is the most important event in Christianity. Since the nineteenth century, some biblical scholars have refused to accept the biblical account of the resurrection because it was produced by people obviously biased in Christ's favor. Interestingly, Christ's followers, by their own admission, did not expect his resurrection. Arriving three days after his death, some of them brought spices to the tomb to anoint his body. Only then did they observe that the stone had been rolled away and the tomb was empty. The fact of the empty tomb was admitted by the Roman guards and also by the Jewish magistrates, who told the Roman authorities that Christ's followers must have stolen the body.

The apostles were deeply skeptical about reports of a resurrection, and the Bible tells us that Christ had to appear before them several times before these doubts were dispelled. Paul writes in 1 Corinthians 15:6 that Christ "appeared to more than five hundred of the brothers at the same time, most of whom are still living, though some have fallen asleep." Paul here appeals to direct historical evidence: the testimony of multiple witnesses who actually saw Jesus alive after his execution. Of this group, Paul says that some are dead but most are alive; in other words, many were in a position to confirm or refute him. In the history of hallucinations, is there a single instance in which five hundred people all saw the same person and were all equally mistaken?

Still, we must ask whether these early Christians were serious about Christ's resurrection, whether they were being truthful about what they saw, and whether it mattered to them. These questions are not difficult to answer. The disciples became so convinced of what they had seen that their dirges of lamentation were replaced with cries of joy. Proclaiming Christ crucified and Christ risen, they launched the greatest wave of religious conversion in history. The number of Christians increased from around one hundred at the time of Christ's death to around thirty million by the early fourth century, when the Roman emperor Constantine himself converted to Christianity. These conversions occurred in the teeth of fierce opposition and the persecution of the greatest empire in the ancient world, the empire of Rome. The early Christians did not hesitate to identify themselves with a man who had been branded a traitor and a criminal. They endured imprisonment, torture, exile, and death rather than renounce their commitment to a resurrected Christ. Even from a secular point of view, the evidence for the resurrection is surprisingly strong. Indeed, coming from so many witnesses with so much to lose, it might even be sufficient to convince an impartial jury in a court of law.

A third reason Christ continues to play a central role in our culture is that he makes claims on our lives that we can reject but not ignore. Christ is the most divisive figure who has ever lived. This is strange because he was a man who never hurt anyone, who lived a blameless life, and whose teachings about love and peace are universally praised. Yet whenever I write about Christ, I receive hate mail. Some of it is directed to me, but most of it seems to be provoked by antagonism toward my subject. If you doubt this, start talking at your next picnic or dinner party in a serious way about Christ. The reaction you get will either be gushingly enthusiastic or coldly hostile. Christ's teachings are so challenging that if we accept them they change our lives. If we reject them, they provoke in us either seething animosity or a willful desire to exclude Christ from our lives, or at least to amend him so that he doesn't make us feel uncomfortable.

Throughout history, people have tried to twist and trim Christ's words to suit their predispositions. This strategy of evasion and sly revisionism is quite common today. We hear from the Jesus Seminar and other sources that Christ didn't concern himself with the afterlife, when in reality he concerned himself with that as much as with any-thing else. We hear from milque-toast Christians and many others that Christ spoke only about divine love, when in reality he also fre-quently spoke about divine condemnation. (Hell is mentioned at least three times in the Sermon on the Mount.) We hear from those who wish to avoid conflict at all costs that Christ was a peacemaker, but he said in Matthew 10:34, "I come not to bring peace but the sword."

This strategy of "cutting Christ down to size" is best illustrated by the example of Thomas Jefferson. Jefferson agreed with many of Christ's moral precepts but was offended by Christ's claim to be divine, to perform miracles, and to secure for men a path to heaven. So Jefferson compiled his own private bible in which he, quite literally, took scissors and cut out all Christ's teachings that he didn't like. The virgin birth? Gone. Miracles? Snip, snip. The resurrection? Out. Hell? Ancient history. The "gospel according to Jefferson" was not published until long after his death, but it illustrates the lengths to which people will go to avoid confronting Christ as he really was.

Continuing in this tradition, Richard Dawkins writes that "the historical evidence that Jesus claimed any sort of divine status is minimal."[7] Yet in the Gospel of John 8:58, Christ says, "Before Abraham was, I am." Not only does Christ claim to have existed before Abraham, but in using the term "I am" he is also invoking God's own self-description as revealed to Moses at the burning bush. Christ also says "I and the Father are one" and "Whoever has seen me has seen the Father." The disciples seem to have gotten the message. They routinely referred to him as Ruler, Messiah, Son of David, King of the Jews, King of Israel, and Lord and Savior. On several occasions, Christ corrects and updates the Jewish scriptures, thus claiming for himself the authority of divine revelation. Christ also purports to forgive sins. Ordinarily an offense can be forgiven only by the person who has been wronged. It requires divine power to forgive sins perpetrated against others, and Christ claims precisely this kind of authority. He also insists, "I am the way, the truth, and the life," and "I am the resurrection and the life." The Jewish leaders of the time understood Christ to be assuming the traits of divinity, and in the Jewish monotheistic tradition, it is blasphemous for a man to claim to be God. That was the basis on which the Sanhedrin issued their death sentence against Christ.

It is impossible to remain neutral about these things. This is the message I have been trying to convey in this book. What can be said about Christ can also be said about Christianity. It matters. It is the very core and center of Western civilization. Many of the best things about our world are the result of Christianity, and some of the worst things are the result of its absence, or of moving away from it. Christianity's central claims about God and the nature of reality are supported by the greatest discoveries of modern science and modern scholarship. There are good intellectual and moral reasons to embrace Christianity. For all its eloquence and vehemence, the atheist attack fails. Despite all this, there remains an all too human resistance on the part of many people to becoming Christians. They want to know what's in it for them. This question may shock some Christians, but it is not a bad one. In a low sense, it can be taken to mean: how will Christianity give me financial success and a problem-free life? Christianity offers no such formula. The lives of Christians, far from being problem free, are often infused with struggle and sacrifice. In a higher sense, the undecided person is quite right to wonder how Christianity will make his life better. After all, he is considering not only whether to believe something but whether to base his life on it. Addressing myself specifically to unbelievers who possess an open mind, I conclude this book by enumerating some concrete ways in which Christianity can improve our lives.

First, Christianity makes sense of who we are in the world. All of us need a framework in which to understand reality, and part of Christianity's appeal is that it is a worldview that makes things fit together. Science and reason are seamlessly integrated in a Christian framework, because modern science emerged from a Christian framework. Christianity has always embraced both reason and faith. While reason helps us to discover things about experience, faith helps us discover things that transcend experience. For limited, fallible humans like us, Christianity provides a comprehensive and believable account of who we are and why we are here.

Christianity also infuses life with a powerful and exhilarating sense of purpose. While atheism in most of its current forms posits a universe without meaning, Christianity makes of life a moral drama in which we play a starring role and in which the most ordinary events take on a grand significance. Modern life is typically characterized by gray disillusionment. Christianity gives us a world that is enchanted once again. This is not a return to the past or a denial of modern reality; rather, it is a reinterpretation of modern reality that makes it more vivid and more meaningful. We now see in color what we previously saw in black and white.

What produces this change of orientation? Christians live *sub specie aeternitatis*, "in the shadow of eternity." Life can be terribly unfair, and this is for many people a natural source of cynicism and frustration. In the *Gorgias* and in other Platonic dialogues, Socrates strives to prove that "it is better to suffer wrong than to do wrong." The proof is a failure because there are bad people in the world who prosper and there are good people who undeservedly come to grief. But Christianity produces an enlargement of perspective that prevents us from being jaded by this realization. Christianity teaches that this life is not the only life, and there is a final judgment in which all earthly accounts are settled. The Christian knows that *sub specie aeternitatis* it is better to suffer wrong than to do wrong.

The business tycoon or law partner who cheats people and runs out on his wife may be viewed as a successful man of the world, but the Christian perceives him, *sub specie aeternitatis*, as a truly lamentable figure. By contrast, the poor peasant who crawls to the altar on his knees—a failure by all the world's standards—is one who is preparing to receive his heavenly reward. *Sub specie aeternitatis*, he is the truly fortunate one. Here we have the meaning of the phrase "the last shall be first." It simply means that the standards of worldly success and divine reward are quite different. Without the perspective of eternity, this necessary inversion of values would be lost to us. Seeing things in a new light, the Christian can face life and whatever it brings with a sense of peace and hopefulness that are rare in today's world.

Contrary to what secular critics say, the Christian does not and cannot hold our life on earth to be unimportant. Indeed, it is of the highest importance. The reason is startlingly obvious, and yet often goes completely unnoticed: it is this life that determines our status in the next life. Our fate for eternity hinges on how we live now. So living *sub specie aeternitatis*, far from being a way to escape the responsibilities of life in this world, is actually a way to imbue life with a meaning that will outlast it. It is to give life much greater depth and significance because it is part of a larger narrative of purpose and truth.

Christianity also offers a solution to the cosmic loneliness we all feel. However successful the secular life, there comes to every thinking person the recognition that, in the end, we are alone. Christianity removes this existential loneliness and links our destiny with God. Our deepest relationship is with Him, and it is a relationship that is never-ending and always faithful. The secular person may wonder what this relationship feels like. It is an enduring experience of the sublime. Have you ever had a moment with someone you love in which you are transported into a transcendent realm that seems somehow outside space and time? Ordinarily, such experiences are rare and never last for long. For the Christian, the sublime is a part of everyday life. Milton terms this a joy surpassing Eden, "a paradise within thee, happier far."[8] Another benefit of Christianity is that it helps us to cope well with suffering and death. *Time* magazine reported on the case of a woman who suffered a series of tragedies. Her husband was laid off. She had a miscarriage. A month later her first cousin was diagnosed with cancer. Then two hurricanes struck her hometown. Finally, one of her best friends died from a brain tumor. Here is the woman's reaction: "We're putting our lives in God's hands and trusting He has our best interests at heart. I've clung to my faith more than ever this year. As a consequence, I haven't lost my joy."[9] Joy under these conditions simply isn't natural, and that is this woman's point—only the supernatural can produce enduring joy in the face of life's tragedies. When we are in pain and feeling hopeless, Christianity raises our spirits. We don't know why we are in this situation, but we have faith that there is a reason, even if only God knows what that is. Perhaps God is trying to teach us something, or to draw us closer to Him by intimating to us our mortality. Christianity also gives us the hope that when someone dies, we will see that person again.

Then there is the matter of our own death. Ordinarily we do our best to avoid thinking about mortality, and many of us resist going to funerals. Funerals remind us of our own extinction, and the notion that we will one day cease to exist is a source of anxiety and terror. But Paul writes, "Oh death, where is thy sting? Oh grave, where is thy victory?" For Christians, death is a temporal end but not a final end. The secular person thinks there are two stages: life and death. For the Christian, there are three: life, death, and the life to come. This is why, for the Christian, death is not so terrifying.

Finally, Christianity enables us to become the better persons we want to be. The decent and honorable things we do are no longer a matter of thankless routine. This isn't just a morality we made up for ourselves. Rather, we are pursuing our higher destiny as human beings. We are becoming what we were meant to be.

Christianity not only makes us aspire to be better, but it also shows us how to be better. In marriage, for example, Christianity teaches that marriage is not merely a contract. If we treat it that way and use it for our own benefit, it doesn't work very well. For Christians, marriage is a covenant not merely between the two parties but also between them and God. The operating principle of Christian marriage is *agape* or sacrificial love. This means that marriage functions best when each partner focuses primarily on the happiness of the other. This can be attempted as a secular proposition but human selfishness makes it very difficult. Christian marriage is much easier, because God is now a central part of the relationship. So when there are hardships in marriage, we pray to God and He gives us grace. Agape is not so much human love as it is God's love shining through us. This is a bountiful resource that is available for the asking, and when we make agape the ground of our marriages and relationships, we find that the whole system works and we are much happier as a result.

We want to be better parents, and what better examples can we provide for our children than the Christian dad and mom practicing the sacrificial love of agape? We want to be good citizens, and can we find a more inspiring model of genuine compassion and charity than Mother Teresa? A man who saw her embrace a leper told her he wouldn't do that for all the money in the world. She replied that she wouldn't either; she was doing it for the love of Christ. This is the same motive that seems to have propelled humanity's greatest acts of heroism and sacrifice.

We want to raise the level of our personal lives, bringing conscience into harmony with the way we live. Christianity gives us a reason to follow this interior guide; it is not simply our innermost desire but the voice of God speaking through us. We want to be good because virtue is God's stamp in our hearts, and one way we relate to Him is by following His ways. As Thomas More said, in the final analysis we are good not because we have to be but because we want to be. Seemingly incorrigible criminals, alcoholics, and drug addicts have reformed their lives by becoming Christians. Earlier in this book I quoted Steven

Weinberg's claim that "for good people to do bad things—that takes religion." Actually, the exact opposite is true: for bad people to do good things—that takes religion.

Ultimately we are called not only to happiness and goodness but also to holiness. Christ says in the Sermon on the Mount, "Blessed are the pure in heart, for they shall see God." What counts for God is not only our external conduct but also our inward disposition. Holiness does not mean merely performing the obligatory rituals on the outside; it means staying pure on the inside. Yet holiness is not something we do for God. It is something we do with God. We couldn't do it without Him. In order for us to be more like Christ, we need Christ within us. In the words of that disheveled prophet John the Baptist, standing waist-deep in the river, "He must increase and I must decrease." Paul says the same thing in Galatians 2:20: "It is no longer I who live, but Christ who lives in me." This is Christ's countercultural challenge to us. In a society based on self-fulfillment and self-esteem, on looking after yourself and advancing yourself, Christ calls us to a heroic task of self-emptying. He must increase and we must decrease. This we do by allowing his empire an ever greater domain in our hearts. Goodness and happiness flow from this.

For the Christian, human joys are a small foreshadowing of the joys that are in store. Terrestrial happiness is only a foretaste of eternity. As the book of Revelation 21:4 puts it, "God will wipe away every tear, and there will be no more death, neither sorrow, nor crying, neither shall there be any more pain, for the former things are passed away." It is in this spirit that the Christian awaits this final moment of destiny, relishing the gift of life while every day proclaiming, "Even so, come, Lord Jesus. We are ready."

ACKNOWLEDGMENTS

MY WIFE, DIXIE, AND MY DAUGHTER, DANIELLE, were my constant support and encouragement. Dixie, an engaged reader and my sharpest critic, is constantly emphasizing how strange Christianity must look from the outside, and this has forced me to think through the issues in terms of first principles. My good friend Bruce Schooley has been involved in every aspect of this book; he has helped me to formulate my ideas and answer objections. My research assistants Michael Hirshman, Gregory Hirshman, and Robb Eastman performed valuable tasks of criticism and fact-checking. Sam Reeves, Benjamin Wiker, and Dick Thompson offered valuable support and advice. Suzanne Thompson was a regular source of articles, my online monitor of what the atheists were up to. Philosopher Daniel Robinson and physicist Stephen Barr were kind enough to read the manuscript, and their suggestions have made it much better. I also want to thank Clark Van Deventer, Harvey Popell, Mike Mason, Rob Brendle, Valerie Schooley, Ray Garza, Bob Botsford, and Dave Menard. Finally I wish to convey my appreciation to Harry Crocker, my friend for many years and the editor of this book, who has shepherded it through the whole process.

NOTES

PREFACE: A CHALLENGE TO BELIEVERS—AND UNBELIEVERS

1. Stephen Jay Gould, *Rocks of Ages: Science and Religion in the Fullness of Life* (New York: Ballantine Books, 1999).

CHAPTER ONE: THE TWILIGHT OF ATHEISM

1. Philip Jenkins, *The Next Christendom: The Coming of Global Christianity* (New York: Oxford University Press, 2002), 3.

2. Brent Staples, "If You're Devout, Get Out," *New York Times Book Review*, November 26, 2000.

3. H. Richard Niebuhr, *The Kingdom of God in America* (New York: Harper and Row, 1959), 193.

4. Data compiled by the Institute on Religion and Democracy, 2005, http://www.ird-renew.org/site/apps/nl/content2.asp?c=fvKVLfMVIs G&b=470745&ct=1571507.

5. Ibid.

6. Peter Berger, *The Desecularization of the World: Resurgent Religion and World Politics* (Grand Rapids, MI: William Eerdmans Publishing, 1999), 12.

7. Vaclav Havel, "Paradise Lost," *New York Review of Books*, April 9, 1992.

8. Philip Jenkins, *God's Continent: Christianity, Islam, and Europe's Religious Crisis* (New York: Oxford University Press, 2007), 29, 32, 57.

9. Paul Bloom, "Is God an Accident?" *Atlantic Monthly*, December 2005.

10. Pippa Norris and Ronald Inglehart, *Sacred and Secular: Religion and Politics Worldwide* (Cambridge: Cambridge University Press, 2004), 5, 23.

11. Jenkins, *The Next Christendom*, 2–3.

12. Ibid., 4, 91.

13. David Martin, *Tongues of Fire: The Explosion of Protestantism in Latin America* (London: Blackwell Publishers, 1993).

14. David Aikman, *Jesus in Beijing: How Christianity Is Transforming China and Changing the Global Balance of Power* (Washington, DC: Regnery, 2004).

15. Philip Jenkins, *The New Faces of Christianity: Believing the Bible in the Global South* (New York: Oxford University Press, 2007).

16. Norimitsu Onishi, "Koreans Quietly Evangelizing Among Muslims in Mideast," *New York Times*, November 1, 2004.

17. Kevin Sullivan, "Foreign Missionaries Find Fertile Ground in Europe," *Washington Post*, June 11, 2007.

18. Wolfhart Pannenberg, *Christianity in a Secularized World* (London: SCM Press, 1989), 43.

CHAPTER TWO: SURVIVAL OF THE SACRED

1. Charles Darwin, *The Origin of Species* (New York: Barnes and Noble Classics, 2004), 73.

2. Richard Dawkins, "What Use Is Religion?" *Free Inquiry*, Vol. 24, No. 5.

3. Cited by Robin Henig, "Darwin's God," *New York Times Magazine*, March 4, 2007; Scott Atran, *In Gods We Trust: The Evolutionary Landscape of Religion* (New York: Oxford University Press, 2002), 264.

4. Daniel Dennett, *Breaking the Spell: Religion as a Natural Phenomenon* (New York: Viking, 2006), 69.

5. E. O. Wilson, *On Human Nature* (Cambridge: Harvard University Press, 1978), 192.

6. Richard Dawkins, *The God Delusion* (Boston: Houghton Mifflin, 2006), 168, 190.

7. Stephen Pinker, *How the Mind Works* (New York: Penguin, 1997), 555.

8. Steven Pinker, "The Evolutionary Psychology of Religion," lecture at MIT conference, October 14, 1998.

9. Pippa Norris and Ronald Inglehart, *Sacred and Secular: Religion and Politics Worldwide* (Cambridge: Cambridge University Press, 2004), 24.

10. Philip Jenkins, *God's Continent: Christianity, Islam, and Europe's Religions Crisis* (New York: Oxford University Press, 2007), 6–7.

11. Eric Kaufmann, "Breeding for God," *Prospect*, November 2006.

12. David Sloan Wilson, *Darwin's Cathedral: Evolution, Religion, and the Nature of Society* (Chicago: University of Chicago Press, 2003).

CHAPTER THREE: GOD IS NOT GREAT

1. Edmund Burke, *The Works of the Right Honorable Edmund Burke* (London: Holdsworth and Ball, 1834), 574.

2. John Horgan, "Keeping the Faith in My Doubt," *New York Times*, December 12, 2004.

3. Andrew Higgins, "As Religious Strife Grows, Europe's Atheists Seize Pulpit," *Wall Street Journal*, April 12, 2007.

4. Richard Dawkins, *The God Delusion* (Boston: Houghton Mifflin, 2006), 3.

5. Richard Dawkins, "The Future Looks Bright," *Guardian*, June 21, 2003.

6. Daniel Dennett, "The Bright Stuff," *New York Times*, July 12, 2003.

7. Cited by George Johnson, "A Free-for-All on Science and Religion," *New York Times*, November 21, 2006.

8. Sam Harris, *The End of Faith: Religion, Terror, and the End of Reason* (New York: W. W. Norton, 2005), 234.

9. Christopher Hitchens, "Bush's Secularist Triumph," Slate.com, November 9, 2004.

10. Richard Dawkins, statement to the Freedom from Religion Foundation, Madison, Wisconsin, September 2001.

11. Edward J. Larson and Larry Witham, "Leading Scientists Still Reject God," *Nature* 394 (1998), 313.

12. Carl Sagan, *The Demon-Haunted World: Science as a Candle in the Dark* (New York: Ballantine Books, 1996), 9.

13. Steven Pinker, *The Blank Slate: The Modern Denial of Human Nature* (New York: Viking, 2002), 2.

14. Harris, 173, 225.

15. Richard Dawkins, *The Blind Watchmaker: Why the Evidence of Evolution Reveals a Universe Without Design* (New York: W. W. Norton, 1996), 6.

16. Carl Sagan, *The Varieties of Scientific Experience: A Personal View of the Search for God* (New York: Penguin Press, 2006), 64.

17. Richard Dawkins, *The Selfish Gene* (New York: Oxford University Press, 1989), v.

18. Daniel Dennett, *Darwin's Dangerous Idea: Evolution and the Meanings of Life* (New York: Simon & Schuster, 1995), 63.

19. Francisco Ayala, "Darwin's Revolution," in John Campbell and J. W. Schoff, eds., *Creative Evolution* (New York: James & Bartlett Publishers, 1994), 4–5.

20. Cited by Kenneth R. Miller, *Finding Darwin's God: A Scientist's Search for Common Ground Between God and Evolution* (New York: Harper Perennial, 1999), 171.

21. Francis Crick, *Astonishing Hypothesis: The Scientific Search for the Soul* (New York: Scribner, 1995), 3; cited in Larry Witham, *The Measure of God: Our Century-Long Struggle to Reconcile Science & Religion* (San Francisco: Harper, 2005), 237.

22. E. O. Wilson, *Consilience: The Unity of Knowledge* (New York: Knopf, 1998), 119–20.

23. Steven Pinker, "Is Science Killing the Soul?" A dialogue with Richard Dawkins and Steven Pinker, London, February 10, 1999.

24. Cited by James M. Byrne, *Religion and the Enlightenment: From Descartes to Kant* (Louisville: Westminster John Knox Press, 1996), 29.

25. Dawkins, *The God Delusion*, 282.

26. Christopher Hitchens, "The Future of an Illusion," in *Love, Poverty and War: Journeys and Essays* (New York: Nation Books, 2004), 334.

27. Ibid., 336; Christopher Hitchens, "Moore's Law: The Immorality of the Ten Commandments," Slate.com, August 27, 2003.

28. Bertrand Russell, *Why I Am Not a Christian: And Other Essays on Religion and Related Subjects* (New York: Simon & Schuster, 1957), 20.

29. Wendy Kaminer, "Our Very Own Taliban," *American Prospect*, online edition, September 17, 2001.

30. Harris, 73.

31. Richard Rorty and Gianni Vattimo, *The Future of Religion* (New York: Columbia University Press, 2005), 33; Richard Rorty, *Achieving Our Country: Leftist Thought in Twentieth-Century America* (Cambridge: Harvard University Press, 1998), 18, cited by Christian Smith, *The Secular Revolution* (Berkeley: University of California Press, 2003), 81.

32. Richard Dawkins, *Unweaving the Rainbow: Science, Delusion, and the Appetite for Wonder* (Boston: Houghton Mifflin, 1998), x.

33. Carl Sagan, *Pale Blue Dot: A Vision of the Human Future in Space* (New York: Ballantine Books, 1994), 55.

34. Rorty, *Achieving Our Country*, 18.

35. Wilson, 248.

CHAPTER FOUR: MISEDUCATING THE YOUNG

1. Richard Dawkins, *The God Delusion* (Boston: Houghton Mifflin, 2006), 315.

2. "Life Is a Cup of Tea," *Economist*, October 8, 2005.

3. Cited by Carl Sagan, *The Demon-Haunted World: Science as a Candle in the Dark* (New York: Ballantine Books, 1996), 6.

4. Richard Dawkins, *The Selfish Gene* (New York: Oxford University Press, 1989), 330–31; Richard Dawkins, "Is Science a Religion?" *The Humanist*, January–February 1997; Richard Dawkins, "The Improbability of God," *Free Inquiry*, Vol. 18, No. 3.

5. Christopher Hitchens, *God Is Not Great: How Religion Poisons Everything* (New York: Twelve Books, 2007), 217, 220.

6. Sam Harris, *Letter to a Christian Nation* (New York: Knopf, 2006), 87.

7. Remarks by Steven Weinberg at the Freedom from Religion Foundation, San Antonio, November 1999.

8. E. O. Wilson, *On Human Nature* (Cambridge: Harvard University Press, 1978), 201.

9. Richard Lewontin, "Billions and Billions of Demons," *New York Review of Books*, January 9, 1997.

10. Daniel Dennett, *Darwin's Dangerous Idea: Evolution and the Meanings of Life* (New York: Simon & Schuster, 1995), 519.

11. Daniel Dennett, *Breaking the Spell: Religion as a Natural Phenomenon* (New York: Viking, 2006), 25.

12. Harris, 51.

13. Jonathan Rauch, "Let It Be," *Atlantic Monthly*, May 2003.

14. Cited by George Johnson, "A Free-for-All on Science and Religion," *New York Times*, November 21, 2006.

15. Cited by Gary Wolf, "The Church of the Non-Believers," *Wired*, November 2006; Dawkins, *The God Delusion*, 315.

16. Dennett, *Breaking the Spell*, 324, 326.

17. Nicholas Humphrey, "What Shall We Tell the Children?" Oxford Amnesty Lecture, 1997.

18. Cited by Jason Boffetti, "How Richard Rorty Found Religion," *First Things*, May 2004.

19. Kenneth R. Miller, *Finding Darwin's God: A Scientist's Search for Common Ground Between God and Evolution* (New York: Harper Perennial, 1999), 19, 184.

CHAPTER FIVE: RENDER UNTO CAESAR

1. Cited in Christa Case, "Germans Reconsider Religion," *Christian Science Monitor*, September 15, 2006.

2. Alan Wolfe, *The Transformation of American Religion: How We Actually Live Our Faith* (Chicago: University of Chicago Press, 2003), 247.

3. George Weigel, *The Cube and the Cathedral: Europe, America, and Politics Without God* (New York: Basic Books, 2005).

4. Edward Gibbon, *The Decline and Fall of the Roman Empire and Other Selections* (New York: Washington Square Press, 1963), 35.

5. Christopher Dawson, *Religion and the Rise of Western Culture* (New York: Image Books, 1991).

6. Rodney Stark, *The Victory of Reason: How Christianity Led to Freedom, Capitalism, and Western Success* (New York: Random House, 2005), 233.

7. J. M. Roberts, *The Triumph of the West* (Boston: Little, Brown, 1985), 37.

8. Sam Harris, "The Myth of Secular Moral Chaos," secularhumanism.org.

9. Theodore Schick, "Morality Requires God ... or Does It?" *Free Inquiry*, Vol. 17, No. 3.

10. Wolfhart Panenberg, *Christianity in a Secularized World* (London: SCK Press, 1989).

11. Celsus, *On the True Doctrine: A Discourse Against the Christians*, trans. R. Joseph Hoffman (New York: Oxford University Press, 1987).

12. Gibbon, 55.

13. Mary Lefkowitz, *Greek Gods, Human Lives: What We Can Learn from Myths* (New Haven: Yale University Press, 2003), 83.

14. Bernard Lewis, *Islam and the West* (New York: Oxford University Press, 1993), 136.

15. Thomas Jefferson, *Notes on the State of Virginia* (New York: W. W. Norton, 1982), 163.

16. Cited by A. James Reichley, *Religion in American Public Life* (Washington, DC: Brookings Press, 1985), 103, 105.

17. Alexis de Tocqueville, *Democracy in America* (New York: Vintage, 1990), Vol. 1, 303.

CHAPTER SIX: THE EVIL THAT I WOULD NOT

1. Erich Auerbach, *Mimesis*, trans. Willard R. Trask (Princeton, NJ: Princeton University Press, 1953), 72.

2. Denis de Rougemont, *Love in the Western World* (Princeton, NJ: Princeton University Press, 1983), 363.

3. Bruce Thornton, *Eros: The Myth of Ancient Greek Sexuality* (Boulder, CO: Westview Press, 1997), 103.

4. Michael Grant, *The Founders of the Western World* (New York: Charles Scribner's Sons, 1991), 16.

5. K. J. Dover, *Greek Homosexuality* (Cambridge: Harvard University Press, 1989), 91.

6. Harold Berman, *Law and Revolution: The Formation of the Western Legal Tradition* (Cambridge: Harvard University Press, 1983), 166.

7. Adam Smith, *The Wealth of Nations* (Chicago: University of Chicago Press, 1976), 362–63.

8. James Boswell, *Life of Johnson* (New York: Oxford University Press, 1933), Vol. I, 567.

9. Rodney Stark, *The Victory of Reason* (New York: Random House, 2005), 65.

10. Ibid., xii.

11. J. B. Bury, *The Idea of Progress: An Inquiry into Its Origins and Growth* (New York: Dover Publications, 1960), 73.

CHAPTER SEVEN: CREATED EQUAL

1. Friedrich Nietzsche, *The Will to Power* (New York: Vintage Books, 1968), 401.
2. Cited by Paul Rahe, *Republics Ancient and Modern* (Chapel Hill, NC: University of North Carolina Press, 1994), Vol. 2, 25.
3. Jacob Cooke, ed., *The Federalist* (Middletown, CT: Wesleyan University Press, 1961), Nos. 55 and 63, 374, 425.
4. Sam Harris, *Letter to a Christian Nation* (New York: Knopf, 2006), 14.
5. Steven Weinberg, "A Designer Universe?" American Association for the Advancement of Science, Washington, D.C., April 1999.
6. Orlando Patterson, *Slavery and Social Death* (Cambridge: Harvard University Press, 1982), 27–28.
7. Paul Johnson, *A History of Christianity* (New York: Touchstone Books, 1995), 427.
8. John Adams, letter to Hezekiah Niles, 1818, htpp://www.teachingamericanhistory.org; see also Bernard Bailyn, *The Ideological Origins of the American Revolution* (Cambridge: Harvard University Press, 1992), 1.
9. Martin Luther King, "I Have a Dream," in James Melvin Washington, ed., *A Testament of Hope* (San Francisco: Harper, 1986), 289–302.
10. Ibid.
11. John Rawls, *A Theory of Justice* (Cambridge: Harvard University Press, 2005).
12. Jeremy Bentham, "An Introduction to the Principles of Morals and Legislation," in John Stuart Mill and Jeremy Bentham, *Utilitarianism and Other Essays* (New York: Penguin, 1987).
13. For an excellent account see Mary Ann Glendon, *A World Made New: Eleanor Roosevelt and the Universal Declaration of Human Rights* (New York: Random House, 2001).
14. Benjamin Constant, *Political Writings* (Cambridge: Cambridge University Press), 102–4, 321.
15. Norman Cantor, *Antiquity: From the Birth of the Sumerian Civilization to the Fall of the Roman Empire* (New York: HarperCollins, 2003), 109.

CHAPTER EIGHT: CHRISTIANITY AND REASON

1. Thomas Aquinas, *Selected Writings* (New York: Penguin, 1998), 244.
2. Sam Harris, "Selling Out Science," *Free Inquiry*, Volume 26, Issue 1.
3. E. O. Wilson, "Let's Accept the Fault Line Between Faith and Science," *USA Today*, January 15, 2006.
4. David Van Biema, "God vs. Science," *Time*, November 5, 2006.
5. Ernest Fortin, "Thomas Aquinas," in Leo Strauss and Joseph Cropsey, eds., *History of Political Philosophy* (Chicago: University of Chicago Press, 1981), 226.
6. Sam Harris, *Letter to a Christian Nation* (New York: Knopf, 2006), 73.
7. Richard Dawkins, *The God Delusion* (Boston: Houghton Mifflin, 2006), 143.
8. This point is effectively made in Stephen Barr, *Modern Physics and Ancient Faith* (Notre Dame: University of Notre Dame Press, 2003), 262.
9. Anselm, "Proslogion," in Anselm, *Basic Writings* (LaSalle, IL: Open Court Press, 1979); see also M. J. Charlesworth, trans., *St. Anselm's Proslogion* (Notre Dame: University of Notre Dame Press, 1979).
10. Christopher Hitchens, *God Is Not Great: How Religion Poisons Everything* (New York: Twelve Books, 2007), 265.
11. Anselm, 150–51, 158.

CHAPTER NINE: FROM LOGOS TO COSMOS

1. Cited by Owen Gingerich, *God's Universe* (Cambridge: Harvard University Press, 2006), 9.
2. Richard Feynman, *The Meaning of It All: Thoughts of a Citizen-Scientist* (New York: Basic Books, 1998), 43.
3. Neil deGrasse Tyson, "An Astrophysicist Ponders the God Question," in Paul Kurtz, ed., *Science & Religion* (Amherst, NY: Prometheus Books, 2003), 74.
4. James Trefil, *Reading the Mind of God* (New York: Anchor Books, 1989), 1.
5. Steven Weinberg, *Facing Up: Science and Its Cultural Adversaries* (Cambridge: Harvard University Press, 2001), 24, 45.
6. Eugene Wigner, "The Unreasonable Effectiveness of Mathematics in the Natural Sciences," in Douglas Campbell and John Higgins, eds., *Mathematics* (Belmont, CA: Wadsworth, 1984), Vol. 3, 117.

7. Feynman, 23–24.

8. See the discussion of al-Ghazali's writings in Pervez Hoodbhoy, *Islam and Science* (London: Zed Books, 1991), 105.

9. Joseph Needham, *The Grand Titration: Science and Society in East and West* (Toronto: University of Toronto Press, 1969), 327.

10. Alfred North Whitehead, *Science and the Modern World* (New York: Free Press, 1953), 13.

11. Alvin Schmidt, *Under the Influence: How Christianity Transformed Civilization* (Grand Rapids, MI: Zondervan Publishing, 2001), 190.

12. John Channing Briggs, "Bacon's Science and Religion," in Markku Peltonen, ed., *The Cambridge Companion to Bacon* (Cambridge: Cambridge University Press, 1996), 172–99.

13. Cited by Robert Nisbet, *History of the Idea of Progress* (New York: Basic Books, 1980), 79.

14. For a detailed account, see Rodney Stark, *The Victory of Reason: How Christianity Led to Freedom, Capitalism, and Western Success* (New York: Random House, 2005).

15. Morris Kline, *Mathematics in Western Culture* (Oxford: Oxford University Press, 1953), 109.

16. Richard Westfall, "Isaac Newton," in Gary Ferngren, ed., *Science and Religion* (Baltimore: Johns Hopkins University Press, 2002), 155.

17. Owen Gingerich, "The Copernican Revolution," in Ferngren, ed., 101.

18. Cited by Gingerich, *God's Universe*, 112–13.

19. Cited by Kitty Ferguson, *The Fire in the Equations: Science, Religion, and the Search for God* (Philadelphia: Templeton Foundation Press, 1994), 143.

20. Gregg Easterbrook, "Science and God: A Warming Trend," *Science*, August 15, 1997.

CHAPTER TEN: AN ATHEIST FABLE

1. Arthur Koestler, *The Sleepwalkers: A History of Man's Changing Vision of the Universe* (New York: Penguin, 1990), 432.

2. Daniel Dennett, *Breaking the Spell: Religion as a Natural Phenomenon* (New York: Viking, 2006), 274.

3. Bruce Jakosky, *The Search for Life on Other Planets* (Cambridge: Cambridge University Press, 1988), 299.

4. Carl Sagan, *Cosmos* (New York: Random House, 1980), 54, 115.

5. Sam Harris, *The End of Faith: Religion, Terror, and the Future of Reason* (New York: W. W. Norton, 2005), 105.

6. David Lindberg, "Medieval Science and Religion," in Gary Ferngren, ed., *Science and Religion* (Baltimore: Johns Hopkins University Press, 2002), 70; see also David Lindberg and Ronald Numbers, *God and Nature* (Berkeley: University of California Press, 1986).

7. Edward Larson, *Evolution: The Remarkable History of a Scientific Theory* (New York: Modern Library, 2004), 95.

8. Thomas Kuhn, *The Copernican Revolution* (Cambridge: Harvard University Press, 1985), 199.

9. William Shea and Mariano Artigas, *Galileo in Rome: The Rise and Fall of a Troublesome Genius* (New York: Oxford University Press, 2003); Richard Westfall, *Essays on the Trial of Galileo* (Notre Dame: University of Notre Dame Press, 1989); Maurice Finocchiaro, ed., *The Galileo Affair: A Documentary History* (Berkeley: University of California Press, 1989); Owen Gingerich, "The Galileo Affair," *Scientific American* 247 (1982), 132–43.

10. David Lindberg, *The Beginnings of Western Science: The European Scientific Tradition in Philosophical, Religious, and Institutional Context, 600 B.C. to A.D. 1450* (Chicago: University of Chicago Press, 1992), 97.

11. Kuhn, 43–44.

12. Ibid., 95.

13. Cited by James Broderick, *Robert Bellarmine: Saint and Scholar* (Westminster, MD: Newman Press, 1961), 360–61.

14. Richard Blackwell, "Galileo Galilei," in Ferngren, ed., 108.

15. Michael Ruse, *Can a Darwinian Be a Christian? The Relationship between Science and Religion* (Cambridge: Cambridge University Press, 2000), 2.

16. Koestler, 485.

17. "Introduction," in Ferngren, ed., xi.

18. Thomas Lessl, "The Galileo Legend," *New Oxford Review*, June 2000.

19. Alfred North Whitehead, *Science and the Modern World* (New York: Free Press, 1953), 2.

CHAPTER ELEVEN: A UNIVERSE WITH A BEGINNING

1. Stephen Hawking, *A Brief History of Time* (New York: Bantam, 1996), 131.

2. Steven Weinberg, *Facing Up: Science and Its Cultural Adversaries* (Cambridge: Harvard University Press, 2001), x.

3. Cited by Steve Paulson, "Religious Belief Itself Is an Adaptation," Salon.com, March 21, 2006.

4. Today scientists have, based on new evidence, revived Einstein's concept of a cosmological constant. None of this invalidates my point, which is that Einstein developed his constant not so much for a scientific reason as to avoid the creation implications of his theory of relativity.

5. Steven Weinberg, *The First Three Minutes: A Modern View of the Origin of the Universe* (New York: Basic Books, 1993), 6, 30.

6. John Barrow, *The Origin of the Universe* (New York: Basic Books, 1994), 3.

7. Robert Jastrow, *God and the Astronomers* (New York: W. W. Norton, 1992), 104–5.

8. Stephen Brush, "How Cosmology Became a Science," *Scientific American*, August 1992.

9. Cited by Morris Kline, *Mathematics in Western Culture* (New York: Oxford University Press, 1953), 260.

10. Hawking, 53.

11. Martin Rees, *Just Six Numbers: The Deep Forces That Shape the Universe* (New York: Basic Books, 2000), 11.

12. The Dalai Lama, *The Universe in a Single Atom* (New York: Morgan Road Books, 2005), 81.

13. Leon Kass, *The Beginning of Wisdom: Reading Genesis* (New York: Free Press, 2003), 26.

14. Northrop Frye, *The Great Code: The Bible and Literature* (New York: Harvest Books, 1982), 106.

15. Leo Strauss, *Studies in Platonic Political Philosophy* (Chicago: University of Chicago Press, 1983), 152.

16. Gerald Schroeder, *Genesis and the Big Bang: The Discovery of Harmony Between Modern Science and the Bible* (New York: Bantam Books, 1990), 91, 160.

17. Arthur Eddington, *The Expanding Universe* (New York: Macmillan, 1933), 124.

18. Cited by Malcolm Browne, "Clues to the Universe's Origin Expected," *New York Times*, March 12, 1978.

19. Jastrow, 107.

20. Bertrand Russell and Frederick Copleston, "The Existence of God," in John Hick, ed., *The Existence of God* (New York: Macmillan, 1964), 175.

21. Victor Stenger, "Has Science Found God?" *Free Inquiry*, Vol. 19, No. 1.

22. J. Y. T. Greid, ed., *The Letters of David Hume* (Oxford: Clarendon Press, 1932), 187.

CHAPTER TWELVE: A DESIGNER PLANET

1. Lee Smolin, *The Life of the Cosmos* (New York: Oxford University Press, 1997), 24.

2. Victor Stenger, *God: The Failed Hypothesis* (Amherst, NY: Prometheus Books, 2007), 161.

3. Steven Weinberg, *Facing Up: Science and Its Cultural Adversaries* (Cambridge: Harvard University Press, 2001), 5.

4. Carl Sagan, *Pale Blue Dot: A Vision of the Human Future in Space* (New York: Ballantine Books, 1994), 7.

5. Paul Davies, *The Mind of God: The Scientific Basis for a Rational World* (New York: Touchstone Books, 1993), 21.

6. John Wheeler, "Introduction," in John Barrow and Frank Tipler, *The Anthropic Cosmological Principle* (New York: Oxford University Press, 1996), 1.

7. Cited by Brad Lemley, "Why Is There Life?" *Discover*, November 2000, 66; see also Martin Rees, *Just Six Numbers: The Deep Forces That Shape the Universe* (New York: Basic Books, 2000), 179.

8. Smolin, 37, 45.

9. Stephen Hawking, *A Brief History of Time* (New York: Bantam Books, 1996), 126.

10. Fred Hoyle, *The Intelligent Universe: A New View of Creation and Evolution* (London: Michael Joseph Publishers, 1983), 218.

11. Freeman Dyson, *Disturbing the Universe* (New York: Harper and Row, 1979), 250–51.

12. Owen Gingerich, *God's Universe* (Cambridge: Harvard University Press, 2006), 38.

13. Robert Jastrow, "The Astronomer and God," in Roy Varghese, ed., *The Intellectuals Speak Out about God* (Chicago: Regnery Gateway, 1984), 22.

14. Victor Stenger, *Not By Design: The Origin of the Universe* (Amherst, NY: Prometheus Books, 1988), 12.

15. Weinberg, *Facing Up*, 238.

16. Richard Dawkins, *Unweaving the Rainbow* (Boston: Houghton Mifflin, 1998), 5.

17. "My Pilgrimage from Atheism to Theism," an interview with Antony Flew by Gary Habermas, *Philosophia Christi*, winter 2004.

18. Smolin, 45.

19. Steven Weinberg, *Dreams of a Final Theory: The Scientist's Search for the Ultimate Laws of Nature* (New York: Vintage, 1993), 38.

20. Smolin, 6, 275, 293.

21. Carl Sagan, *The Demon-Haunted World: Science as a Candle in the Dark* (New York: Ballantine Books, 1996), 211.

22. E. O. Wilson, *Consilience: The Unity of Knowledge* (New York: Knopf, 1998), 53.

23. Stephen Barr, *Modern Physics and Ancient Faith* (Notre Dame: University of Notre Dame Press, 2003), 157.

24. Davies, 81.

25. Stenger, *God: The Failed Hypothesis*, 131.

CHAPTER THIRTEEN: PALEY WAS RIGHT

1. Jacques Monod, *Chance and Necessity* (London: Collins Press, 1972), 167.

2. William Paley, *The Works of William Paley* (Oxford: Clarendon Press, 1938), Vol. 4, 1.

3. Richard Dawkins, *The Blind Watchmaker: Why the Evidence of Evolution Reveals a Universe Without Design* (New York: W. W. Norton, 1996), 5.

4. I. Bernard Cohen, *Revolution in Science* (Cambridge: Harvard University Press, 1985), 299.

5. David Quammen, "Darwin's Conundrum," *Harper's*, December 2006.

6. This data is cited in Larry Witham, *Where Darwin Meets the Bible: Creationists and Evolutionists in America* (New York: Oxford University Press, 2002), Table 3, 274.

7. Francisco Ayala, "Darwin's Greatest Discovery," *American Scholar*, winter 2006, 131.

8. E. O. Wilson, *On Human Nature* (Cambridge: Harvard University Press, 1978), xiii.

9. Stephen Jay Gould, "In Praise of Charles Darwin," in C. L. Hamrun, ed., *Darwin's Legacy* (New York: Harper & Row, 1983), 6–7.

10. Douglas Futuyma, *Evolutionary Biology* (Sunderland, MA: Sinauer Press, 1986), 3.

11. Cited by Witham, 23.

12. Charles Darwin, *The Descent of Man* (Chicago: University of Chicago Press, 1982), 507.

13. Jared Diamond, *The Third Chimpanzee: The Evolution and Future of the Human Animal* (New York: HarperPerennial, 1992), 32.

14. Gertrude Himmelfarb, *Darwin and the Darwinian Revolution* (Chicago: Ivan Dee, 1996), 397.

15. Cited by Adrian Desmond and James Moore, *Darwin* (New York: W. W. Norton, 1991), 585.

16. Ernst Mayr, *What Evolution Is* (New York: Basic Books, 2001), 121.

17. Jonathan Weiner, *The Beak of the Finch: A Story of Evolution in Our Time* (New York: Vintage Books, 1994), 6.

18. "The crust of the earth is a vast museum, but the natural collections have been made only at intervals of time immensely remote." Charles Darwin, *The Origin of Species* (New York: Barnes and Noble, 2004), 146.

19. Kenneth Miller, *Finding Darwin's God: A Scientist's Search for Common Ground between God and Evolution* (New York: HarperPerennial, 1999) 53.

20. Cited by David Sloan Wilson, *Darwin's Cathedral: Evolution, Religion, and the Nature of Society* (Chicago: University of Chicago Press, 2003), 7.

21. Stephen Jay Gould, "Darwinian Fundamentalists," *New York Review of Books*, June 12, 1997.

22. Franklin Harold, *The Way of the Cell: Molecules, Organisms, and the Order of Life* (New York: Oxford University Press, 2001), 235.

23. Richard Dawkins, *A Devil's Chaplain: Reflections on Hope, Lies, Science, and Love* (Boston: Houghton Mifflin, 2003), 28.

24. Harold, 10–11.

25. Neil deGrasse Tyson and Donald Goldsmith, *Origins* (New York: W. W. Norton, 2004), 236.

26. Richard Dawkins, *The God Delusion* (Boston: Houghton Mifflin, 2006), 137.

27. Steven Pinker, *How the Mind Works* (New York: W. W. Norton, 1997), 184; Steven Pinker, "Is Science Killing the Soul?" a discussion with Steven Pinker and Richard Dawkins, London, February 10, 1999.

28. Pinker, *How the Mind Works*, 305.

29. Michael Ruse, *Can a Darwinian Be a Christian? The Relationship between Science and Religion* (Cambridge: Cambridge, University Press, 2000), 73.

30. Darwin, *The Descent of Man*, 304.

31. John Barrow and Frank Tipler, *The Anthropic Cosmological Principle* (New York: Oxford University Press, 1996), 289.

32. Stephen Barr, *Modern Physics and Ancient Faith* (Notre Dame: University of Notre Dame Press, 2003), 78–79, 111.

CHAPTER FOURTEEN: THE GENESIS PROBLEM

1. Daniel Dennett, *Darwin's Dangerous Idea: Evolution and the Meanings of Life* (New York: Simon & Schuster, 1995), 21.

2. Carl Sagan, *The Demon-Haunted World: Science as a Candle in the Dark* (New York: Ballantine Books, 1996), 304.

3. John Maddox, "Down With the Big Bang," *Nature* 340 (1989), 425.

4. Cited by Hugh Ross, *The Creator and the Cosmos: How the Latest Scientific Discoveries of the Century Reveal God* (Colorado Springs: NavPress, 2001), 77.

5. Stephen Hawking, *A Brief History of Time* (New York: Bantam Books, 1996), 49.

6. Steven Weinberg, *The First Three Minutes: A Modern View of the Origin of the Universe* (New York: Basic Books, 1993), 154.

7. Lee Smolin, *The Life of the Cosmos* (New York: Oxford University Press, 1997), 183, 264.

8. Cited by Kenneth Chang, "In Explaining Life's Complexity, Darwinists and Doubters Clash," *New York Times*, August 22, 2005.

9. Barry Palevitz, "Science vs. Religion," in Paul Kurtz, ed., *Science & Religion* (New York: Prometheus Books, 2003), 175.

10. Christian Smith, *The Secular Revolution: Power, Interests, and Conflict in the Secularization of American Public Life* (Berkeley: University of California Press, 2003).

11. Ernst Mayr, "Evolution and God," *Nature*, March 1974, 285.

12. Franklin Harold, *The Way of the Cell: Molecules, Organisms, and the Order of Life* (New York: Oxford University Press, 2003), 254.

13. Francis Crick, *Life Itself* (New York: Simon & Schuster, 1981).

14. John Maddox, *What Remains to Be Discovered: Mapping the Secrets of the Universe, the Origins of Life, and the Future of the Human Race* (New York: Free Press, 1998), 281.

15. John Brockman, ed., *Intelligent Thought: Science versus the Intelligent Design Movement* (New York: Vintage, 2006), 58.

16. Richard Dawkins, *The Blind Watchmaker: Why the Evidence of Evolution Reveals a Universe Without Design* (New York: W. W. Norton, 1996), 240, 317.

17. Steven Pinker, *How the Mind Works* (New York: W. W. Norton, 1997), 162.

18. Richard Lewontin, "Billions and Billions of Demons," *New York Review of Books*, January 9, 1997.

19. Paul Davies, *God and the New Physics* (New York: Touchstone Books, 1983), 31.

20. Francis Collins, *The Language of God: A Scientist Presents Evidence for Belief* (New York: Free Press, 2006), 229.

21. Owen Gingerich, *God's Universe* (Cambridge: Harvard University Press, 2006), 6–7, 111.

22. Cited by Roger Highfield, "Do Our Genes Reveal the Hand of God?" *Daily Telegraph*, March 20, 2003.

23. Steven Weinberg, "Free People from Superstition," remarks to the Freedom from Religion Foundation, *Freethought Today*, April 2000.

24. William Provine, "Progress in Evolution and Meaning in Life," in Matthew Nitecki, ed., *Evolutionary Progress* (Chicago: University of Chicago Press, 1988), 64.

25. John Polkinghorne, *One World: The Interaction of Science and Theology* (London: SPCK Publishing, 1986), 62.

26. Roger Penrose, *The Road to Reality: A Complete Guide to the Laws of the Universe* (New York: Knopf, 2006), 1028.

CHAPTER FIFTEEN: THE WORLD BEYOND OUR SENSES

1. Immanuel Kant, *Critique of Pure Reason* (New York: St. Martin's Press, 1965), 17.

2. Susan Jacoby, *Freethinkers: A History of American Secularism* (New York: Metropolitan Books, 2004), 4.

3. Sam Harris, *The End of Faith: Religion, Terror, and the Future of Reason* (New York: W. W. Norton, 2005), 29.

4. Vern Bullough, "Church and State," *Free Inquiry*, Volume 16, No. 2.

5. Paul Bloom, reply to letters, *Atlantic Monthly*, March 2006.

6. Steven Weinberg, *Facing Up: Science and Its Cultural Adversaries* (Cambridge: Harvard University Press, 2001), 43, 103.

7. E. O. Wilson, *Consilience: The Unity of Knowledge* (New York: Knopf, 1998), 60–61.

8. Cited by Bryan Magee, *The Philosophy of Schopenhauer* (New York: Oxford University Press, 1983), 70.

9. George Berkeley, *A Treatise Concerning the Principles of Human Knowledge* (New York: Penguin, 1988), 61.

10. Leonard Peikoff, *Objectivism: The Philosophy of Ayn Rand* (New York: Random House, 1961), 33.

11. http://www.ase.tufts.edu/cogstud/papers/Dsouza.htm.

12. Cited by Bryan Magee, *Confessions of a Philosopher* (New York: Modern Library, 1997), 43, 105.

13. Wilson, 46–47.

14. Peter Berger, *The Desecularization of the World: Resurgent Religion and World Politics* (Grand Rapids: W. B. Eerdmans, 1999), 13.

15. Kant, 29.

CHAPTER SIXTEEN: IN THE BELLY OF THE WHALE

1. Arthur Schopenhauer, *On the Will in Nature* (Oxford: Berg Publishers, 1992), 110–11.

2. Stephen Jay Gould, *Rocks of Ages: Science and Religion in the Fullness of Life* (New York: Ballantine Books, 2002), 4.

3. Richard Dawkins, *A Devil's Chaplain: Reflections on Hope, Lies, Science, and Love* (Boston: Houghton Mifflin, 2003), 150; Richard Dawkins, "Is Science a Religion?" speech to the American Humanist Association, 1996; "God vs. Science," *Time*, November 13, 2006.

4. Michael Ruse, *Can a Darwinian Be a Christian? The Relationship between Science and Religion* (Cambridge: Cambridge University Press, 2000), 96.

5. Christopher Hitchens, *God Is Not Great: How Religion Poisons Everything* (New York: Twelve Books, 2007), 141; Richard Dawkins, *The God Delusion* (Boston: Houghton Mifflin, 2006), 91.

6. David Hume, *An Enquiry Concerning Human Understanding* (Oxford: Clarendon Press, 1777 edition reprint), 165.

7. Carl Sagan, *The Varieties of Scientific Experience* (New York: Penguin Press, 2006), 231.

8. Daniel Dennett, "Why Getting It Right Matters," in Paul Kurtz, ed., *Science & Religion* (Amherst, NY: Prometheus Books, 2003), 158.

9. Neil deGrasse Tyson and Donald Goldsmith, *Origins* (New York: W. W. Norton, 2004, 19.

10. Karl Popper, *The Logic of Scientific Discovery* (New York: Routledge, 2002).

CHAPTER SEVENTEEN: A SKEPTIC'S WAGER

1. Blaise Pascal, *Pensées* (New York: Oxford University Press, 1999), 153.

2. Stephen Jay Gould, *Rocks of Ages: Science and Religion in the Fullness of Life* (New York: Ballantine Publishing, 1999), 12–16.

3. Carl Sagan, *Billions and Billions: Thoughts on Life and Death at the Brink of the Millennium* (New York: Random House, 1997), 166.

4. Richard Dawkins, *The Selfish Gene* (New York: Oxford University Press, 1989), 330.

5. Christopher Hitchens, "Mommie Dearest," Slate.com, October 20, 2003.

6. Cited by Ray Monk, *Ludwig Wittgenstein* (New York: Penguin Books, 1990), 301.

7. Ludwig Wittgenstein, *Tractatus Logico-Philosophicus* (London: Routledge, 2006), 88.

8. Bryan Magee, *The Philosophy of Schopenhauer* (New York: Oxford University Press, 1997), 118.

9. Michael Novak, "Reply," *American Spectator*, December 2006–January 2007, 45.

10. Pascal, 62.

11. Abu Hamed al-Ghazali, *The Alchemy of Happiness* (Armonk, NY: M. E. Sharpe Publishers, 1991), 42–43.

12. Pascal, 153–56.

13. Carl Sagan, *The Varieties of Scientific Experience: A Personal View of the Search for God* (New York: Penguin, 2006), 167.

14. Pascal, 56–57, 158, 169.

15. Christopher Hitchens, *God Is Not Great: How Religion Poisons Everything* (New York: Twelve Books, 2007), 212.

16. Richard Dawkins, *The God Delusion* (Boston: Houghton Mifflin, 2006), 103–4.

17. Pascal, 163.

18. Peter Kreeft and Ron Tacelli, *Handbook of Christian Apologetics* (Downers Grove, IL: Intervarsity Press, 1994), 387.

CHAPTER EIGHTEEN: RETHINKING THE INQUISITION

1. Steven Weinberg, *Facing Up: Science and Its Cultural Adversaries* (Cambridge: Harvard University Press, 2001), 242.

2. Sam Harris, *The End of Faith: Religion, Terror, and the Future of Reason* (New York: W. W. Norton, 2005), 35.

3. Steven Pinker, *How the Mind Works* (New York: W. W. Norton, 1997), 555.

4. Steven Pinker, *The Blank Slate: The Modern Denial of Human Nature* (New York: Viking, 2002), 189.

5. Bertrand Russell, *Why I Am Not a Christian* (New York: Simon & Schuster, 1957), 202.

6. Robert Kuttner, "What Would Jefferson Do?" *American Prospect*, November 2004, 31.

7. Richard Dawkins, *A Devil's Chaplain: Reflections on Hope, Lies, Science, and Love* (Boston: Houghton Mifflin, 2003), 161.

8. Daniel Dennett, *Breaking the Spell: Religion as a Natural Phenomenon* (New York: Viking, 2006), 72.

9. James Carroll, *Crusade: Chronicles of an Unjust War* (New York: Metropolitan Books, 2004), 2, 5.

10. Cited by Bernard Lewis, *The Muslim Discovery of Europe* (New York: W. W. Norton, 1982), 18.

11. Jonathan Riley-Smith, *The Crusades: A Short History* (New Haven: Yale University Press, 2005), xxxiii, 12, 15–16, 18–20, 22.

12. Henry Kamen, *The Spanish Inquisition: A Historical Revision* (New Haven: Yale University Press, 1997), 10, 17–18, 30, 41, 59–60, 305.

13. Harris, 255. His source for the 100,000 figure is Robin Briggs, *Witches and Neighbors: The Social and Cultural Context of European Witchcraft* (New York: Viking, 1996).

14. Carl Sagan, *The Demon-Haunted World: Science as a Candle in the Dark* (New York: Ballantine Books, 1996), 413.

15. Richard Dawkins, *The God Delusion* (Boston: Houghton Mifflin, 2006), 21.

16. Christopher Hitchens, *God Is Not Great: How Religion Poisons Everything* (New York: Twelve Books, 2007), 18, 21.

17. Harris, 239.

CHAPTER NINETEEN: A LICENSE TO KILL

1. Fyodor Dostoevsky, *The Brothers Karamazov* (New York: Vintage, 1991), 589.

2. Richard Dawkins, *The God Delusion* (Boston: Houghton Mifflin, 2006), 273, 279.

3. Steven Weinberg, *Dreams of a Final Theory: The Scientist's Search for the Ultimate Laws of Nature* (New York: Vintage Books, 1993), 259.

4. Jung Chang and Jon Halliday, *Mao: The Unknown Story* (New York: Knopf, 2005).

5. Stéphane Courtois, et al., *The Black Book of Communism: Crimes, Terror, Repression* (Cambridge: Harvard University Press, 1999), 590.

6. This parallel is more comprehensively drawn in Allan Bullock, *Hitler and Stalin: Parallel Lives* (New York: Vintage Books, 1993).

7. Daniel Dennett, *Breaking the Spell: Religion as a Natural Phenomenon* (New York: Viking, 2006), 299.

8. Sam Harris, *The End of Faith: Religion, Terror, and the Future of Reason* (New York: W. W. Norton, 2005), 79, 101, 259.

9. Adolf Hitler, *Mein Kampf* (Boston: Houghton Mifflin, 1999), 65.

10. Bullock, 381.

11. Hitler, 177–85.

12. *Hitler's Table Talk* (New York: Enigma Books, 2000).

13. Christopher Hitchens, *God Is Not Great: How Religion Poisons Everything* (New York: Twelve Books, 2007), 237.

14. Richard Evans, *The Third Reich in Power* (New York: Penguin, 2005), 256.

15. Ibid.; see especially 230, 237, 250–51.

16. Richard Weikart, *From Darwin to Hitler: Evolutionary Ethics, Eugenics, and Racism in Germany* (New York: Palgrave Macmillan, 2004), 9.

17. Friedrich Nietzsche, *Basic Writings of Nietzsche* (New York: Modern Library, 2000), 783.

CHAPTER TWENTY: NATURAL LAW AND DIVINE LAW

1. Richard Dawkins, *The God Delusion* (Boston: Houghton Mifflin, 2006), 31.

2. Christopher Hitchens, "Why I'm Rooting Against the Religious Right," OpinionJournal.com, May 5, 2005.

3. Daniel Dennett, *Breaking the Spell: Religion as a Natural Phenomenon* (New York: Viking, 2006), 55, 279.

4. Dawkins, *The God Delusion*, 227.

5. "Is Science a 'Satisfying Replacement' for Religion? A Conversation with E. O. Wilson," *Research News and Opportunities in Science and Theology*, July–August 2003.

6. Frans de Waal, *Good Natured: The Origins of Right and Wrong in Humans and Other Animals* (Cambridge: Harvard University Press, 1996), 209.

7. Carl Sagan, *Cosmos* (New York: Random House, 1980), 169.

8. Carl Sagan, *The Demon-Haunted World: Science as a Candle in the Dark* (New York: Ballantine Books, 1996), 296.

9. Hans Küng and Karl-Josef Kuschel, eds., *A Global Ethic* (New York: Continuum Press, 1993).

10. James Q. Wilson, *The Moral Sense* (New York: Free Press, 1993).

11. Donald E. Brown, *Human Universals* (New York: McGraw-Hill, 1991).

12. Richard Dawkins, *The Selfish Gene* (New York: Oxford University Press, 1989).

13. Cited by Stephen Jay Gould, *Ever Since Darwin: Reflections on Natural History* (New York: W. W. Norton, 1977), 262.

14. Dawkins, 230.

15. Ernst Mayr, *What Evolution Is* (New York: Basic Books, 2001), 259.

16. C. S. Lewis, *Mere Christianity* (San Francisco: Harper, 2001), 9–10.

17. For a discussion of the impartial spectator, see Adam Smith, *A Theory of Moral Sentiments* (Indianapolis: Liberty Fund, 1982).

CHAPTER TWENTY-ONE: THE GHOST IN THE MACHINE

1. Daniel Dennett, *Freedom Evolves* (New York: Viking, 2003), 1.
2. Victor Stenger, *God: The Failed Hypothesis* (Amherst, NY: Prometheus Books, 2007), 84.
3. "The Nonbeliever," *New York Times Magazine*, January 22, 2006; Dennett, *Freedom Evolves*, 1.
4. Jerome Elbert, "Does the Soul Exist?" in Paul Kurtz, ed., *Science and Religion* (Amherst, NY: Prometheus Books, 2003), 251.
5. Cited by John Horgan, *The Undiscovered Mind: How the Human Brain Defies Replication, Medication, and Explanation* (New York: Touchstone, 1999), 247.
6. E. O. Wilson, *Consilience: The Unity of Knowledge* (New York: Knopf, 1998), 119.
7. Richard Dawkins, *The Selfish Gene* (New York: Oxford University Press, 1989), 3, 201.
8. Steven Pinker, *The Blank Slate: The Modern Denial of Human Nature* (New York: Viking, 2002), 41–42.
9. Steven Pinker, *How the Mind Works* (New York: W. W. Norton, 1997), 52; see also Steven Pinker, "Is Science Killing the Soul?" a discussion with Steven Pinker and Richard Dawkins, London, February 10, 1999.
10. Francis Crick, *The Astonishing Hypothesis: The Scientific Search for the Soul* (New York: Touchstone, 1995), 30, 32, 57, 170.
11. Max Bennett and Peter Hacker, *Philosophical Foundations of Neuroscience* (London: Blackwell, 2003).
12. David Hume, *A Treatise of Human Nature* (New York: Penguin Books, 1985), 300.
13. Arthur Schopenhauer, *The World as Will and Idea* (London: J. M. Dent, 2004), 19–20.
14. Bryan Magee, *Confessions of a Philosopher* (New York: Modern Library, 1997), 378.
15. Pinker, *How the Mind Works*, 314.
16. Paul Davies, *God and the New Physics* (New York: Touchstone Books, 1983), 62.
17. J. B. S. Haldane, *Possible Worlds* (London: Chatto and Windus, 1927), 209.

18. Stephen Hawking, *A Brief History of Time* (New York: Bantam Books, 1996), 12–13.

CHAPTER TWENTY-TWO: THE IMPERIAL "I"

1. William Shakespeare, *Hamlet*, Act 1, Scene 3, in *The Complete Works of William Shakespeare* (New York: Barnes and Noble, 1994), 676.
2. Augustine, *Confessions* (New York: Penguin Books, 1961), 146.
3. Charles Taylor, *The Ethics of Authenticity* (Cambridge: Harvard University Press, 1991), 27.
4. Augustine, 28.
5. Cited by Roger Masters, *The Political Philosophy of Rousseau* (Princeton: Princeton University Press, 1968), 11.
6. James Byrne, *Religion and the Enlightenment: From Descartes to Kant* (Louisville, KY: Westminster John Knox Press, 1996), 201.
7. Dante, *Inferno* (New York: Anchor Books, 2000), 97.
8. C. S. Lewis, *The Four Loves* (New York: Harcourt Bruce & Company, 1988), 7.
9. Barbara Dafoe Whitehead, *The Divorce Culture* (New York: Vintage, 1996), 67.
10. Rousseau, *Emile* (New York: Basic Books, 1979), 391.
11. Lewis, 114.
12. Alan Wolfe, *The Transformation of American Religion: How We Actually Live Our Faith* (Chicago: University of Chicago Press, 2003), 251.

CHAPTER TWENTY-THREE: OPIATE OF THE MORALLY CORRUPT

1. Karen Armstrong, *A History of God: The 4,000-Year Quest of Judaism, Christianity, and Islam* (New York: Ballantine Books, 1993), 378.
2. Karl Marx, "Contribution to the Critique of Hegel's Philosophy of Right," in *The Portable Karl Marx* (New York: Penguin, 1985), 115.
3. Sigmund Freud, *The Future of an Illusion* (New York: W. W. Norton, 1961).
4. "The Discreet Charm of M. Sarkozy," dialogue between Nicolas Sarkozy and Michel Onfray, *Harper's*, July 2007.
5. See, e.g., James Haught, "My God, How the Money Rolls In," *Free Inquiry*, December 2006–January 2007, 51.
6. R. C. Sproul, *The Holiness of God* (Wheaton, IL: Tyndale House, 1985), 53.

7. Cited by Walter Kaufmann, *The Portable Nietzsche* (New York: Viking, 1968), 627.

8. S. T. Joshi, ed., *H. L. Mencken on Religion* (Amherst, NY: Prometheus Books, 2002), 38.

9. Victor Stenger, *God: The Failed Hypothesis* (Amherst, NY: Prometheus Books, 2007), 240.

10. Thomas Nagel, *The Last Word* (New York: Oxford University Press, 1997), 130.

11. Michael Novak, *Belief and Unbelief: A Philosophy of Self-Knowledge* (New Brunswick, NJ: Transaction Publishers, 1994), xxii.

12. George Williams, *Plan and Purpose in Nature: The Limits of Darwinian Evolution* (New York: Basic Books, 1966), 157.

13. Stephen Jay Gould, cited in "The Meaning of Life," *Life*, December 1988; see also Stephen Jay Gould, *Ever Since Darwin: Reflections on Natural History* (New York: W. W. Norton, 1977), 13.

14. Santiago Zabala, "Introduction," in Richard Rorty and Gianni Vattimo, *The Future of Religion* (New York: Columbia University Press, 2005), 11–12.

15. "I can indeed hardly see how anyone ought to wish Christianity to be true, for if so the plain language of the text seems to show that men who do not believe, and this would include my father, my brother, and almost all my best friends, will be everlastingly punished. And this is a damnable doctrine." Charles Darwin, *The Autobiography of Charles Darwin* (London: Collins, 1968), 87.

16. Adrian Desmond and James Moore, *Darwin* (New York: W. W. Norton, 1991), 387.

17. Benjamin Wiker, *Moral Darwinism: How We Became Hedonists* (Downers Grove, IL: InterVarsity Press, 2002).

18. Ibid., 27.

19. Cited by Desmond and Moore, 260.

20. Julian Huxley, *Essays of a Humanist* (London: Penguin, 1966), 223.

21. Aldous Huxley, "Confessions of a Professed Atheist," *Report*, June 1996.

22. Cited by Jeremy Driscoll, "The Witness of Czeslaw Milosz," *First Things*, November 2004.

23. These themes are advanced in Friedrich Nietzsche, *The Will to Power* (New York: Vintage, 1968); see especially 129, 136.

24. Bertrand Russell, *Why I Am Not a Christian* (New York: Simon & Schuster, 1957), 26.

25. Christopher Hitchens, *God Is Not Great: How Religion Poisons Everything* (New York: Twelve Books, 2007), 283.

26. Augustine, *Confessions* (New York: Penguin Books, 1979), 169.

27. Sam Harris, *The End of Faith: Religion, Terror, and the Future of Reason* (New York: W. W. Norton, 2005), 177.

28. Peter Singer, *A Darwinian Left: Politics, Evolution, and Cooperation* (New Haven: Yale University Press, 2000).

29. Steven Pinker, "Why They Kill Their Newborns," *New York Times*, November 2, 1997.

30. Steven Pinker, *The Blank Slate: The Modern Denial of Human Nature* (New York: Viking, 2002), 269.

31. Wiker, 100.

CHAPTER TWENTY-FOUR: THE PROBLEM OF EVIL

1. Christopher Hitchens, *God Is Not Great: How Religion Poisons Everything* (New York: Twelve Books, 2007), 3.

2. Steven Weinberg, *Dreams of a Final Theory: The Scientist's Search for the Ultimate Laws of Nature* (New York: Vintage Books, 1993), 250.

3. Steven Pinker, *How the Mind Works* (New York: W. W. Norton, 1997), 560.

4. Richard Dawkins, *River Out of Eden: A Darwinian View of Life* (New York: Basic Books, 1995), 133.

5. Jacques Monod, *Chance and Necessity* (New York: Random House, 1971), 145–46, 180.

6. Steven Weinberg, *The First Three Minutes: A Modern View of the Origin of the Universe* (New York: Basic Books, 1977), 154.

7. William James, *The Varieties of Religious Experience* (New York: Penguin, 1986), 51, 141, 526–27.

8. C. S. Lewis, *The Problem of Pain* (New York: Macmillan, 1962), 89.

9. Peter Kreeft, *Making Sense Out of Suffering* (Ann Arbor, MI: Servant Books, 1986), 135.

CHAPTER TWENTY-FIVE: JESUS AMONG OTHER GODS

1. William Shakespeare, "The Merchant of Venice," in *The Complete Works of William Shakespeare* (New York: Barnes & Noble, 1994), 409.

2. Richard Dawkins, *A Devil's Chaplain: Reflections on Hope, Lies, Science, and Love* (Boston: Houghton Mifflin, 2003), 150.

3. Bernard Lewis, *The Middle East* (New York: Touchstone Books, 1997), 234.

4. For a good overview, see Huston Smith, *The World's Religions: Our Great Wisdom Traditions* (San Francisco: Harper, 1991).

5. Blaise Pascal, *Pensées and Other Writings* (New York: Oxford University Press, 1999); see especially 37, 52–53.

6. For a discussion of these ideas, with source manuscripts, see Ainslie Embree, *Sources of Indian Tradition* (New York: Columbia University Press, 1988).

7. Isadore Twersky, *A Maimonides Reader* (New York: Behrman House, 1972), 99.

8. Christopher Hitchens, *God Is Not Great: How Religion Poisons Everything* (New York: Twelve Books, 2007), 100.

9. In Matthew 5:48 Jesus says, "Be ye therefore perfect, even as your father which is in heaven is perfect."

10. John 12:24.

11. Carlos Fuentes, *The Buried Mirror: Reflections on Spain and the New World* (New York: Mariner Press, 1999), 146.

12. Richard Dawkins, *The God Delusion* (Boston: Houghton Mifflin, 2006), 253.

13. C. S. Lewis, *Mere Christianity* (San Francisco: Harper, 1980), 147.

14. "When Christopher Met Peter," a dialogue between Christopher Hitchens and Peter Hitchens, *The Guardian*, May 31, 2005.

15. J. Gresham Machen, *What Is Faith?* (Carlisle, PA: Banner of Truth Trust, 1991), 154.

16. D. James Kennedy, *Why I Believe* (Waco, TX: Word Books, 1980), 137.

CHAPTER TWENTY-SIX: A FORETASTE OF ETERNITY

1. John Stott, *Basic Christianity* (Grand Rapids, MI: William Eerdmans, 1971), 18.

2. Maurice Chittenden, "Jesus Faked Death on Cross," *Times of India*, April 10, 2006.

3. Christopher Hitchens, *God Is Not Great: How Religion Poisons Everything* (New York: Twelve Books, 2007), 114.

4. Robert Funk, "The Coming Radical Reformation," http://www.westarinstitute.org, July/August 1998.

5. For a summary of this scholarship, see Charlotte Allen, *The Human Christ* (New York: Free Press, 1998).

6. Jeff Sheler, "Is the Bible True?" *U.S. News & World Report*, October 25, 1999.

7. Richard Dawkins, *The God Delusion* (Boston: Houghton Mifflin, 2006), 92.

8. John Milton, *Paradise Lost* (New York: W. W. Norton, 1975), 279.

9. Pamela Paul, "The Power to Uplift," *Time*, January 17, 2005.

INDEX